D0442864

DAY
OF
FURY

By the same author:

Excursion to Russia
They Seek a Living
Duet for Three Hands (with Cyril Smith)
The Poisoning of Michigan
From Cradle to Grave

JOYCE EGGINTON

DAY
OF
FURY

The Story of the Tragic Shootings
That Forever Changed the Village of
Winnetka

WILLIAM MORROW AND COMPANY, INC.
NEW YORK

Copyright © 1991 by Joyce Egginton

All rights reserved. No part of this book may be reproduced or utilized in any form or by any means, electronic or mechanical, including photocopying, recording, or by any information storage or retrieval system, without permission in writing from the Publisher. Inquiries should be addressed to Permissions Department, William Morrow and Company, Inc., 1350 Avenue of the Americas, New York, N.Y. 10019.

It is the policy of William Morrow and Company, Inc., and its imprints and affiliates, recognizing the importance of preserving what has been written, to print the books we publish on acid-free paper, and we exert our best efforts to that end.

Library of Congress Cataloging-in-Publication Data

Egginton, Joyce.
    Day of fury: The story of the tragic shootings that forever changed the village of Winnetka / by Joyce Egginton.
        p.   cm.
    ISBN 0-688-09085-0
    1. Dann, Laurie, 1957–   . 2. Murderers—Illinois—Biography. 3. Mass murder—Illinois—Case studies. 4. Children—Illinois—Crimes against—Case studies. 5. Obsessive-compulsive neurosis—Case studies.   I. Title.
HV6248.D24E34   1991
364.1′523′097731—dc20   91–6937
                                                                                      CIP

Printed in the United States of America

First Edition

1   2   3   4   5   6   7   8   9   10

BOOK DESIGN BY M&M DESIGNS

For Stephen-Paul
who held the Christ light for me

AUTHOR'S NOTE

Approximately one hundred and fifty people were interviewed for this book. All of them gave freely of their time, many of them on several occasions, to discuss events which awakened painful memories. I am deeply grateful for their understanding and cooperation in a project which may be the first of its kind to examine, in very personal terms, the effects of a deeply intrusive trauma on an unprepared community. Trauma is always easier to bury than to talk about. The emotional pain of reliving intolerable events can be overwhelming, which makes my debt to those who submitted to lengthy interviews all the greater. Some people, understandably, requested anonymity. These, therefore, are pseudonymns: Virginia Dean, Jessica and Sandra Feldman, Emily Fletcher, Judith Gilbert, the Johnstons, Leonora Kahn, Jennifer and Robert Malcolm.

Nothing else has been changed. I am indebted to the many professionals who gave me their insights into the events of May 20, 1988. Winnetka's police chief, Herbert Timm, was unusually generous in permitting access to his files and in sharing his memories. So was his staff, especially Lieutenant Joseph Sumner and Sergeant Patricia

McConnell. Police from neighboring villages were equally helpful, particularly Detective Floyd Mohr of Glencoe.

Dr. Donald S. Monroe, Winnetka's superintendent of schools, and Clarine Hall, former village president, added enormously to my understanding of the village's unique characteristics. So did the clergy from the Winnetka area: the Reverend Frank M. McClain, rector, and the Reverend Andrew Dietsche and Jan Wood, assistants, of Christ Episcopal Church; the Reverend David G. Goodman, pastor of Winnetka Bible Church; the Reverend Robert K. Hudnut and the Reverend Marcia T. Heeter, pastors of Winnetka Presbyterian Church; the Reverend Paul S. Allen, pastor of Winnetka Congregational Church; the Reverend Thomas Raftery, pastor of the Sacted Heart Catholic Church; the Reverend Thomas Ventura, pastor of Saints Faith, Hope and Charity Catholic Church; the Reverend Jason L. Parkin of the Church of the Holy Comforter, Kenilworth; Rabbi Robert D. Schreibman of Temple Jeremiah, Northfield; and the Reverend Richard E. Augspurger of the Institute for Living Pastoral Counseling Center, Winnetka.

Medical specialists who helped to heal the wounds of May 20 were generous with their time and knowledge. My thanks to Dr. Ira Sloan, chairman of the Department of Psychiatry at Evanston Hospital, to his vice chairman, Dr. Eitan Schwartz, and Dr. Ronald Rozensky, clinical psychologist at Evanston Hospital; to Dr. Raymond Silverman, director of psychiatric services at Highland Park Hospital; to Dr. Mary Giffin of the Irene Josselyn Clinic, Winnetka; and to Dr. James Garbarino, president of the Erikson Institute, Chicago, for their insights into the effects of trauma upon children; also to Dr. Richard Lasky, faculty member and director of the Institute for Psychoanalytic Training and Research, for additional psychiatric evaluation.

I am grateful to these physicians and surgeons for sharing some of the rarely discussed aspects of their lives and work: Dr. John C. Alexander, chief of cardiovascular and thoracic surgery at Evanston Hospital; Dr. Charles Brown, clinical assistant professor of surgery at the University of Chicago; Dr. Charles Drueck, director of the Trauma Program at Evanston Hospital; Dr. Willard A. Fry, professor of clinical surgery at Northwestern University Medical School; Dr. Joseph R. Hageman, director of the Pediatric Intensive Care Unit at Evanston Hospital; Dr. Avram R. Kraft, Dr. Edward J. Margulies, and Dr. Phillip Rosett, general surgeons in private practice; Dr. Stephen F. Sener, thoracic surgeon attending at Evanston Hospital; and Dr. David P. Winchester, head of general surgery at Evanston Hospital.

Many other people from the Winnetka area, some of whom prefer to be nameless, contributed generously to my research. My agent, Jane Cushman, and my editor, Lisa Drew, were as ever in the background and to the forefront, inspiring, encouraging, and when necessary, driving, in the most supportive manner and with the best of intentions.

–J.E.

Murder is a deeply contaminating crime. Every life it touches is changed.

—P. D. James

This could happen to any community in the world, but it happened in Winnetka, and this village became a microcosm of human experience.

—Herbert Timm, police chief

ONE

Emily FLETCHER was always one of the last to leave church. By the time she had packed away the Sunday-school things and helped the young children into their coats, most of the worshipers at the main service had usually left the building. Being Sunday-school superintendent was one of several voluntary jobs which helped to fill the gap of Emily's widowhood, and she did it with conscientious enthusiasm. At an age when most people are ready to retire, she was determined to keep busy and be useful. She never left the Sunday school until everything was orderly; then she would often meet relatives or friends for lunch.

This immutable pattern of her Sundays was interrupted at about noon on April 10, 1988, by the appearance of a young woman who walked purposefully across the church parking lot as Emily was about to get into her car to drive home. Afterward, when it became important for her to remember the date, she was able to pinpoint it with certainty because this was the one Sunday in April when she did not have a lunch appointment. It struck her that the stranger made an interesting picture as she walked

13

toward her, with her brown hair and her full brown cotton skirt rippling in the spring breeze. The scene impressed itself upon Emily's mind like an instant photograph and left a lasting image there, partly because of the unexpectedness of the encounter, but largely because of what happened less than six weeks later: an unforgettable horror which would always remind her of this first glimpse of the girl in brown.

By the time she was ready to leave church there were only two or three cars remaining, other than her own immaculate Cadillac. The young woman was heading toward this little group of cars in a way which Emily sensed could mean trouble. It was a curious reaction for her, indeed anyone, to have in this quiet village, so peaceful and protected, because nothing really bad ever happened in Winnetka.

The young woman did not look threatening, but there was something strange about her manner. As she neared the cars she asked in a peremptory tone, "Can anyone give me a ride to Wilmette?"

She did not introduce herself. She did not say please. She simply flung the question in Emily's direction.

Wilmette was barely three miles south—like Winnetka, one of a string of lakefront villages which form an affluent exurbia to Chicago, popularly known as the city's north shore. It was a pleasant morning, cool and sunny, and Emily's instinctive reaction was that this girl could easily walk. Or else be more polite in her request. She appeared to be in her twenties, was casually dressed, had sturdy legs, and was wearing flat-heeled shoes with knee socks, and a light jacket. Although two generations older, Emily would have walked rather than beg a ride from someone she did not know. The brusqueness of this stranger's manner irked her, and Emily was wary of giving rides to hitchhikers. She was wondering whether to ignore the question when she noticed the girl heading toward a rather frail elderly couple, also about to get into a car. Emily knew them well. They had been faithful members of her church for many years. She regarded them as very gentle people, who were so innocent and trusting that they might easily be taken advantage of.

"I must protect the Johnstons," Emily thought. Although small, slender, and alone, she believed she could cope with a bad situation better than they.

14

"I'll take you there," she said.

The young woman settled into Emily's front passenger seat as though she had a right to it.

"I walked up here and I'm too tired to walk back," she explained.

There was nothing submissive or appreciative about her manner; it was clearly she, not Emily, who was in charge. She had a very determined expression, almost stern, but her voice was pleasant. As Emily turned into Green Bay Road, the main highway which links the north shore villages, her passenger made a sudden, astonishing statement.

"I have been thinking of committing suicide."

Over the years Emily had heard many confidences from young people. It took a lot to shock her; she also realized that a troubled person was more likely to confide a death wish to a stranger than to a close friend. She did not even think about her response. It was immediate and vehement, out of the depths of her faith.

"No, you mustn't do that. It won't solve anything. You will only wake up with the same set of problems. You can't walk away from them simply by dying."

Emily staunchly believed that there had to be accountability in the hereafter; as she often expressed it, "I can't imagine Adolf Hitler getting a free ride." She also felt that suicide was immoral, arguing that "you don't slip out of life like that. It's cheating. And you don't cheat your way out of anything. Ever."

The girl looked at Emily in surprise, as though it had not occurred to her that there might be anything beyond the oblivion of death. Then she lapsed into silence.

Emily tried another tack to get her passenger to talk about herself.

"Where do you live?"

"In Glencoe," the girl replied, naming the lakefront village immediately north of Winnetka.

"What's your name?"

"Laurie. But I like to be called Melissa." She did not add a surname.

"And what do you do?"

"I'm a baby-sitter."

It was an unexpected response. In these exclusive north shore villages there are two kinds of baby-sitters: young teenagers

15

who are available only when there is a gap in their complex social lives, and more experienced household helpers from less affluent neighborhoods. A young woman whose family had the means to live in Glencoe was most unlikely to be a full-time baby-sitter. Stranger yet for someone of her social background, this girl in brown made no attempt to elevate her title to something like tutor or governess. Instead, she seemed defiantly proud of her work. She answered Emily with a toss of her head, daring the older woman to question her reply.

Emily knew better than that. It crossed her mind that this girl might have deliberately gone into a church parking lot looking for a ride not because she minded walking to Wilmette but because she felt desperate and needed someone to talk to, someone with compassion and faith. The suicide threat might have been more of a cry for help than a statement of intent.

There's not much counseling a person can give in a ten-minute drive, so Emily attempted to establish some kind of relationship with her passenger, one which the young woman could take up at any time she felt the need. She gave her name and told about her affiliation with the church. She also tried to elicit some information. Was this girl satisfied with her life? Was there something else she would like to do?

Yes, the girl replied, she would like to take some journalism courses at Northwestern (a prestigious university close by) and become a writer.

"Then you should," Emily encouraged her. "You can be anything you want to be. All you have to do is work at it. And writing is a wonderful career."

By now they were in Wilmette. The girl directed Emily to the residential section where she said she was visiting friends. She got out of the car at a street corner and said good-bye.

"Good-bye, Melissa," Emily smiled back.

Over the next days and weeks Emily thought a lot about Laurie-Melissa. She kept hoping to hear from her. But as time passed she realized that this was unlikely; the young woman had been so absorbed in herself that she had no interest in anyone else.

Emily prayed that her passenger would find a purpose in life, and recover from her depression.

DAY OF FURY

*   *   *

About three weeks after Emily's strange encounter, Robert and Jennifer Malcolm advertised in the north shore's weekly newspaper, *Winnetka Talk*, for a full-time baby-sitter. They had a one-year-old daughter, and needed a responsible woman to come to their house five days a week, from 8:00 A.M. to 6:00 P.M., while Jennifer went to work. They had several responses, one of which seemed particularly promising, and they asked this woman to come for an interview. A few days later, during the first week of May, there was a telephone call from another applicant who seemed to be equally qualified. She gave her name as Laurie Wasserman.

Robert Malcolm took the call. He was immediately impressed by Laurie because she passed all his criteria. She spoke English as her native language, she seemed to be well educated, and she said she had worked professionally with children. He kept her talking for some time, assessing her personality. In the insurance business it was part of his job to spend hours on the telephone every day, weighing the truth of people's stories. He prided himself on being able to read voice syntax so well that it was hard for a caller to fool him. On the basis of his conversation with Laurie, he felt strongly that he and Jennifer should interview her.

Laurie told him that she had been a teacher (which appealed to him because Jennifer once taught too), that she also had nursing training and a lot of baby-sitting experience, and could supply excellent references. She said she lived nearby, in Glencoe, and that the working hours would suit her beautifully because she did not want a live-in situation, and had her own car. She explained that she was looking for a job because the family for whom she had been working as a nanny was moving to another part of the country.

Robert explained to her that he and his wife had already promised to see another applicant, and that if they did not hire this woman, they would ask Laurie to come for an interview.

Laurie seemed so eager to get the job that on May 11 she telephoned again. This time she spoke to Jennifer, who was as impressed as her husband had been.

"Her credentials were wonderful," Jennifer recalled. But although Laurie seemed overqualified, she never once asked about

17

salary. In an area where good baby-sitters are hard to come by and parents can well afford to pay, her lack of interest in money was strange. Jennifer assumed they would talk about it when they met, and reassured Laurie that she would have an answer for her within a few days. She could scarcely believe that she had been fortunate enough to find two highly qualified candidates vying for this rather lowly dead-end job.

On May 14 Laurie called again. Jennifer was beginning to feel irritated by her persistence, probably because the call came in the early morning when she was rushing to get to work, and when she still hadn't decided about the first candidate. She explained that this was an awkward time, asked Laurie to call back later, and was surprised to get an aggrieved response. The tone of Laurie's voice changed abruptly and she sounded very put out, as though she expected Jennifer to drop everything—her breakfast, the baby, the demands of her job—and concentrate on her. Yet she was unwilling to leave a telephone number for Jennifer to return her call. Through these various conversations, the Malcolms had no idea where Laurie was calling from.

At about this time they interviewed the first applicant and decided to hire her. On the morning of May 20, six days after her last conversation with Laurie, Jennifer went in her car to pick up this new baby-sitter. She had her infant daughter with her, and was driving the two of them back to her home when she ran into a police blockade toward the northern end of Winnetka. There was great panic and excitement in the village, and word was going around that a crazy woman had walked into the Hubbard Woods elementary school carrying a gun, and had shot some children. In this peaceful setting the tale seemed too bizarre to be true. But the local radio stations soon confirmed it, preempting other programs to spread the news. After a few hours they broadcast the perpetrator's name: Laurie Dann. This meant nothing to the Malcolms until later in the evening when radio and television reporters filled in the details. Laurie Dann, it emerged, had been born Laurie Wasserman and was the pleasantly spoken woman they had seriously considered as a baby-sitter for their child.

Emily Fletcher did not make the connection until she picked up her *Chicago Tribune* the following morning and saw the photographs of Laurie Dann. Immediately she recognized the girl in brown. On the previous day she had been preoccupied with concern for her youngest grandchild, a fourth grader, who had been very frightened to hear that children were shot in a neighborhood school. After reassuring herself that he would be all right, Emily told his mother, her daughter, about her own experience with Laurie Dann. Her daughter was horrified.

"Mother, you must promise me that you will never again give a ride to a stranger!" she said.

On the morning of Friday, May 20, about an hour before Jennifer Malcolm ran into the police roadblock in Winnetka, Leonora Kahn left her home in Glencoe to do some errands. After making a detour to drop off a pile of newspapers for recycling she headed toward the Old Orchard Shopping Center in Skokie, a route that would take her past Winnetka.

"I was in Glencoe, at Park Avenue, turning south into Green Bay Road," she recalled. "The light was in my favor, and as I finished making the turn I looked in my mirror and saw a white car bearing down on me. There was a woman driver who must have come through the red light, straight down Green Bay Road at tremendous speed. She swerved to overtake me, and sped on. I said to myself, 'That lady is crazed. In a few minutes I'm going to see her car up a tree. She must be on something.' I was thinking of drugs, of course."

A little farther down Green Bay Road, between Glencoe and Winnetka, Leonora had often noticed a policeman in a patrol car parked at the side of the road. She watched out for him as she continued her journey. "I'm not sure what I was going to tell him, except to chase this woman who was driving so dangerously. She was going too fast for me to get her license plate. But this one time I needed him, the policeman wasn't there.

"At about one P.M. I was at the Old Orchard Shopping Center when a saleslady said to me, 'Have you heard about what just happened in Winnetka?' And she told me about a madwoman who had walked into the Hubbard Woods School and fired a gun into a classroom full of children.

"I said to her, 'I know who did it. She almost killed me on her way there.'"

Later, when Leonora heard that Laurie Dann had driven to Winnetka in a white Toyota, there was no doubt in her mind that this was the woman who had almost crashed into her. Not only did the car description fit, but also the time and the route that Laurie must have taken. From then on Leonora would never cease to wonder whether the bloodshed of May 20 could have been prevented if only the police patrolman had been in his usual place.

Similarly, Emily Fletcher would always wish there had been a way of knowing that the stranger in her car was even more disturbed than her odd behavior indicated. And the Malcolms would be traumatized by the knowledge that they came very close to hiring a murderer as the baby-sitter for their only child.

TWO

THE WINNETKA family that was about to move out of state had not employed Laurie Dann for at least three months. She was never their full-time baby-sitter, as she led the Malcolms to believe; she had cared for their five children only when the parents, Marian and Padraig Rushe, went out socially. They knew her as Laurie Porter. Sometimes she romanticized her name and signed herself Lori.

She was good with children, especially the younger ones. She would get down on the floor with them, play games, tell them stories. She seemed to relate to them better than to adults, with whom she was shy and rather awkward. The Rushe youngsters adored her. The family was Irish and had settled in Winnetka after Padraig's company transferred him to its Chicago office. They lived in an upper-middle-class house typical of many in this family-oriented village: spacious, detached, and immaculate, surrounded by a well-kept lawn, with a basketball hoop above the two-car garage.

Around the end of 1986 they advertised in the local newspaper for a baby-sitter, and Laurie responded. She seemed ideal.

She lived nearby, had a pleasant manner, was experienced with children and old enough to be fully responsible. Further, she was available when the Rushes most needed her. They were still feeling their way in American society and had developed a social life which was centered on Chicago's Irish community. Most of the community's social events took place at weekends, and Laurie was one of those rare sitters who was readily available at such times. She even said that weekend jobs suited her because her boyfriend always worked on Saturdays or Sundays, and when she couldn't see him she was glad of the chance to make extra money. She indicated that they were saving to get married.

Laurie told the Rushes that she had a weekday job at Evanston Hospital, and that she lived with her parents on Sheridan Road, Glencoe, one of the most exclusive neighborhoods along the north shore. Padraig sometimes drove her there after an evening of baby-sitting, and noted a well-kept ranch-style house of handsome proportions on a winding, leafy road of sedate and opulent mansions. He never met any of her relatives.

She worked for the Rushes over a period of about eighteen months, never giving them the slightest cause for concern. She was always prompt, responsible, and thoughtful; so satisfactory that they recommended her to several friends. Then around the end of 1987, for no apparent reason, Laurie dropped out of their lives. Marian did not worry about this for several weeks because her sister was visiting from Ireland, happy to baby-sit when necessary. After the sister left, Marian telephoned Laurie's home several times, but could get no reply. Finally the phone was answered by a man who stated that Laurie was out of town. No other explanation was offered. Marian presumed this man to be Laurie's father, and wished he had told her more. After that she gave up calling.

On one of her last visits to the Rushe home Laurie had confided that her boyfriend had given her an engagement ring, a family treasure which had been his mother's. She explained that she could not yet show the ring to Marian because it was being restyled by a jeweler, but that she expected to have it shortly. She seemed excited about the plans for her wedding, which, she said, would take place the following June of 1988.

After a few weeks, when Laurie ceased to respond to her phone calls, Marian assumed that she had advanced the date of her wedding and moved away. The terse statement from Laurie's father seemed to confirm this. It was out of character for her to disappear without saying good-bye to the children, but what other explanation could there be?

On Wednesday, May 18, 1988, Laurie unexpectedly showed up on the Rushes' doorstep. Marian had given up hope of seeing her again, and was shocked by her appearance. Normally petite and pretty, Laurie had put on about forty pounds in weight. Her complexion was pasty, and there were dark circles under her eyes. Her brown hair no longer hung soft and loose about her shoulders, but had been cut short, tinted auburn, and frizzed into an ugly "perm." This took away her girlishness, gave a hardness to her face, and emphasized her heavy jawline. In every respect she seemed to have given up caring about herself; instead of the fresh, clean "preppie" clothes which were her usual style, she looked slovenly. Poor Laurie, Marian thought, her romance must have come to an end and she's so depressed about it she has let herself go.

But no, not according to Laurie. Marian invited her in, and during an hour of conversation Laurie talked enthusiastically about her wedding plans. She explained that she was still unable to show Marian her engagement ring because she did not like what the jeweler had done to it, so had sent it back for a second restyling. She would be married next month, and have a honeymoon in the Virgin Islands.

Marian expressed concern at not hearing from her. Laurie responded that she had been ill, suffering from the effects of allergies, and that there had been a death in the family. Neither of the women commented on the change in her looks.

Marian suspected there was something Laurie wasn't telling her. Could she be pregnant? But this wasn't that kind of weight gain; besides, she did not look well. Yet, if she did not want to talk about her personal problems, Marian felt it would be an intrusion to ask. At the same time Laurie's news of an imminent wedding gave Marian the chance to explain something which might otherwise have been difficult: that she would no longer need Laurie's services because the family was moving to New York, where her husband's company was about to transfer him. Laurie did not seem at all distressed about this. She implied that

23

it suited her because she did not plan to continue baby-sitting after her marriage, and she went on to ask a few polite questions about the Rushes' moving plans.

She was eager for news of the children and asked if she might take the two youngest out for a farewell treat. She suggested a children's carnival which, she said, was to be held at Evanston Hospital that Friday, May 20. She explained that this event was for small children only, and therefore ideal for six-year-old Patrick and four-year-old Carl. There was no question of including the three older Rushe children, who would be in school. Marian agreed on condition that Laurie bring the little ones back before lunch so that Patrick could attend the afternoon kindergarten session at Hubbard Woods School. Laurie agreed to pick them up at nine in the morning, and to be back by eleven.

There were a lot of things about Laurie which, at that time, Marian would have found hard to believe. She had no inkling that this perfect baby-sitter whom she trusted had created a fantasy world for herself which bore no relation to her real life. Her name had never been Porter. She had never worked at Evanston Hospital. She did not have a fiancé, let alone a prospect of marriage. There was no ring at the jeweler's. There were no plans to visit the Virgin Islands. And it was not allergies that had made her look so bloated, but a severe eating disorder, as well as the medication she was taking for a deep-seated psychiatric illness.

Laurie had told the Rushes that she was single, but she was in fact divorced. She had avoided mentioning her marriage because it ended with her rejection by a man she had loved and depended upon to be her lifelong provider, and with the passage of time this hurt had deepened rather than diminished. Laurie could not cope with rejection. It made her feel so isolated and angry that in her disturbed state of mind she became vengeful. Being married gave her an identity; being divorced diminished her, which is probably why she fantasized about being married again. Part of the fantasy was that she need no longer be a baby-sitter because there would be someone other than children to love her.

Laurie Dann did not baby-sit for money. That's why the pay was unimportant to her. She did it for affection; because hugs and kisses come readily from little children to anyone who takes

24

time and trouble with them. This was the theory of her ex-husband, Russell Dann, and it fitted the known facts better than any other explanation. He also revealed that she did not particularly like children, and was afraid of having her own. In their brief and childless marriage, he was the only one who wanted to be a parent. After they separated, Laurie's need to satisfy her emotional hunger found a sad substitute for marriage in baby-sitting, a relationship in which little was asked of her but which offered the possibility of unconditional love.

If Marian Rushe had known this (but how could she?), she would have understood how devastated Laurie was to learn that the Rushes did not need her anymore. Laurie had appeared unconcerned, but her feelings of rejection must have been bitter. In a desperate attempt to find a substitute family, she made her second telephone call to the Malcolms as soon as she left the Rushe home that day, stressing her eagerness to look after their baby daughter and inventing so many credentials for herself that she left Jennifer wondering why such an expert in child care would settle for baby-sitting.

The way in which Laurie made this latest job application was strikingly similar to her introduction to the Rushes eighteen months earlier. Both times she answered a local newspaper advertisement. Both times she presented herself as a responsible young woman who had professional experience with children. Both times she seemed unusually anxious to get the job. There was, however, one serious discrepancy. She told the Malcolms that she could supply an excellent reference from her last employers, the family that was about to move out of town. But while the Rushes would recommend her as Laurie (or Lori) Porter, she had introduced herself to the Malcolms as Laurie Wasserman. How would she deal with this inconsistency? And why did she keep changing her name?

By May 20, when she returned to the Rushe home to pick up Carl and Patrick for a last outing, she must have realized that there was very little hope of a substitute job with Robert and Jennifer Malcolm. Jennifer had been cool and abrupt when she last called, and she could not bring herself to telephone a fourth time. At the age of twenty-eight Laurie Wasserman Dann—the only daughter of wealthy parents and the recipient of a generous divorce settlement—was alone, frightened, sick, friendless, and barely holding herself together. When Laurie walked into the Rushes' kitchen that Friday morning, Marian caught no hint of her inner turmoil, but the woman she knew as Laurie Porter was crazed enough to kill.

It was a bright clear morning which promised a beautiful day, and Laurie was appropriately dressed for a casual outing. She wore light tan shorts with a much-washed yellow T-shirt, and flat-heeled shoes of soft black leather on her bare feet. A subsequent police report described them as ballet slippers, but they were sturdier than that, with rubber soles flexible enough for the hard running she might have to do. Her T-shirt was the kind of garment that a medical student might have given in fun, years ago; across the front was a logo of a skeleton encircled by the words COLLEGE OF MEDICINE, UNIVERSITY OF ARIZONA. She was carrying a large Mickey Mouse cup of brightly colored plastic and a paper plate on which there were several Rice Krispie treats, the home-made kind with marshmallow, which she had covered with transparent plastic wrap.

She arrived at the Rushe house at 8:45 A.M., just as eleven-year-old Robert and nine-year-old Mary Rose were leaving for the short walk to Hubbard Woods elementary school. They exchanged cheerful greetings with her by the kitchen door. Marian Rushe broke off from clearing breakfast dishes to help Patrick and Carl into their outdoor clothes. She had not expected Laurie for another fifteen minutes and the two little ones weren't quite ready. While Marian was bustling around, Laurie picked up a one-gallon plastic milk container from the kitchen table and poured some of the milk into her Mickey Mouse cup.

"I'm taking this in case the children get thirsty," she remarked.

This struck Marian as odd. Unrefrigerated milk would not stay fresh on such a warm day. She wanted to suggest taking fruit juice instead but then became distracted and forgot to mention it.

"Okay, I guess we can leave now," Laurie told Patrick and Carl. Her manner was cheerful, with no hint of the fact that she had been up for most of the night.

Marian walked them out to Laurie's car, a white Toyota Cressida which she did not recollect seeing before. She was gratified to note how solicitously Laurie secured the children's seat belts, and how very clean was the interior of her car. After strapping the children side by side on the back seat, Laurie drove off. Marian went back indoors, glad of two uninterrupted hours in which to get some chores done. She felt happy and relieved that Laurie had come back to say good-bye to the children.

Back in the kitchen, she was about to put the milk jug away when she noticed that its contents were a strange yellowish color. She smelled the milk, tasted a little, and judged it to be all right. Perhaps one of the children had dumped orange juice into it, she thought as she put it in the refrigerator.

Marian was in the basement laundry room doing the family wash when Laurie returned with the children. Although she had agreed to bring them back by eleven, this was only a few minutes after ten o'clock. Laurie reported that she had made a mistake about the carnival, that when she arrived at the hospital she discovered that it was scheduled for another day, so she took Patrick and Carl to the park instead. Her error about the date was understandable; what seemed odd was that on this farewell visit with the children she had not spent much more than an hour with them. As she came into the house Marian noticed that she was carrying a yellow plastic bag and a small packet of matches, which she placed on the console table in the hall. Afterward, when every little detail became important, Marian would remember that the folder containing the matches was imprinted with the name of a Mexican restaurant in Chicago. La Something-or-other, she thought it was.

Marian remarked that she was doing the laundry, and went back downstairs. Patrick and Carl followed her. So did Laurie, bringing the yellow plastic bag, which she then set down on a table in the basement recreation room.

"Are Mary Rose and Robert coming home for lunch?" she inquired.

"No," Marian replied. "They've gone on a field trip and won't be back until later."

Most Hubbard Woods children went home for lunch. This was a small school in a safe neighborhood to which youngsters walked or bicycled. Like the two other elementary schools in Winnetka, Crow Island and Greeley, it operated on the presumption that life had not changed since the fifties; that all the children came from close-knit, happy families in which fathers were the only ones who went out to work, while mothers stayed home fixing nutritious lunches, making cookies for bake sales, and supporting the Parent-Teacher Association. As Marian Rushe typically did.

Later, police investigators would speculate as to whether Laurie heard the whole of Marian's response about the field trip, or whether she dismissed that part of the answer because all she wanted to know was where Robert and Mary Rose were likely to be when she carried out the next part of her plan. Or perhaps Laurie's inquiry about the two older children was merely an innocent question, asked for the sake of making conversation. She did not even mention the oldest Rushe child, a thirteen-year-old daughter, who was in another school.

It would remain a mystery, to be conjectured about forever after: whether Laurie intended to take revenge on the Rushe children because she felt abandoned by their parents, or whether her actions that morning were just blind insanity, aimed at whoever happened to cross her path. Once Patrick and Carl were in her care she had not even attempted to take them to Evanston, knowing very well that there was no carnival at the hospital. Instead she had driven them in the opposite direction, due north, to visit two schools in Highland Park, where she would use them as a cover to carry out a diabolical plan of her own.

After the three returned from their trip, Marian went on with her wash, totally unaware of Laurie's disturbed state of mind. Patrick and Carl settled in the recreation room next to the laundry, and Laurie seemed prepared to play with them for a while when suddenly she picked up her yellow plastic bag and mumbled something about having to get an item from her car. As she moved there was a rattling sound from the bag, as of glass bottles clinking together. Marian assumed that Laurie had gone to prepare a treat for the children, something to eat or drink perhaps, so she encouraged them to stay downstairs with her until Laurie returned.

Immediately after Laurie had walked up the basement stairs, Marian heard a small "pouf" like the noise of a gas jet being lit.

Then a smoke alarm on the main floor began to sound and some-one, probably Laurie, shouted "Fire!" Marian hurried toward the staircase, intending to go up and investigate, and was horrified to see the stairs in flames. Within seconds thick black smoke was pouring into the basement. One of her first thoughts was fear for Laurie, that she might have been trapped in the fire.

There was no other exit from the basement, and as part of a recent renovation, the windows in the recreation room had been replaced by glass bricks. The Rushes had not realized it at the time, but this "improvement" turned the area into a firetrap. The only remaining window was a small metal-framed casement high up in the laundry room.

It was much too narrow for Marian to squeeze through but at least she could get the children to safety. She hustled them into the laundry room, grabbed the leg of a disused crib which was stored there, and used it to smash the glass. After picking out the shards from around the frame, she hoisted Patrick on her shoulders, and told him to climb out and run to ask a neighbor to call the fire department. As soon as he was safely outside, she held Carl up to the window and urged him to join his older brother.

Afterward Marian told the police that getting the children out was all that mattered to her; that she did not expect to survive. Within minutes the electricity failed and she was alone in the dark laundry room, made blacker by smoke billowing in from the stairway. She knew that even if Patrick got the fire department right away, the chances of her being rescued were very slender. The stairs were impassable and there wasn't room enough for any-one to pull her out through the laundry-room window. When the firemen came they might be able to enlarge the window space by smashing some of the surrounding concrete, but she would surely be burned to death before they could get to her.

She might be able to buy a little time, she thought, by taking the wet laundry out of the washing machine and wrapping it around herself. She could also climb up and put her head and shoulders out of the broken window. The rest of her body would be badly burned, but provided she didn't collapse from smoke inhalation, there was a faint chance of the firemen putting out the flames before they engulfed her. Marian was an athletic woman, a familiar figure on the village tennis courts, but of only average strength. Desperately she yanked at the window frame with all the force she could muster. Then she yanked again. And again.

Suddenly it gave a little. Fiercely she pulled and pulled until she had torn most of the metal frame away from the concrete wall. Afterward police and firemen would be in awe of the superhuman strength she had summoned, of the wrenching and tearing with her bare hands, of the adrenaline which must have surged through her body. Tugging and yanking in the choking darkness she eventually managed to detach part of the frame to create enough extra window space for her to squeeze through. She then piled up several suitcases, climbed on top of them, heaved herself up and out into the window well.

The Winnetka fire department did not arrive until several minutes later. Patrick had run to the neighbor's house, only to find that the sole occupant was a Polish maid who did not speak enough English to understand what he was saying. Seeing how agitated he was, the maid took him to another neighbor's for help, all of which caused a delay in the emergency call being made. By the time firemen arrived the house had been badly damaged, and Marian Rushe had already rescued herself. They found her lying on the lawn, exhausted, with one arm badly lacerated.

"Is anyone still in the house?" they asked her.

"My baby-sitter," she gasped. "I'm afraid she may not have got out in time. Can you find her?"

At risk to his life, one of the firemen entered the burning building and searched around. There was no sign of Laurie, but there was evidence of arson—of the kind of burn pattern that would result from gasoline being poured down the basement stairs, then ignited. Afterward, when she had recovered a little, Marian realized that the white Toyota was no longer in her driveway. She wondered why Laurie had left without a word, after saying that she would be right back. She must have seen the stairs in flames. Knowing that three people were trapped in the basement, why hadn't she gone for help? And how did the fire start, anyway?

There were no obvious answers to the questions. Even after she thought about the matches and the yellow plastic bag, the reality of what had happened was beyond Marian's comprehension.

THREE

If LAURIE had slept at all on the night before she set fire to the Rushes' house, it was only briefly. Afterward, when her photograph appeared in all the Chicago-area newspapers, to be recognized by Emily Fletcher and others, an Evanston bus driver identified her as one of his last passengers in the early hours of May 20. He remembered her well because she behaved so strangely, as though she did not care whether she went home or not.

Evanston is both a suburb of Chicago and a self-contained town of almost eighty thousand. Its northern section is a tranquil and elegant neighborhood of distinctive turn-of-the-century architecture, with the ivied brick and stone buildings of Northwestern University occupying prime sites close to the Lake Michigan shore. The next community to the north is Wilmette, the southernmost of the north shore villages, and beyond Wilmette the exclusive enclaves of Kenilworth, Winnetka, Glencoe, and Highland Park.

The south side of Evanston, where the bus driver picked up Laurie, is a very different area. It abuts the northern fringes of

Chicago, is graceless in design, garish and shabby. Late at night it is a place where shadowy figures are seen in darkened door-ways, where street gangs argue over territorial rights, and where no young woman in her right mind would walk alone.

Laurie was doing just that—pacing by an unlit park—when the bus driver first saw her. It was about 11:50 P.M. on May 19, and she was walking up and down, up and down the deserted street, as though treading an imaginary line of predetermined length, counting the exact number of paces before turning around and precisely retracing her steps. There was a bus stop by the park, and the driver watched her as he paused there, wondering what on earth this girl was doing in such a lone and dangerous spot. She was moving her lips as though talking to herself, count-ing the paces perhaps, completely self-absorbed. She had to be crazy, he thought.

On his next trip around Evanston, the driver was surprised to see the same young woman waiting for his bus on Oakton Street, near the park where he had first noticed her. By now it was 12:40 A.M. and he was driving south on his last round trip of the night, heading toward Howard Street Station at the boundary between Evanston and Chicago, the southern terminus of his route. She boarded the bus and offered him a dollar, the standard fare, requesting a transfer.

"That'll be another quarter," he told her.

"I don't have a quarter," she replied, rummaging through her pockets. Watching her with some curiosity, he noticed that she was not carrying a purse. Her beige pants and dark-blue wind-breaker were rumpled, and she looked (in his phrase) "as though she had a lot on her mind." He wondered whether she was homeless.

When the bus reached Howard Street Station at 12:53 A.M. she did not attempt to get off.

"Is there a truck stop near here?" she asked the driver.

"No. But there's a Dunkin' Donuts open all night at Howard and Western. If you want to stay on the bus I'll drop you off there on my way back."

He assumed she meant to hitch a ride from a truck driver, and for all anyone knows she probably did, because it was far too late for her to make the twelve-mile trip to her parents' home in Glencoe by public transport.

It was about one o'clock when, retracing his route for the last time that night, the bus driver left her outside the Dunkin' Donuts which they had passed several minutes earlier. This was a neon-lit oasis on a street corner in a neighborhood the police describe as rough. Even if she was lucky enough to get a ride from there, Laurie could not have reached home until close to 1:45 A.M.

Seven hours later she showed up at the Rushes' house in Winnetka, apparently carefree, eager to take Patrick and Carl out for their treat.

When the police began to piece together everything they could discover about Laurie Dann, the question arose as to whether the bus driver might have mistaken the identity of his strange passenger. By then all kinds of people were claiming to have seen her in places where she could not possibly have been. But the bus driver's tale had the ring of authenticity. After seeing Laurie's photograph, he was positive that this was the girl on his bus, and a regular passenger on that late route concurred. The driver's most convincing evidence, however, was his description of the unusually preoccupied and precise way she paced the sidewalk by James Park. He could not have known, because it had not yet been published, that Laurie Dann had a psychiatric condition known as obsessive-compulsive disorder. Ritualistically she counted paces, counted lampposts, counted the cracks in the sidewalk, avoided touching metal, and went out of her way to touch other things, all to such excess that at times the compulsive repetition of inconsequential actions became so important to her that nothing else mattered. Not even her own safety.

It was not by chance that Laurie arrived at the Rushe home at 8:45 that morning. Nine was the time Marian Rushe had suggested, but Laurie intended to be four miles north in Highland Park before nine o'clock. And it was an important part of her plan to pick up Patrick and Carl first.

Highland Park was the north shore village where most of the Dann family lived. Laurie spent her childhood there, and returned after her marriage to Russell Dann. The two of them bought a house on Hastings Avenue, a quiet curving street in a modern development where the houses are sufficiently different from one another to be individual, yet obviously part of the same master plan. The young Danns chose a generously sized split-level of superior design, surrounded by an attractively landscaped yard, the kind of home that few couples can afford before they are middle-aged. In their twenties Laurie and Russell were already comfortably off.

When he married her in September of 1982, Russell was already a junior executive in a highly successful company built up by his father and uncle, Dann Brothers, Inc., one of the largest insurance brokers in the Chicago area. He had two older siblings, Scott and Susan ("Susie"), who were twins—all three of them reared to work hard, to play hard, and to enjoy the considerable rewards of a prosperous family business. With their slimly athletic bodies, olive complexions, and striking brown eyes, they bore a strong resemblance to one another and had a very close relationship. Scott was a senior executive at Dann Brothers; Susie was married to Jeffrey ("Jeff") Taylor of the Cole Taylor Bank, another prestigious Chicago institution. None of these in-laws had felt very much at ease with Laurie, but they had included her, as Russell's wife, in their social circle.

On one occasion, because Laurie was always offering to baby-sit, Susie had asked her to watch her small children for about fifteen minutes while she did an errand in the neighborhood. Although their two homes were in the same village, Laurie had arrived more than an hour later. She was pale, tearful, and holding one arm close to her body with the wrist hanging limply. She said she had an automobile accident on her way to Susie's house, and that her arm was hurt. She seemed badly shaken.

"She looked so pathetic I wanted to hug her," Susie related. "I suggested seeing a doctor but she refused. Whenever I saw her for two or three days after that her body was quivering and she was clutching her arm. She put on a terrific act and was totally believable. Finally Russell insisted on taking her to a doctor, whereupon she put her arm down, smiled, and said, 'There was no car accident. I just told that to Susie because I was late.'"

At Russell's instigation, he and Laurie had separated in October 1985. For a time, first one and then the other of them lived alone in the house on Hastings Avenue; later he moved to a duplex apartment and she returned to her parents' home in Glencoe.

During this period Susie Taylor began to receive harassing telephone calls. Sometimes a woman's voice would taunt her, "Susie, Susie, your children are going to die." Sometimes there was silence on the line. After the Taylors complained to the police, calls were traced to the Dann house on Hastings Avenue and Laurie was arrested for telephone harassment. She denied the charge. No legal action was taken because it could not be proved that she was responsible, since Russell's possession of a key to the house meant that other people could have had access to the phone.

Susie suspected that the phone threats were Laurie's way of taking revenge on the Dann family. "Also I think she was jealous of me because I have a happy marriage and three children, and she didn't."

She related: "We had hang-up phone calls for one and a half years after that. Then we had noises on the phone. Then she disguised her voice with death threats. I always hung up as soon as I recognized her voice. One time when I was particularly frustrated I said, as though to someone else, 'Did you get that on tape?' She did not ring for some time after that. But for quite long periods she would call our house night after night, always in the middle of the night. These were silent calls because by this time she realized that if we could not identify the caller we couldn't prosecute. But I have no doubt it was Laurie."

This was an extremely stressful period for the Taylors. They became even more fearful for their children when they learned that Laurie had purchased a handgun. They appealed to the local police, and to the state's attorney's office in their county but could get no satisfaction. In Illinois any adult who has not been institutionalized for mental problems or who does not have a criminal record can legally buy any number of handguns, and Laurie satisfied the law on all counts.

During the winter of 1987–1988 the Taylors had been relieved to hear that she had moved to Madison, Wisconsin. But from time to time they still received anonymous telephone calls. Between April 21 and May 11, 1988, the number of calls intensified, one of them with a disguised woman's voice again threatening death to the Taylor children. Susie took that call, and felt certain she was listening to Laurie. Early in May of 1988 Jeff filed new complaints with the state's attorney's office and the Glencoe police, stating that he was very worried about his family's safety. At both offices he was told that the Federal Bureau of Investigation had Laurie under surveillance for other suspected crimes, and was moving toward an arrest.

"We felt a sense of relief that the FBI was on to her," he related. "We did not know, and apparently they didn't either, that she had just left Madison and returned to the north shore. If we had been told she was back in the neighborhood, we would have hired a private detective to watch our children."

He was right to be so concerned. On that morning of May 20, before Laurie set fire to the Rushe house, it was part of her plan to eliminate the Taylor children, also by burning them to death.

It was Laurie's understanding that Jeff and Susie's two older children, Brian and Adam, attended the Ravinia School in Highland Park. Her information was a little out of date. Brian was still a student there but Adam had transferred to another school in the village.

On May 20, immediately after picking up Patrick and Carl Rushe in Winnetka, Laurie drove directly to the Ravinia School. She pulled up on the quiet street in front of the weathered brick building at 8:55 A.M., shortly after the beginning of the school day. Her timing was perfect. At that moment the school was full of children but none of them was wandering around the building. Soon there would be activity in the hallways, but from 8:45 until lessons began at nine, children were required to be with their teachers in their homerooms. During those fifteen minutes, and perhaps only at that time, an outsider could enter the school unseen and walk freely down the corridors with little likelihood of being stopped and questioned.

Even so, Laurie was fearful of being recognized. She had attended the Ravinia School as a small child and some of the current mothers were her contemporaries; there was also the embarrassing possibility of bumping into Susie Taylor. So she attempted to disguise herself.

Having instructed the Rushe children to wait for her in the car, she walked into the school carrying one of the several yellow plastic bags she had equipped with incendiary devices. Paul

Grant, a second-grade teacher who later saw her in a hallway, noted that it was a drawstring shopping bag from Herman's World of Sporting Goods. He also felt sure she was wearing a wig.

"It was a real cheap wig, reddish color, more orange than red, shaped in a Buster Brown cut, as though someone had put a bowl on top of her head and snipped around it."

Grant was certain that she wore a skirt or culottes of light-blue denim, suggesting that, unseen by the Rushe children, she may have put on the wig and pulled a blue skirt over her light tan shorts as she left her car. But from everything else that happened, there is no doubt that the woman he saw was Laurie Dann.

Grant left his classroom at 8:58 A.M. to take eighteen second graders upstairs to the audiovisual center to see a film. In a hallway on the main floor, near an outside door, there was a large refrigerator box of heavy cardboard which some of the third-grade children had made into a playhouse. It had been part of a social-studies exercise in creating a community, and now the project was finished, the box had been left outside a classroom for someone to take home. As he led his class down the hallway, Grant saw a woman back out of the hole in the box that had been cut for a doorway, hurry to the swing doors by the teachers' lounge, hurl them open, and dash out into the street.

Her movements were so strange and swift that he took a good look at her as she fled. That was why he was sure about the blue skirt and the wig. It struck him that she must be very familiar with the building to hurry out of it so decisively. He assumed she was a kindergarten mother who had brought her child to school late, then lingered to peep inside the playhouse before hurrying on. He noticed the odd way she ran with her left hand tucked under her right armpit. At the time he merely thought it peculiar; later he believed he knew the reason.

"She was carrying a gun. I did not see it. I cannot prove it. But I'm positive she was."

He passed by the playhouse seconds after she backed out of it. His class followed. As he reached the top of the stairs, close to the principal's office, the last children in line came abreast of the playhouse. Two of them called out to him, "Mr. Grant, someone put a fire in that box!"

He told the class to go on, and ran back downstairs. Inside the playhouse some material was smoldering. The fire was in such an early stage that he was able to blow it out. Hearing the commotion, Principal Paul Zavagno hurried downstairs.

Grant related: "The two of us tipped over the box and saw the remains of a yellow plastic bag containing two or three one-liter lab bottles with handwritten labels describing flammable chemicals. I remember seeing the names of heptane and butanol. In the bottom of the bag was something like charcoal lighter fluid. We looked at one another and gasped. Suddenly this wasn't an accidental fire we were dealing with, but a deliberate attempt to blow up the school."

Zavagno hurried back to his office to call the Highland Park fire department. A team arrived there within minutes. Grant watched as two firemen examined the bottles of chemicals.

In a horrified tone one of them said to the other, "All of that is highly toxic stuff which could have been burning, and to think we came in here without oxygen!"

No one saw Laurie drive away from the school. With two small children in the back of her car she looked like one of the many young mothers who would have been in the neighborhood at that time. Her next call was at a nearby day-care center, where the youngest Taylor child, five-year-old Lisa, was enrolled. It was on Clavey Road, Highland Park, just around the corner from her old home on Hastings Avenue, in a single-story brick building owned by the Young Men's Jewish Council.

She was well prepared for this visit. Three days earlier she had called at the center posing as a potential client, inquiring about the hours it was open and the services it provided. After she left, a small card-index file containing the names and addresses of all the children who were enrolled there was inexplicably missing from the office, and could not be found.

When she returned at about 9:30 A.M. on May 20, Laurie had two little boys in tow. With Patrick and Carl Rushe affectionately clinging to her, she was again taken for a young mother who was seriously interested in the center and had come back with her children to look around. The only thing odd about her was that she was carrying a red plastic gas can. Mrs. Jean Leivick, director of the center, watched from her office window as the three of them walked up to the building. Then she hurried out to confront Laurie at the front door.

"You can't bring that can in here," she said.

Laurie set it down on the path by the door, and took Patrick and Carl Rushe inside. There she spoke with a woman teacher, explaining that she intended to sign up her children for the summer program. Another teacher had a brief conversation with Laurie by her classroom door, and noticed that she smelled strongly of gasoline. A third teacher watched the encounter from her classroom and decided that she didn't like the look of Laurie, although she wasn't sure why.

Having used the Rushe children to justify her visit, Laurie sent them out to play. There were swings and climbing equipment at the side of the day-care center, and the little boys were eager to use them. Later in the day Patrick told police that he thought he was at a park in Evanston because that's what Laurie told him—a supposition which set off an official search for bombs in every park up and down the north shore.

Patrick also gave a graphic account of how he watched Laurie go back to her car, take out a light blue plastic garbage bag, and put it on like a dress. Patrick noticed that she had already cut a hole in it for her head. When she pulled it down, her T-shirt and shorts were completely covered. The children giggled.

"You look funny," Patrick said.

"I do?" she asked.

As though unsure of herself, she removed the bag.

While the Rushe children played she went back to the day-care center, undisguised. Again she was carrying a red plastic gas can. Once more Jean Leivick intercepted her at the front door, and gesturing toward the can, repeated, "You can't bring that in here."

Laurie responded that she was looking for assistance because her car was out of gas. Firmly Jean Leivick walked her out to her white Toyota and helped her pour the contents of the can into its tank. Like Marian Rushe, she was impressed by the cleanliness of the vehicle, and noticed that it was identified by a Glencoe sticker. She waited outdoors while Laurie beckoned the two children to the car, and continued to watch until she drove away.

Jean Leivick wanted to hurry this strange woman off the premises, but she was much more effective than that. Like Paul Grant at the Ravinia School, she prevented an explosion that could have killed every child in the place.

While she had the Rushe children in her car, Laurie made one more murder attempt. She offered them milk from her Mickey Mouse cup, urging them to drink it as she drove along. Before leaving their home she had poured an arsenic solution into the gallon jug on the kitchen table, not the orange juice that their mother assumed. Both boys sipped from the cup but, disliking the taste, quietly dribbled the milk onto the clean red carpet in the back of the Toyota. Meantime, intent on getting back to Winnetka, Laurie drove down Green Bay Road so recklessly that as she sped through a Glencoe stoplight, Leonora Kahn saw only the vague shape of a woman driver, and had no idea that there were two small children snuggled up together on the backseat.

When a Winnetka police investigator gently questioned Patrick and Carl Rushe that afternoon, it was evident that they had no sense of danger until after Laurie had returned them to their mother, and the basement fire broke out. Patrick gave a lively description of being taken to a children's playground and of seeing his baby-sitter dressed in a garbage bag. He thought she had put it on to amuse him. Why else?

FOUR

WINNETKA IS the prettiest of the north shore communities. With its gracious homes, its Tudor-style storefronts and elm-shaded streets, it has developed over more than a century into an idealized version of what its founders intended: a New England village transplanted to the Midwest. It began to grow on the shore of Lake Michigan soon after the region's previous inhabitants, the Potawami Indians, were dispatched to less fertile territory west of the Mississippi, leaving few memorials to themselves except in the name of the place, and that came about almost by chance.

One of the first white settlers of substance was a wealthy leather merchant from Vermont, Charles Peck, who had the public spirit and foresight to beautify the area by importing a wide variety of flowering trees and shrubs, and to lay out a large village green which would serve as a community gathering place for generations to come. Most of the surrounding villages were developing by happenstance, but Peck ensured that this one would be exquisitely planned. At that time, the early 1850s, a pattern was being set for naming the new north shore communities after their founders: Evanston to honor Dr. John Evans, Wilmette for the French-Canadian Antoine Ouilmette. Hence, at an informal gathering of Peck's friends, Pecktown was seriously proposed.

At this point his wife, Sarah, is reported to have declared: "No, the place shall not be called Pecktown; it shall be called Winnetka." Although no one has since been able to find the reference, Sarah Peck insisted that she had come across the word in a book of American Indian stories, and that it meant "beautiful land." Friends protested that Winnetka was too difficult to remember or to pronounce; nevertheless, the name stuck, and the village prospered. More than a century later it had become so affluent and idyllic that on appropriate occasions (as when they were making public speeches in one another's presence) villagers would unofficially describe it by yet another name, one which typified their feelings about a place that their collective wealth had made so orderly and pleasant, so secure and insulated, that none of the ugliness in the outside world seemed likely to intrude. They referred to it as Camelot.

Chicago is sixteen miles and a whole world away. The Chicago of 1988 had a reputation for some of the most deprived public schools in the nation, an excess of violent crime, and a society with deep divisions between rich and poor, black and white. Although some of the poor were living in unspeakable slums near the heart of the city, the unofficial boundaries of their housing projects were so well understood that few white people ever crossed them, and then at their peril. "I wouldn't go into the projects alone, not even with my gun," a Winnetka policeman remarked, with good reason. Yet not many blocks from the projects are the stock exchange and the corporate offices, the Art Institute and the symphony, those strongholds of financial power and international culture from which the privileged families of the north shore draw their being.

Many of Winnetka's breadwinners are corporate executives who work in Chicago. A comfortable ride on a double-decker train bridges the gap between their two worlds, bringing them back every evening from the pressures of the city to the bucolic quiet of Camelot. It is a very traditional life for most of the fourteen thousand inhabitants, based on the Protestant ethic of church and home and family. Except that these are not ordinary churches and homes. There are chapels decorated with religious art of museum quality, and parish meeting rooms furnished like the lounges of grand hotels. There are houses like colonial mansions and Tudor manors and French chateaux; great dwellings in quarried stone and russet brick which look as though they were built to shelter an art collection rather than a single family; houses with turrets like burgeoning castles, with Greek columns and elegant porticos, or, more modestly, with wraparound porches and gingerbread trims.

Architects who designed these places seem to have extended themselves to blend traditional European design with modern American comforts. Every week the real-estate advertisements in the local newspaper give a different variation of the theme: "Impeccable Tudor with huge family room and wet bar . . . newly renovated Georgian with European kitchen . . . distinctive ten-room country French home in prime estate area of Winnetka . . ." Or, better yet: "Visit many countries in one magnificent home—French exterior, English library and dining room, Spanish living room and American garden/family room . . ."

In the village's antique shops there is furniture of extraordinary quality to go with the houses. Some of it is early Georgian, as old as the republic. Some of it is adapted to suit the anachronistic decor of the north shore: Staffordshire figurines supporting electric lamps, a 150-year-old French farmhouse table with its legs deliberately shortened. ("Yes, some people think it's a pity but they didn't make coffee tables in those days," a saleswoman explains, as though apologizing for the aberrations of an earlier generation.)

Winnetka's charming little shops attract buyers from many surrounding villages, since the ambience is so pleasant and the help so solicitous. In several of the stores customers are soothed by complimentary coffee or herbal tea, and by an invitation to come back, whether or not they have bought anything. Even if the purchase is only a bag of groceries, it is served with a smile and an offer to carry the goods out to the customer's car.

None of this comes cheaply. But even the middle class who settle in the village, and who at first tend to go bargain hunting elsewhere, soon succumb to the life-style. As one such woman explained: "When we came here from Wisconsin I was shocked at the price of things. But the service is incomparable. When it snows, Eckart's hardware store will promptly deliver my rock salt. Or I will call them and say I have lost my cookie cutter, and they have one ready when my little boy goes to get it. Money does not change hands. I get the bill at the end of the month. Or I call one of the clothing stores and say I want a spring blazer and will be coming by in ten minutes. When I get there, they have a selection set out for me in the fitting room.

"All the dress stores know all the women, and what they like to wear. They will call you when something in your style comes in. If you have a problem with something you buy, you can take it back. You don't need a sales receipt. If your child is invited to a birthday party, it is understood that you buy the present from the Village Toy Shop because the people there will know what everyone else is giving, and make sure there are no duplicates. If a child doesn't like one of his presents, his mother will know where it can be exchanged.

"I also go to a dentist and a doctor in the village. They're the same people that we meet on the village green, so we know one another socially. When one of my children had pneumonia the doctor opened his office on a Sunday morning. And when I was ill the man at White's Drug Store made two trips to pick up my old prescription and deliver a new one. All this costs a bit extra, but I would rather spend a few more dollars in Winnetka than have cold, impartial service elsewhere."

The village green continues to be the center of community activity, just as Charles Peck intended. It is the scene of egg hunts at Easter, kite-flying contests in summertime, and annual solemn gatherings around the monument to Winnetka's war dead. ("On Memorial Days I always shed a few tears and feel my children have been exposed to something very special," one mother said.) Winnetka is also one of the few places where the Fourth of July is celebrated in the same spirit of innocence and patriotism that was felt across America at the turn of the century. Everyone shows up wearing a carnival hat and carrying a flag. There are family races, fireworks, lots of ice cream, and a parade around the green while a band plays Sousa.

All these events are believed to be social levelers, and so they are, except that the poorest people in Winnetka are middle class and virtually all the residents are white. In 1988, the year that Laurie Dann put the village ignominiously on the map, the median annual income for a Winnetka family was $95,000, more than three times the national average. Kenilworth, the lakeshore village immediately to the south, was listed as the wealthiest community in the nation, and the edge that Kenilworth had on Winnetka was very slight indeed.

In an inversion of the usual small-town formula, the people who live in these villages do not work there, and most of those who work there—shopkeepers, schoolteachers, secretaries, police—cannot afford to live there, commuting from the urban sprawl west of the lakeshore. Yet there has long existed between these two Winnetka communities, the providers and the payers, an unusually close relationship which has made the village special. For as long as anyone there can remember, the driving force has been a mutual dedication to doing things "the Winnetka way," a phrase that defies definition to those who don't belong, and is implicitly understood by those who do.

Winnetka's residents, who pride themselves on preserving one another's anonymity, include some of the most famous names in America: men who travel the world as heads of international corporations, entertainers who are accustomed to having their names in neon lights and want to come home to a place where they and their privacy are respected. A longtime resident commented: "In this village, if you think you recognize a person's last name, you probably do. But you do not ask. Not long after we moved here I asked a woman what her husband did, and she told me. I was so embarrassed because his name was known all over the world."

Most Winnetkans live somewhat lower down the social ladder. Many who grew up here return to the village as young marrieds, having failed to discover any other place which offers so much to its inhabitants: such a wealth of community services, such friendliness and mutual respect, such excellent schools for their children, such sensitively zoned use of open space to protect their property investments, so much of the flavor of small-town America as they remembered it from childhood and have romanticized it ever since. For this they will pay almost twice the price that a similar house would cost in a less affluent suburb of Chicago, and fix it up a little at a time.

"All we could afford in Winnetka was a small house with so many holes in it that every room had to be redone," one young mother related. "For the same money we could have bought a lovely home on the South Side of Chicago, but the neighborhood wouldn't be so safe and our children would not have the same advantages."

To help pay for the advantages this mother did a full-time job in a beauty parlor, where she was often aware of the gulf between her life-style and that of her clients. Most of them are highly educated, few of them work, many serve on the boards of charitable institutions and spend a lot of time entertaining and being entertained. One client told her, with the delight of one who had made an important discovery, that she had finally found a way to keep track of all the details of her complex social life: She had hired a secretary.

"I am in awe of all this," the young mother commented.

She, meantime, was worrying about how to get around the fact that it wasn't acceptable for her child to take a lunch box to school. There seems to be no place in the Winnetka school system for working mothers or latchkey children, or for families who do not remain intact.

"What is unusual about this community is that most couples stay married," one nonworking mother observed. "I know of no single parents. They cannot afford to live here. Even if they could, they would feel isolated. With schools structured the way they are, so that children come home for lunch, the unspoken message is that there is something wrong if they cannot, and that the world should not be that way. There would be a lot of implicit disapproval."

This woman, who had not grown up on the north shore, sometimes worried about the vision of life that was being given to her children.

"Winnetka is almost too good to be true," she said. "It's like the America you grow up believing is the norm, but which is not. It is homogeneous in terms of ethnic groups, picturesque, quiet, and terribly comfortable. But part of me is uncomfortable with it. I wonder if we are doing our children any favors, bringing them up in this sheltered environment, where they never see poverty and everyone is so nice. Then another part of me says it's absurd to be thinking like that."

Leaders of church youth programs struggle with this dilemma, and sometimes try to solve it by taking a group of Winnetka youngsters to a slum neighborhood where they will spend
a day making themselves useful, painting a tenement or planting
a garden. Parents see this as a meaningful experience, and their
children are briefly excited by it. But there is never any doubt
about the future for these intelligent young people with their natural good looks and their impeccable orthodontia. By way of some
of the best schools in the nation, they will go to excellent col-
leges, and then work their way up (more swiftly than most because of family connections) to prestigious professional
appointments or directorships in successful corporations.

All this takes driving ambition and hard work. Many of Winnetka's breadwinners put in long, stressful hours making multi-
million-dollar decisions which have to be right, always knowing
that at the end of a draining day they can leave the raw edges of
the city behind and come home to Camelot. Until Laurie Dann
shattered the peace of this place, Winnetka represented serenity,
continuity, and the promise that social and racial upheavals which
disrupt other communities could never happen here. It is a special
little enclave with an invisible wall of security around it (as cir-
cumscribed, in a very different way, as the boundary around Chicago's slums); an entire village run like a private estate, where
the police are expected to keep out anyone suspicious. When a
car is seen in the neighborhood which looks too old or battered
to belong, the driver will be stopped by one of Winnetka's ever-
present and quietly benevolent patrolmen and asked to explain
his business.

Winnetkans do not have to shovel snow from their sidewalks
or carry their garbage cans out to the street; all this is done for
them. There are no bars in the village, no neon signs, no vagrants
or beggars. The children's play equipment on the village green is
pristine; no graffiti or broken swings. The village beaches, tennis
courts, baseball fields, ice-skating rinks, and municipal golf course
are as beautifully maintained as if they belonged to a country
club.

This wonderful little world is held together by a strong community spirit and a tradition of public service. It is quite common
to see corporate executives umpiring children's baseball games on
a Saturday afternoon, or top-ranking professionals volunteering

47

their expertise in the village schools. When the Episcopalians have a rummage sale, the Catholics help out. When there is a death in the family, neighbors take food and comfort to the bereaved.

"Winnetkans are very involved in the community's well-being," explained Clarine Hall, who was village president in 1988. "They will support causes, and speak out at public meetings. They are willing to pay high local taxes, but in return they expect outstanding services. We have many highly intelligent, opinionated people in Winnetka, but even when they differ they are committed to working together. In some other parts of the United States people complain that nobody cares about anybody else. That wouldn't happen here. We respond to the needs of our neighbors and are sensitive to their well-being."

In politics, economics, and religion, Winnetka is conservative, a Republican exurb of a traditionally Democratic city. The villagers who have attained considerable wealth, either by inheritance or their own driving ambition, tend to assume that prosperity is the just reward for righteous living and that the poor would be better off if only they would work harder, and they resist any change to this order of things. In the village churches, which are able to offer a broad spectrum of programs because they are so generously supported, it is often hard for the clergy to preach the social gospel. Privately they agonize over the extent to which the needs of the outside world can be held before Winnetkans, and the extent to which the needs of their own parishioners can be honestly examined and addressed. Winnetkans think of their community as idyllic, but behind the comfortable facade there is probably as much marital discord, infidelity, alcoholism, drug abuse, and child abuse as in the rest of America. But here the private tragedies are more difficult to deal with because to acknowledge them would be to deny the dream on which these people have built their existence.

It was this very topic which the clergy were discussing on the morning of Friday, May 20, 1988. There is a fraternal association of the village's priests and ministers which meets once a month to talk about matters of mutual concern, a group so broadly ecumenical that it includes the rabbi from a neighboring community serving Winnetka's Jewish minority. Its convener for 1988 was the Reverend David G. Goodman, senior pastor of Winnetka Bible Church. This May meeting was held in a downstairs room on his church premises and, ironically as it turned out, focused on the setting up of a telephone network of clergy and social workers to respond to crises in the schools.

For several years the teenage suicide rate along the north shore had been considerably above the national average. A September 1980 issue of *Time* magazine had described the area as America's "suicide belt" and quoted a nineteen-year-old girl student: "Growing up here, you're handed everything on a silver plate, but something else is missing." She defined the something as parental "love, understanding, acceptance of you as a person."

Another side of the story was the extent to which children were pressured to succeed, even from their kindergarten days. From time to time a teenager who didn't measure up, or who felt unloved, would take the tragic way out. Years after the event Winnetka was still haunted by the memory of an attractive young girl who had gone into the local forest preserve and hanged herself. Nobody knew why. Recently a high school junior from the village had died when she drove home from a party under the influence of alcohol and smashed her car into a tree. And an adolescent boy from a nearby north shore community, seeking the ultimate thrill, had been the victim of an accidental, autoerotic suicide. Such stories recurred too often. The clergy's concern was not only for the bereaved families but for the traumatized classmates, and they talked about ways in which they might work with the police and school communities to help ease the pain.

They were almost ready to break for lunch on this bright May morning when Goodman's administrative assistant, Caroline Smith, burst into the room. She was very agitated. "We have just had a call from Hubbard Woods School," she gasped. "There has been a shooting, and some of the children are seriously wounded."

Afterward she recalled: "They just couldn't believe it. They had me telephone the police station to verify the report. The police weren't giving out any information at that time, but from the way they reacted we knew it had to be true."

After a brief prayer for the victims the clergy dispersed. Some of them felt uncertain about where they could be of most help, whether by their telephones or on the scene. The Reverend Robert K. Hudnut, pastor of Winnetka Presbyterian Church, went directly to the school because of his concern about the principal, Richard Streedain, who was a regular member of his congregation.

"I wanted to be there for Dick, in case he needed me," Hudnut said. He arrived as the ambulances were leaving and saw Streedain standing outside the school trying to give orders, his face as white as his shirt had been, and his shirt drenched with the blood of a child he had just carried out to an ambulance.

Some of the clergy followed Hudnut to the school, others returned to their churches. David Goodman went to his house across the street and tuned in to the local television news. On the plastic screen he was shocked to see a scaled-down version of the familiar tree-shaded streets around Hubbard Woods School, crowded with police and ambulances and anxious parents—among them a young mother from his church watching in horror as children were being carried out on stretchers. He telephoned her home and was relieved to hear that she was back there and that her child was not among the injured. Then he, too, hurried to Hubbard Woods.

By this time television crews were all over the neighborhood, and news media helicopters were hovering overhead. The police had strung yellow tape barriers around the school to keep back sightseers, and the surrounding streets were clogged with cars and people. In Goodman's shocked mind the scene superimposed itself on the one he had just watched in his living room. Later he described the sensation: "I thought to myself, 'I am walking into a television set, and this scene is not real, and this place is not Winnetka.'"

FIVE

THE REVEREND Thomas Raftery could not attend the clergy meeting that Friday morning. He was at his Church of the Sacred Heart in the Hubbard Woods section of Winnetka, saying a Mass of the Resurrection for Lawrence Carney. It was a big funeral attended by about 150 people. Larry Carney had worked for twenty-one years as a village fireman and paramedic, had been active in village politics, and was widely known in the area. He was fifty-nine when he died a bizarre and tragic death. Early the previous Sunday he and his son Brian, also a professional fire-fighter, had taken their boat out from Winnetka's public beach to go salmon fishing on Lake Michigan. It was a clear spring morning with a forecast for only occasional showers, but when they were half a mile from shore a heavy storm blew up. They pulled in their fishing lines, and were heading for home when Larry Carney was struck by lightning.

The flash sent a massive electrical shock through his body, setting his clothes on fire and knocking him unconscious. It sent his son sprawling, gouged holes in the bottom of the boat, damaged its engine, and disabled its marine radio. Although in deep shock, Brian put all his professional training into practice. He scrambled back on his feet, poured water on his father to extinguish the flames, and administered cardiopulmonary resuscitation. Somehow he managed to get the boat back to shore, screaming for help all the way. His heroic efforts were in vain; his father died the next day in Evanston Hospital. As Larry Carney was being rushed to the emergency room, paramedics from Winnetka and the neighboring village of Glencoe continued to try to revive him. His death was a very personal loss for them, and his funeral a deeply emotional event.

Almost everyone in Winnetka's fire department was there. So were police and firemen from miles around. Traffic control for the funeral procession had been the main concern of Winnetka's police chief, Herbert Timm, before he left his office that morning to attend the mass. The Church of the Sacred Heart is on Tower Road, a main thoroughfare connecting Green Bay Road (which hugs the lake) to the interstate highway running parallel to it, several miles inland. It was essential to keep the traffic on Tower Road moving as well as to accommodate the funeral procession which, after leaving the church, was scheduled to go west on Tower Road to the Catholic cemetery in Northbrook, four miles away. To avoid congestion the police chief had posted patrolmen to block off some of Tower Road's access streets in the immediate vicinity of the church, a routine decision which was to have enormous consequences on the subsequent events of that day.

Toward the end of the funeral mass, as if on cue, there was a clanging and screeching of fire trucks speeding along Tower Road.

"What a nice gesture for the fire crew to give a final salute," Village President Clarine Hall remarked to Fire Chief Ronald Colpaert as she came out of church. "Ron, do you always do that for a fallen comrade?"

"I wish that's what it was," Colpaert responded uneasily. "But there's a house fire in the village."

He knew only the bare facts: a basement blaze at a house on Forest Glen Drive, two blocks from the church. There was not yet any suspicion that this was an act of arson, caused by Laurie Dann in a crazed attempt to eliminate Marian Rushe and two of her children. The Rushes were members of Father Raftery's parish ("nice, nice people" in his description); afterward he was shocked to realize that in those hushed and solemn moments when he was serving communion, Marian Rushe must have been wrenching at her basement window frame, fighting for her life.

Hearing the sirens Fire Chief Colpaert had slipped out of church as the communion was ending. Seconds later Police Chief Herb Timm joined him on Sacred Heart's broad stone steps. It was 10:20 A.M. and the mass, which had started at 9:30, would be over in a few minutes. Colpaert was listening intently to his portable radio.

"How bad is the fire?" Timm asked.

"Pretty bad," Colpaert told him.

Timm had parked his car on a side street whose exit was about to be blocked by the funeral procession. Realizing that it would be some time before he could drive across Tower Road to the police station, he walked briskly in the opposite direction to the nearest pay phone, barely a block away. It was an open phone in the Hubbard Woods Pharmacy, sandwiched between the candies and the magazines, right by the street door.

The emergency line to the station was busy. He pushed the buttons for one of the station's inside lines, and repeated the question he had asked Colpaert.

"How bad is the fire?" He was concerned about the need to divert some of his patrolmen from the funeral procession to the area of the blaze, where they might be needed to control traffic. But his staff had something even more immediate for him to deal with: "We have just had a report of a shooting at Hubbard Woods School."

"I'll go right there," he said. And he sprinted the half block back to his car.

Police in the north shore villages are often called upon to cope with trivial events, and the petty demands upon them are constant: A neighbor's dog is scratching up my lawn; please send someone to remove it. There's a squirrel in my chimney; can you get it out? I'm at the railroad station, it's raining and there are no taxis; can a policeman drive me home? I have a flat tire and the gas station is closed; will you get someone to fix it? Or: What will the weather be like in central Iowa when I drive there tomorrow?

Herb Timm and his staff received more of these calls than of real emergencies, so it was natural for him to suppose that a school shooting meant a mischief-maker with a BB gun. Or a domestic argument over child custody that had spilled over onto school premises, although surely not badly enough for anyone to be hurt. However, Winnetka's police force was expected to provide service, and in his courteous, gentlemanly fashion, Herb Timm set the style. Even among the other north shore police chiefs (all of whom regarded themselves as public servants, in the literal sense) he stood out as a man of taste and refinement, with a low-key approach and a warm, caring manner.

He started to drive the few blocks to Hubbard Woods School, but by now the funeral procession was leaving Sacred Heart for the cemetery, and his own patrolmen were preventing Timm from crossing Tower Road. As he waited on a side street for the funeral cars to pass, a Glencoe police car came rushing past him with all its lights on, causing a break in the procession while it tore across. Anxiously Timm followed the Glencoe car to the school, a low building of weathered brick which blended into this quiet neighborhood of well-kept detached homes.

Herb Timm was horrified by the scene he walked into: Richard Streedain, the principal, and Donald Monroe, Winnetka's school superintendent, running out of the school building toward two waiting ambulances, each carrying a limp and wounded child, their own shirts darkly stained with the children's blood. Timm would never forget the shock and terror on these men's faces.

"Are there any others?" he asked.

"Yes, there are more inside," Monroe told him. Hurrying into the building, Timm noted Sergeant Patricia McConnell shepherding a bewildered-looking young woman (evidently a material witness) into one of the unmarked squad cars, a blue Chevrolet. He did not stop to speak with either of them; he trusted Patty McConnell's instincts. Barely three months earlier he had promoted her to head his investigations unit, a bold move considering the fact that she was the first and only policewoman in his force. At thirty-three, Patty was slender, athletic, and attractive, with shoulder-length golden-brown hair, a fresh complexion, and a warm and ready smile. Her typical plainclothes outfit was the blue jeans, white sneakers, white T-shirt, and hooded blue sweatshirt she wore that day. She could have passed for a college student or a young mother, except that she was carrying a gun. A woman teacher caught a glimpse of her hurrying down a hallway, and froze in horror. Patty did not know it then, but the death and destruction she had come to investigate had just been caused by a woman close to her age, also casually dressed, also with a gun in her hand. To a traumatized observer Patty looked like her accomplice.

After setting fire to the Rushe home, Laurie Dann had driven the three and a half blocks to Hubbard Woods School, walked calmly into the building, pulled two handguns out of her shorts, and, for no apparent reason, fired at the first children she saw. Then she had gone into Room 7 and fired again. And again. No one had seen her arrive and, in the ensuing chaos, no one saw her drive away. She left no clue as to whether she was a lone assassin or part of a conspiracy, whether she had a target in mind or was firing randomly, much less why she wanted to kill children. In its entire history, the Winnetka police force had never been faced with a case of such magnitude and horror. For months afterward, whenever Police Chief Herb Timm talked about it, he would say that the events of this day changed his life and that of the entire community forever.

Less than an hour earlier Patty McConnell had been eating breakfast with her police partner, Detective Robert Kerner, at a local diner. They were congratulating themselves on a job well done, having just arrested a man who had eluded them for six months. At 6:30 that morning they had finally tracked him down to a condominium in Palatine, a Chicago suburb ten miles west of Winnetka, and had gone there in plain clothes and an unmarked squad car. As he was preparing to leave for work, they were able to arrest him on a charge of passing bad checks. Since he did not have bond money, they had taken him to Winnetka police station and put him in a cell. Now they were relaxing. Friday was payday for the two of them, so after breakfast they decided to deposit their paychecks at the Winnetka Bank. On the short drive there, they heard fire sirens.

"That must be a big fire because they're sending more trucks," Patty commented to her partner.

A few minutes later, in line for the bank's drive-up window, they heard a news flash on the car radio: a shooting at Hubbard Woods School. It was about 10:40 A.M., and seconds later they were at the scene, a few minutes ahead of Chief Timm.

"We pulled up in front of the school, right by the main entrance," Patty recalled. "Don Monroe, the school superintendent, was sitting on the steps, waiting for the ambulance, with a little girl in his arms. There was blood all over her and over the front of his shirt. Right next to him was a teacher holding another little girl, also bleeding. I think I said, 'My God, what happened?' And he said, 'There's more inside.'

"The whole scene was like surreal. It was beautiful outside, sunny and breezy. Bob and I ran into the hallway and met a huge group of people in confusion. Teachers and children running around. Some of them were crying. They told us that a woman had come into the school with a gun and opened fire. Then we heard ambulances arrive.

"We went into Room Seven. There were children on the floor bleeding. Soon the paramedics arrived and began working on them. Another policeman, Rich Carlson, had just got there ahead of us. He had been outside the funeral directing traffic when he heard about the shooting on his radio. He had already found a witness, a young woman named Amy Moses. He said to me, 'This lady is a teacher and she saw everything. Maybe you want to take her with you.' She was slender and quiet and shy and very nervous; her hands were fluttering.

"I said to her, 'Amy, I am Sergeant McConnell and I am a detective. Do you know the woman who did the shooting?' She said, 'No, but I can describe her.'

"By this time the Glencoe ambulance had joined the Wilmette ambulance outside the school, and they were taking the children away. Bob and I got into our squad car with Amy in the back seat. She gave us a detailed description of a heavyset young woman with kinky reddish-brown hair, wearing baggy shorts and a T-shirt with a medical-school emblem.

"We began searching the streets. No one had seen her in a car, so we thought we were looking for someone on foot. Amy was doing everything she could to help us, and was trying to tell us what happened in the classroom. But she kept breaking down and sobbing, 'Oh, my God, she killed Nicky. I wish she had killed me instead.'"

While their chief was trying to get through to the police station on the drugstore telephone, Patrolmen Richard Carlson and Craig Tisdale were directing traffic at the corner of Gordon Terrace and Tower Road, the crossroads by the Sacred Heart Church. Shortly before the funeral service ended they received a fire call on their police radio. Tisdale hurried to the Rushes' house in response to it, leaving Carlson on traffic duty. Between five and ten minutes later, as the procession of cars finished pulling out of the church's parking lot, Carlson received another urgent radio message, this time about the shooting at Hubbard Woods School. Intent on keeping Tower Road free for the procession to the cemetery, he had been restricting the flow of traffic from the side streets, with no way of knowing that one of the cars he held back was the white Toyota Cressida driven by a crazed Laurie Dann as she tried to make her getaway from Hubbard Woods School. Her best escape route from the school would have been down Gordon Terrace onto Tower Road, where a left turn would have led her directly to the interstate highway. Since no one had a description of her car she could have been well on her way into Wisconsin if only Rich Carlson had not been standing at the crossroads, keeping the road clear for all those police and firemen who were respectfully following Larry Carney's casket to the cemetery.

Seeing the roadblock and all those uniformed law enforcers, she panicked, did a fast U-turn, and then lost her bearings. Seconds later Carlson got the radio message, left his post, and was the first policeman at the school, arriving there one minute after the alarm call to the police station. If Laurie had waited those few seconds she could have made her getaway. Instead, seeing Carlson and assuming that the police were already on the lookout for her, she made the move which would inevitably lead to her capture.

Carlson's initial reaction to the radio message was the same as his chief's: that an older child with a BB gun was probably making a nuisance of himself at the school.

"I hopped in the car and was there in fifteen seconds," he recalled. "I pulled up at the school and saw the principal holding a child who had been shot. His eyes were kind of wide. He was standing there with the child in his arms, trying to tell me how many people were hurt and how badly. He said, 'A woman came into the school and started shooting. There's two or three other children hurt, maybe more.'

"I asked him, 'Where is she now?'

"He said, 'I don't know. She left.'

"Then Amy Moses came out of the building. She was upset and excited but coherent. She said, 'This woman just came into my classroom, sat down, pulled out a gun, and started shooting.' She gave a pretty good description of her which I began putting out over the radio as she was telling me; you could hear her voice in the background.

"By this time I could hear the sirens and other police were arriving—first Craig Tisdale, who had come directly from the fire with Sergeant Brewer, then Patty McConnell and Bob Kerner, and then the chief. They were all there within five minutes. It was very quick, but it seemed like a long time. I told Patty that she should talk to Amy Moses, so she put her in the back seat of the squad car and drove off. All at once there were paramedics, ambulances, the fire department, and more police officers, and the chief was telling me to grab the door and make sure no unauthorized people went in or out of the building."

Chief Timm had gone directly to Room 7. Only about ten minutes earlier Amy Moses, a substitute teacher who often worked with this group of second graders, had been instructing them about bicycle safety. In this well-protected, semirural neighborhood, children were required to learn the rules of the road before being allowed to ride their bicycles to school. Having passed the test, eight-year-old Nicholas Corwin had ridden alone to school that day for the first time, and was feeling excited and proud of the achievement. He had left his new bicycle secured to one of the bicycle stands outside the building, and was looking forward to the short ride home for lunch.

Whether Laurie Dann chose Room 7 for a reason, or at random, may never be clear. But when she disrupted Amy Moses's lesson and opened fire, she killed Nicky Corwin outright. Herb Timm found him lying on the floor, unnaturally still, his face ashen, the pupils of his eyes dilated. Someone had stripped off his shirt, exposing a small deep wound in the chest. A teacher told Herb Timm that she had tried to feel a pulse on the child, and thought she had succeeded until she realized that what she felt was the trembling of her own body.

The first team of paramedics had just arrived and, in the process of triage, was estimating which of the wounded children were the most critical. Some were bleeding so badly that a few seconds' delay in getting them to the hospital could be fatal. The chief paramedic pointed to Nicky Corwin, and turned to Timm for guidance. In the absence of a doctor, a police officer has the authority to pronounce death, and without quite believing that all this was happening around him, Herb Timm did so.

"In the background I could hear children in other classrooms crying and screaming," Timm recalled. "But in this room there was only moaning and whimpering. One child said to me, 'My tummy hurts so bad. I can't breathe. Am I going to die?' And I said to him, 'No, you'll be just fine.' But to this day I don't know how all these kids survived.

"I saw another child running around with wounds in his throat. A paramedic was saying to him, 'You are going to be all right, and you have probably not had so much attention in a long time.' It was good to hear him reassure the child like that. But it was a horrifying sight, even for a police officer. For a few minutes I had to get out of the room.

"The rest of the school was in incredible panic. Children screaming. Teachers running back and forth. I went into the classroom next door and thought at first it was empty. But then I heard a slight scuffle and noticed a table with about ten kids hiding under it. I told them that I was a police officer and that it was safe for them to come out. 'Mister, are you sure?' they asked. Their eyes were as big as watermelons. They were thoroughly scared.

"From the police point of view, there was a great deal to be done immediately. This was a crime scene and it had to be isolated. We had to gather evidence. We had to secure the building. We couldn't let the children go running out into the neighborhood, perhaps to be confronted by the same woman again."

*　　*　　*

Unaware of the crisis, Clarine Hall had driven directly from the Sacred Heart Church to the village hall where she had an appointment with Winnetka's public-works director. Being village president was almost a full-time voluntary job, which this always elegantly dressed woman performed with graceful competence. As soon as Ron Colpaert told her that the sirens were sounding for a real fire, she recalled that the Glencoe fire department had been standing by that morning so that Larry Carney's former colleagues could be his pallbearers, and made a mental note to send a letter of thanks to Glencoe's village president.

At Winnetka's village hall she had barely begun her meeting with the public-works director when a staff member burst into the room. "Clarine, I think you should know. There's been a shooting and five children have been hurt."

Incredulous, she rushed into the village manager's office.

"Bob, what happened?" she asked.

Robert Buechner looked troubled. "I don't know. We're trying to find out." In the course of his eighteen years as village manager, Buechner had developed a keen ear for the different sounds of Winnetka's fire and ambulance sirens, and in a ten-minute period he had identified first the pumper truck, then the ambulance, then the ladder truck, then the rescue-squad truck speeding beneath his office window. These were followed by another siren which he didn't recognize, and which must therefore belong to a fire truck from a neighboring village. He guessed Wilmette. With so much equipment being brought in, he knew the emergency had to be serious.

He had been unable to contact the police station or fire department, either on the telephone or on the intercom. He kept punching buttons and getting busy signals. Finally, just after Clarine Hall burst into his office, he was able to reach the police.

"They say there has been a fire at Hubbard Woods and a shooting at the school," he told her. "Several children are hurt. We'd better get up there, Clarine."

Father Raftery was on his way back from the cemetery when he heard the news bulletin on the funeral director's car radio. There were no details, no mention of injuries, just the fact that there had been a shooting at the school. The driver wondered aloud whether a teacher had gone berserk. Sensing that the incident might be serious, Father Raftery suggested, "Let's go there and find out."

The driver turned onto Tower Road, but stopped at the junction with Gordon Terrace.

"Perhaps you should walk from here," he said. "We had better not show up at the school in a hearse."

SIX

ALTHOUGH SHE had failed to set a fire at the Highland Park day-care center, Laurie Dann probably felt confident that she had eliminated two of her former sister-in-law's children and three members of the Rushe family. Her next target was Hubbard Woods School where two more Rushe children were enrolled. After hurling her homemade fire bomb down Marian Rushe's basement stairs, she drove directly to the school, crossing Tower Road near the Sacred Heart Church. Larry Carney's funeral mass was not yet over, so the crossroads would have been fairly clear, and the three-block drive would have taken her only a few minutes. Laurie must have passed right by Patrolman Richard Carlson, who would have been waiting around to direct traffic when the mourners came out of church.

If he saw her car it would not have aroused his suspicions. It fitted into the neighborhood, an imported sedan in the upper price range, immaculately maintained. With its sparkling white exterior, crimson upholstery, and open sun roof, this car left no doubt that its owner was well-to-do. Even the license plate,

NW 000, was right for Winnetka. It implied ownership by someone of substance, Norman Wasserman in this case, Laurie's father, a self-made man whose successful accountancy business had
provided his family with a house in Glencoe near the lake, a condominium in Boca Raton, Florida, and the privileged life-style of
the north shore. The car was his, bought for the use of his wife,
Edith, borrowed by Laurie who was having trouble with her
Honda. If she had been driving the Honda on this day, she would
have been more conspicuous. It was a battered little blue car
whose interior (according to one of her in-laws) often resembled
a rat's nest.

Typical north shore cars never look untidy, or in need of a
wash. Many of them, like the Wassermans' Toyota Cressida, carry
personalized license plates which hint at the villages where their
owners live. In the old-guard WASP communities of Kenilworth
and Winnetka the message is discreet: the owner's initials only.
The new money of Glencoe and Highland Park tends to express
itself in license plates spelling names like ERWIN, MINDY, and
PATSY. But these divisions are not always clear, given the social
striving of new money to acquire the patina of old. Norman Wasserman had worked his way up from a blue-collar Jewish background, but like his lakefront Sheridan Avenue address, this car
gave him the image of inherited wealth.

So when Laurie parked it outside the Hubbard Woods
School, no one was in the least suspicious. No one saw her pull
up, and even after the havoc she created, no one saw her drive
off. She entered the school by one of the main doors, and aroused
no suspicion until a woman teacher saw her walk toward a boys'
bathroom on the main floor.

"Can I help you?" the teacher asked. Without responding,
Laurie disappeared around a corner of the hallway, and the
teacher did not pursue her. She felt it fair to assume that this was
a visitor who had lost her way and, the building being quite small,
that she would soon find it.

This trusting attitude toward visitors was indigenous to the
atmosphere at Hubbard Woods. Like the two other primary
schools in the village, Crow Island and Greeley, it was run in
such an easygoing, friendly fashion that if parents wanted to know
what their children were learning they were welcome to stroll into

the building and sit in on a class. There was no need to ask ahead of time, and the doors were always open. Educational researchers from out of town were also frequent observers, eager to gain a firsthand impression of one of the best primary-school systems in the country. By any standards, the quality of education in Winnetka was special, the finely honed result of an earlier generation's decision to create such an excellent public-school system that a private-school option would never seem necessary. Money had not been spared in the process. Over more than half a century several dynamic educators had been attracted to Winnetka and given the freedom to develop some of the most progressive teaching methods in America.

The school Laurie Dann walked into was staffed by carefully chosen professionals who had been encouraged by their principal, Richard Streedain, to use their own imaginations and autonomy. They formed a mutually supportive team who, in the face of unpredictable horror, would act magnificently.

"Hubbard Woods is a showplace of a school, and Dick Streedain is the principal that teachers along the north shore would kill to work for," a primary-school teacher in a nearby community observed. "By 1988 he had assembled a wonderful staff, and his school was on the cutting edge of all the good things that were going on in education. He had created the ideal atmosphere for an elementary school, a place where children were taught to think for themselves, and to pursue their own interests assertively. At that time there were a number of good schools along the north shore, but Hubbard Woods was outstanding. That school had everything ."

If it had been a lesser place, the events of May 20 would have left a much deeper wound. Even as it was, the trauma of that day was so terrible that for everyone who was there the healing process seemed likely to take years.

After her false start toward a boys' bathroom, Laurie headed into Room 7, Amy Deuble's class. It was at the end of one of the two long corridors on the main floor, and had one door on to the hallway (by which she entered) and a door on the opposite side of the room opening directly on to the playground. There were twenty-four children in that classroom of second graders, but that

Friday morning their energetic young teacher, Amy Deuble, was absent. She had taken a day's personal leave, which put Amy Moses, who was well known to the children as a substitute teacher, in charge. Amy Deuble had written her a memorandum about the bicycle-safety test which was scheduled for that morning, and had noted: "Nicky Corwin is a real help." Now that he had just turned eight Nicholas Brent Corwin preferred to be known as Nick, but among his classmates the childish name stuck. With his new bicycle at school for the first time, he would be one of those required to take wobbly rides around the playground.

There was also to be a written test, and as Amy Moses was handing out the papers, Laurie Dann walked in. It was about 10:30.

"May I help you?" Amy asked.

"No," Laurie replied.

"Are you here to observe?"

Ignoring the question, Laurie sat down facing the children. Assuming that this casually dressed adult was a college student who had come to sit in on a class, Amy gave her a copy of the test. Later she explained why. The unknown visitor looked "lifeless and hard" and "I really wanted to show her that Bike Day was a big event in these children's lives. I wanted to pass on the enthusiasm I had and sort of spark her, let her know that teaching is energy, loving, caring."

Without comment, Laurie picked up the test paper, dropped it, and left the room. Amy Moses went on with the lesson. She was slightly built, almost fragile in appearance, with short dark hair, a soft voice, and such large brown eyes that she often reminded people of a frightened young doe. At twenty-nine, recently divorced and childless, she was intent on establishing herself as a full-time teacher and was studying for a master's degree in education. Her colleagues at Hubbard Woods had confidence in her career choice; she was so gentle and comfortable with children.

The second graders were gathered in groups on their little orange chairs, so intent on the test that they barely noticed Laurie Dann's sudden departure. Exactly why she walked out of the classroom at that moment will never be clear. While some of the damage she did that day was clearly planned, much of it was random. At random she picked upon a six-year-old boy who was in the corridor, standing by the water fountain. His name was Robert Trossman; he was a stranger to her, as she was to him.

"Don't you have to go to the bathroom, little boy?" she demanded. Grabbing him by the arm, she propelled him into a boys' washroom—not the bathroom she had been about to enter earlier but one diagonally across the hallway from the classroom she had just left. There she pulled out a gun, a .22 semi-automatic Beretta pistol, and fired it at the terrified child. Her first shot hit the wall. Her second struck him in the right side of the chest, went through his body, and exited from his lower back.

Meantime two other boys had come into the bathroom. Laurie tried to shoot them too, holding the Beretta against a seven-year-old's head, but this time it misfired, ejecting some bullets onto the floor. She had concealed two other fully loaded guns in her shorts, a .32 Smith and Wesson revolver, and a .357 Smith and Wesson Magnum. The .357 was by far the most powerful of her guns, and it was fully loaded with six live rounds. Laurie was also carrying a packet of spare .357 bullets, but when she tried to use the Magnum it jammed. While she struggled with it the children who had not been wounded fled from the bathroom. Frustrated, Laurie tossed the .357 into one washbasin and its packet of bullets into another. This panic action prevented the damage she did that day from being infinitely worse.

"If she had shot the Magnum it would have been terrible," commented Police Chief Timm. "The three fifty-seven has such a high velocity that it will go through walls and blow people to pieces. She had loaded that gun with target ammunition, which has the same caliber as the regular ammo but not the same projectile. At short range it would still have blown limbs off and killed every child she hit. I've no idea why she left the Magnum in the bathroom, or why she didn't go back for it before she left the building. But we are lucky she made that mistake."

The first warning of disaster came from the two children in the bathroom who had escaped being shot. They ran into the classroom immediately across the hallway and told the special-education teacher, Mary Lind, that "there's a lady in the boys' bathroom with a gun." Mary Lind's class had been doing reading tests and the quietness of that atmosphere had already been interrupted by strange popping sounds from across the hallway.

"It was not the kind of bang-bang gunfire you hear on TV shows," said Judith Gilbert, the teacher's aide who was working with Mary Lind. "It was more like the popping of balloons. Whenever a child has a birthday in Amy's class the children blow up balloons and pop them, and that's what we thought it was. Except that it seemed louder than usual."

Mary Lind had hurried to the bathroom to investigate the two children's story, leaving Judy Gilbert in charge of the class. Laurie was nowhere to be seen, but Mary found little Robert Trossman still standing there, dazed and bleeding from the chest.

"I've been shot. Am I going to die?" he asked her.

She ran down the hallway to the principal's office, screaming for someone to call the paramedics and police. Then she ran back to the bathroom to help Robert, but he had already left. Somehow he had managed to walk back to his first-grade classroom alone. Part of him was reacting automatically, as though nothing abnormal had happened. Holding a book over the bullet hole in his chest he carefully closed his classroom door behind him, exactly as he had been taught. Then he collapsed. Sobbing, he repeated the question to his teacher, Alice Horowitz, "I've been shot. Am I going to die?"

Her shocked reaction was that someone in the school was gunning for Robert, and might come back to kill him. She took his shirt off, wadded and pressed it against his body to staunch the flow of blood, told all the children to get down on the floor and, expecting Robert's attacker to break into the room at any moment, stretched her own body across his to protect him.

Nearby, in the special-education class, Judy Gilbert also took the initiative of protecting the children. "Get down on the floor and DON'T MOVE!" she ordered them. After they had lain there for a while they heard more popping. Only this time, holding their breaths in terror, they knew it wasn't balloons.

After leaving the boys' bathroom, Laurie had gone back into Room 7. "Gather all the children in a corner of the room," she ordered.

"What?" Amy Moses asked incredulously.

"Put all the children in a corner."

It was such an inappropriate demand, so imperiously given, that Amy reacted with a blunt "No." Busy with their test, most of the children were unaware of this exchange.

"I have a gun," Laurie told Amy. "It's real, and I have another one." And she produced the snub-nosed Beretta she had used on Robert Trossman.

Amy did not react as Laurie expected. She thought this strange visitor was fooling around; that the Beretta was only a toy. It looked too tiny to be real. Amy put her hand on Laurie's wrist to grab the pistol, and in the struggle some bullets were discharged on the floor. Horrified, Amy ran to the classroom door, opened it, and yelled into the hallway, "There's a woman in here with a gun. Get help!"

Shaking herself free from Amy's grasp, Laurie pulled her remaining gun, the .32 Smith and Wesson revolver, from the drawstring waistband of her shorts. In that moment when she came so close to being murdered, Amy was unable to realize her own danger but focused instead on the expanse of pale flesh she saw as Laurie produced the second gun.

"My God, she isn't wearing any underwear" was the incongruous thought that crossed her mind.

When Police Chief Timm reconstructed this episode he felt that Laurie's primary objective had been to kill Amy, putting all twenty-four children in Room 7 at her mercy. In refusing to let Laurie intimidate her into ordering them into a corner, he was convinced, Amy saved many lives. As it was, the children remained in eight small groups in different parts of the room. At short range Laurie fired several shots into the three groups on her right, then fled.

Amy watched in horror as, one after another, five children collapsed, bleeding. She still could not believe in the reality of the scene. "They're making a movie and they forgot to tell me" was the thought that ran through her mind. "They just forgot to tell me." But even as she was thinking this, another part of her consciousness knew that the blood, and the children's screaming, and the awful stillness of Nicky Corwin, were painfully real.

*   *   *

There are several versions of Laurie's departure from the school, and they all conflict. Amy Moses thought that she left Room 7 by the playground door. Some of the children in her class described seeing Laurie go out the other door into the school hallway. In the chaos of the next few minutes the rumors flew: That she had gone into another classroom to shoot more children. That she was still in the building, hiding somewhere. That she was a Hubbard Woods mother, or an ex-teacher, gone mad. That she had an accomplice with more guns. That she was part of a conspiracy to make hostages of children from wealthy families.

A hasty head count revealed that one little girl from Room 7 was missing. Had Laurie grabbed her in the flight that nobody saw? Somehow the child must be found. It was also essential to get the wounded children to the hospital, to inform their parents, to call the police, to calm the panic, to secure the building, to make sure that nobody else got hurt: so many things to be done, and everyone who had to do them was in shock.

The first calls to go out from the school were to the village police station and to the office of Dr. Donald S. Monroe, Winnetka's superintendent of schools. Preserved on tape, the call to the police station recorded a woman's voice on the edge of panic: "There's been a shooting at Hubbard Woods School!"

"A shooting?" The police dispatcher's response was full of incredulity and disbelief. "And there's been an injury, ma'am?" Evidently he, too, was expecting to hear a story about a BB gun.

"Yes!"

At that point the school knew only of the shooting of Robert Trossman in the boys' bathroom. The same terse report, that a child had been shot, was phoned to Monroe's office on Oak Street, ten blocks away.

"I didn't stop to ask who or when or why. I reacted immediately, ran to my car, and drove as fast as I could to the school," Monroe related.

By that time a second call had gone to the police station, reporting the other shootings in Amy Moses's class. As the caller proceeded to give details, the police dispatcher heard background noises of children crying out, and of adults trying to calm them with "Come on in, honey. It's all right." Most of the unhurt children from Room 7 had fled out into the playground, then back into the building by another door to take refuge in the principal's office. Many of them were hysterical. It said much for Richard Streedain's easy relationship with the youngsters in his school that his room was the place where they felt safest.

Streedain had dashed down the corridor to Room 7. At least two women teachers followed him. They found Nicholas Corwin dead, and three other children seriously wounded. The little orange chairs were tumbled about the room, and there were pools of blood on the floor along with a lot of bullets. Another victim, eight-year-old Peter Munro, had run into a nearby kindergarten classroom, bleeding from a wound in his abdomen.

Lindsay Fisher, aged eight, and Kathryn Miller, aged seven, appeared to be the most seriously hurt. Streedain picked up Lindsay and ran down the hallway with her to the front door where he sat on the steps, cradling her in his arms, waiting for an ambulance. She was bleeding terribly from wounds in the chest and abdomen, and her blood quickly seeped across the front of his fresh white shirt. On this fine day he was not wearing a jacket.

Judy Gilbert had begun to half carry Kathryn Miller from Room 7. About three feet down the hallway the child collapsed. Fearful that the killer was still in the building, Judy protected her with her own body. Then she picked her up and began to carry her out to the front steps. The weight was almost too much for such a slightly built woman, and she staggered a little as she ran. Still conscious, Kathryn was whimpering, "I want my mommy."

At that moment Donald Monroe arrived. Dick Streedain was just coming out of the front entrance with Lindsay Fisher in his arms. Seeing Judy Gilbert immediately behind him, burdened with Kathryn, Monroe took the child from her. "I just kind of scooped her up." Soon his shirt, too, was deeply stained with blood.

Later Streedain noted that he sat on the steps holding Lindsay for 4 minutes 38 seconds before an ambulance arrived, helplessly watching her blood drain away. She was limp and unconscious. "It seemed like two hours," he said. While he was waiting, several police officers drove up, including Chief Timm. They came from different directions, and one after another plied him with questions he couldn't answer. Who did it? Where did she go? How many more children are hurt?

One of the first ambulances came from Glencoe. Like the Glencoe fire trucks, it had been standing by for Winnetka emergencies during Larry Carney's funeral mass. Unfamiliar with the one-way traffic regulations of Hubbard Woods, the driver had to back up to the school entrance. There Dick Streedain walked up to one of the paramedics and gently handed over Linds y while Don Monroe carried Kathryn into the same ambulance, negotiating its high step with difficulty. She was crying, and he was trying to reassure her.

"It's all right, honey. You are going to be okay."

But all the way to Evanston Hospital Kathryn kept asking John Fay, the Glencoe paramedic who held her head in his lap: "Am I going to die? Am I going to die?" And more out of faith than certainty he kept responding, "You'll be all right. You'll be all right."

Only a week earlier John Fay had attended a medical lecture on the treatment of gunshot wounds. This was not an emergency that seemed likely to arise in the north shore's protected villages; nevertheless, he felt the knowledge might be useful. Glencoe's public-safety department has an unusual system which requires its officers to be cross-trained as policemen and firefighters. Several of them, like Fay, are also qualified paramedics. While this alternation of duties involves extensive training, it provides a variety of work which is otherwise lacking in a small community. John Fay, a soft-spoken young man with mild blue eyes, particularly enjoyed the caring side of his job: working on an ambulance or a fire truck. A few years earlier he had begun to study for the Catholic priesthood, but had left the seminary, married, and become a public-safety officer instead.

On the morning of May 20 he was off duty, shopping in Glencoe. Missing his checkbook, he decided to stop by his office to see if he had left it there. As soon as he walked into the building the public-safety commander shouted at him, "Go on the ambulance! There has been a shooting at the Hubbard Woods School." There was such an urgency about the command that Fay had to ask someone else to tell his wife, who was waiting outside, and minutes later he was standing by the school, still in his street clothes, gently taking Lindsay Fisher from Dick Streedain's arms.

She appeared to be dying. Inside the ambulance he ripped open her shirt and was shocked by the sight of a child's body torn by bullet wounds. Her abdomen was rigid, indicating massive internal bleeding, and he could not hear any breathing sounds on the side of her worst injuries. Without hesitation he followed the advice he had heard in the lecture, to let gravity work, and he told his colleague to "put her on the injured side so the blood will pool, and then you can maintain an airway in the other lung."

Another crucial decision had to be made. It is part of every paramedic's training to do some essential emergency work in the field, such as starting intravenous injections in cases of severe hemorrhage. The standard procedure is to replace some of the lost blood with a fluid, Ringer's lactate, through a vein in the arm. He had the equipment and the expertise, but Lindsay's condition was so desperate that he doubted he had the time. So he told the driver to set off at full speed to Evanston Hospital.

On the five-mile drive he agonized over his decision. Cradling Kathryn Miller in his arms, murmuring reassurances to her, he said a private prayer for both children. In the emergency room he felt it necessary to explain why he had done no more for Lindsay: "I feel badly because I didn't start an IV, but she was bleeding so terribly that I decided to rush here instead."

When he left the hospital it was uncertain whether Lindsay would survive. But he was consoled by an emergency-room nurse who told him: "The average time it takes to start an IV in a pediatric case is seven minutes, and you didn't have that long."

John Fay felt a surge of gratitude. "I thanked God that I didn't have so much pride as to try to save that child myself."

SEVEN

PEOPLE WERE pouring into Room 7. Teachers, police, new teams of paramedics. It was a strange, terrible, incongruous scene. In this small classroom with the children's mobiles hanging from the ceiling and an alphabet wound around the walls, crayons and bullets were mingled on the floor, chairs and desks were in disarray, and there were pools and splashes of blood everywhere. Added to all this were the bloodied items of children's clothing, left piece by piece where they fell as paramedics cut them from the tiny injured bodies. Amy Moses was standing by the doorway, sobbing.

Police Chief Herbert Timm had gone into the room and made his judgment about Nicholas Corwin. He had seen death so often that he recognized it immediately, even before the paramedic who was acting as triage officer had turned to him, shaking his head. The slender, dark-haired child had been stripped to the waist, exposing a small hole, the exit wound, in the center of his chest. He had been shot in the back with a single bullet. Kneeling beside him, the paramedic had checked for vital signs in vain;

now he wanted his team to work on those who could be saved. The sight of this dead child lying on the classroom floor with all the confusion going on around him was so profoundly disturbing that a teacher said plaintively, "Please cover Nicky. Please cover him."

The police chief had already ordered him covered, and had instructed one of his officers to guard the body. Somebody brought a blanket, gray with little yellow flecks. Less than four feet away Judy Gilbert was kneeling on the floor with eight-year-old Peter Munro's head in her lap, he writhing in pain from an abdominal wound while a paramedic was attaching an IV line. Peter was gasping that he couldn't breathe. Another paramedic brought him an oxygen mask. Nearby, eight-year-old Mark Teborek was being given emergency treatment for a bullet wound to his neck and chest. He, too, wanted to know if he was going to die.

Overwhelmed, Herb Timm stepped outside into the hallway. This was a very emotional moment for him. Eight years earlier he had lost one of his own children, a daughter who lived only five days. He and his wife had held her while she died. She was still so real to him that whenever he saw other children who were born about the same time—playing, toddling, starting kindergarten, then going to grade school—he would say to his wife or to himself: This is what Heather would have been doing. To this day some sharply awakened memory could thrust his mind back into that agony of irrevocable loss. If Heather had lived she would have been in the same age group as the children in Room 7. The thought was so painful that he had to push it out of his mind, as forcefully as if it were a physical presence, and to remind himself that he was a police officer with a job to do.

From teachers in the hallway he had learned only that the shooting was done by a woman whom nobody at the school had recognized. Timm reasoned that she could have acted alone or as part of a conspiracy. She, or others working with her, could be taking their murderous intentions to other schools in the area. Sergeant Patricia McConnell was hustling Amy Moses into a squad car to search the neighborhood for her. As other police officers arrived he sent them to comb through the building and the surrounding streets.

In police terms, the school was now a crime scene and everywhere this woman had been must be isolated. Room 7. The hallway. The boys' bathroom where Robert Trossman was shot, and where the police were surprised to find Laurie's .357 Magnum and a packet of ammunition casually flung into washbasins. It was vital to preserve fingerprints and other clues. Timm was looking ahead to a murder trial when every piece of evidence would be important.

First he needed the help of teachers to identify the injured children and to inform their parents. Shaken and panic-stricken, some were tearfully embracing one another in the hallways. He went up to two of the women and enlisted their help. Then he gave orders for all other children to be kept in their classrooms until the police could be certain that it was safe for them to leave the building. The missing child from Room 7 had to be accounted for, and was. At the time of the shooting she had run, terrified, out of the playground door and straight home.

Timm's next priority was to set up a command post. The principal's office was full of frightened second graders from Amy Moses's class, but it had telephones and desk space, which made it seem ideal.

"Don, I need that office," he said.

Donald Monroe hesitated. Throughout his eleven years as Winnetka's school superintendent, he had insisted that the best interests of the children should always be paramount. This was his guiding principle, for no other reason than that he knew it was right. He was a middle-aged man with a quiet voice and mild blue eyes, but he could not easily be crossed and this building was his territory.

"Not right now, Herb," he said. "The kids are in there and they need to stay there." He didn't want to add to their terror by having them walk past all those panic-stricken people in the hallway into an unfamiliar classroom. But there were classrooms to spare because children in the fourth and fifth grades had gone to Chicago on a field trip, among them two of the five Rushe children and Nicky Corwin's older brother, Michael.

A few minutes later Herbert Timm repeated his request. He could have used his authority to take over the office but it was the Winnetka way to be gentlemanly even under stress. The school's telephone switchboard was already overloaded and the portable phones the police were bringing in to augment it would soon prove inadequate. Seeing the difficulty, Monroe reluctantly agreed to let the police take over the principal's office, and a dispossessed Streedain quietly took the second graders to an empty classroom.

The police chief had warned both men that none of these traumatized children could go home until one of his officers had spoken with them. Only they and Amy Moses had seen the shootings, and anything they could tell might be important. He promised a woman detective who would be gentle with them, thinking of Patty McConnell.

Timm was trying to convey all this, and to think of the many other things he needed to do when he heard someone in the crowd by the principal's office say, "Oh, my God, there's Mrs. Corwin." And for a moment, he froze.

On this beautiful May morning Linda Corwin had been playing golf. Unable to reach her by phone, a staff member at the school had called her husband, Joel, an attorney, at his office in Chicago. Joel was told only that there had been an emergency at Hubbard Woods School, and that he and his wife were needed there. He got a message to the golf club, and Linda was at the school within minutes.

Seeing the fire trucks as she approached the building, she wondered whether a boiler had exploded. As a recently elected member of the village school board, she would expect to be informed about such an accident. She did not think about danger to her child, not even when Dick Streedain answered her question about what had happened.

"This crazy woman came into the school and started shooting kids," he told her.

At first she thought he was making a rather poor joke. Then she saw the blood on his shirt and the look in his eyes; saw also Judy Gilbert's bloodstained clothes and haunted expression. With a sudden dreadful insight she thought of Nick, the second of her three sons, the loving little boy who earlier that morning had crept into bed between her and Joel while they were still asleep, excited about riding his new bicycle to school, eager to share his anticipation with them.

"Don't tell me! It's the worst, isn't it?" she asked Streedain.

"Yes, it's the worst," he said quietly.

She wanted to go into Room 7 to see her son, but was gently led to a seat in the hallway. For some time she sat there sobbing, waiting for her husband. Although there was a confusion of people in the area, everyone left a respectful amount of space around Linda Corwin. No one knew quite what to say to her.

"I just gave her a hug," said Clarine Hall, the village president, who had arrived at the school several minutes earlier. "I knew that nothing I could say could possibly respond to the hurt she was feeling."

Police Chief Timm put his hand on Linda's arm. "I'm so sorry," he told her. Months later he was still agonizing over his inability to be more responsive. "I knew her pain," he explained. "Having lost one of my own children, it was as much as I could say to her. Even that was very difficult for me. Then I just had to walk away." Before doing so, he made sure that someone was there to look after her.

Donald Monroe had the same concern. "Call the rabbi," he said to a teacher's aide who belonged to the same Jewish congregation as the Corwin family.

Although all the phone lines had been jammed, this call to Rabbi Robert Schreibman went through promptly. He was in his office at Temple Jeremiah in Northfield, a few blocks from Winnetka's western boundary. A couple of appointments there had taken up enough of his morning for him to miss the clergy meeting at Winnetka Bible Church, and he had not yet heard the news.

"Bob, there's been a shooting at Hubbard Woods. Nicky Corwin is dead. You have to get here now."

The voice was so urgent and panicky that he immediately ran out to his car. He knew the Corwin family well. Linda sang in the temple choir. Her children were in his religious school, and he thought of Nicky as "a very nice little boy, talented, sweet, with a lot of leadership qualities." It was beyond his comprehension that this child should have been killed.

He parked as close to Hubbard Woods School as the gathering traffic of police cars and ambulances would allow, and ran the last few yards. There was another cleric hurrying in the same direction, a small man like himself: Father Thomas Raftery on his way back from the cemetery after burying Larry Carney, not yet knowing why the rabbi was running yet intuitively aware that something terrible had happened, so terrible that he might innocently have intensified the agony of it by driving up to the school in a hearse. A teacher, waiting by the front door, was struck by the image of these two dignified little men, running. Recognizing them, a policeman who was guarding the school entrance ushered them into the hallway.

Both the priest and the rabbi embraced Linda Corwin. She was sobbing quietly, but seemed numb. A few minutes later her husband arrived, anxious to know what the crisis was about. Rabbi Schreibman intercepted him, struggling for a way to break the news.

"It's bad," he said quietly.

"What do you mean, it's bad?"

As gently as he could, the rabbi told Joel that his son was dead. Then he took him to Linda, stayed with the two of them briefly, and left them to grieve together. From teachers and police in the hallway he learned that Nicky's body had been moved to Highland Park Hospital.

After a while the Corwins wanted to go there. Joel was prepared to drive the six miles, but the rabbi insisted on taking them in his car. Walking ahead of them to clear the way, he was shocked to see television news cameras being set up outside the school.

"Don't take any pictures right now," he asked a cameraman. "Please allow these parents their privacy." He was surprised and impressed when the photographer agreed.

Seeing Nicky's body at the hospital was more difficult for Rabbi Schreibman than he could have imagined. "He was lying there so peacefully. It was impossible to believe he was dead. I didn't want to believe it and I knew of no faith, my own or any other, which could give me a satisfactory religious answer to the question, Why Nicky? Some people might reason that God had other purposes for him, or that He was testing our faith, but I still don't know what any of these explanations means. There really was no answer. We could only pray for strength to accept the unacceptable."

DAY OF FURY

*   *   *

That day no one was able to accept it. Ambulance workers, doctors, clergy, police—all who were close to this child's death had to struggle with their own denial of it. Some felt constrained to work against all medical wisdom and experience to try to save him. Those who were parents themselves, or who had suffered untimely losses, took Nicky's death the hardest. They wanted so badly to disbelieve in it.

After the first ambulances had left for Evanston Hospital, more paramedics arrived from neighboring villages, and one of them could not resist turning back the blanket covering Nicky and checking for a heartbeat. Ambulance workers are trained not to accept death until all body functions have completely ceased, and the electrodes this paramedic put on Nicky's chest registered a faint cardiac activity, an almost imperceptible quivering instead of the normal rhythmic pumping. This can happen after death has become inevitable and has essentially taken place, a diminishing flutter of the heart like a spent generator trembling to a halt, but it was enough to give the paramedic hope that the child might be saved. He made radio contact with his headquarters and was ordered to Highland Park Hospital. This is in the opposite direction from Evanston Hospital, whose resources were already stressed by the fact that all four children who had just been taken there required major surgery.

The police officer who had been instructed to guard Nicky's body was having to deal with so many other aspects of the crime scene, and there was so much confusion in Room 7, that neither he nor Chief Timm was aware of this new ambulance team's decision until they saw the child's body being carried to an ambulance.

"That body is not to be moved," Timm insisted.

He was thinking entirely like a police officer. Nicky was dead, of that he had no doubt, and this was homicide. In a murder case the most critical piece of evidence is the victim's body, which must not be disturbed until forensic experts have examined and photographed it. Timm's evidence technicians had not yet arrived, yet this body was being moved not only from the crime scene but out of his jurisdiction. Highland Park Hospital is in Lake County, and Winnetka and Evanston in Cook County.

Timm was appalled at this violation of police authority, at the jurisdictional problems he would have to face, at the prospect of losing a murder conviction because after all the heroic attempts to save this unsalvageable life, there might not be enough medical proof left to determine exactly how it was lost. Some of the other wounded children might also die, turning this into a mass-murder investigation of national notoriety. Within the village especially, there would be outraged demands for justice, and any impediment to the police work could be disastrous. All this went through his mind, and some of it he tried to argue, before the ambulance set off. But he was overridden.

Later Timm was given an insight which assuaged his anger. He was told that the paramedic who overrode his determination of death had formerly served in Vietnam where he had the painful experience of helping to remove children's bodies from a bombed school. At Hubbard Woods this half-buried memory was so vividly awakened that he could not resist trying to do what he had been unable to do then, to restore the life of a mortally wounded child.

His reaction was not unique. At Highland Park Hospital it was echoed in startling ways by medical staff who had long been inured to death but who could not accept this savage murder of an innocent child. For some, as for the paramedic, it recalled earlier tragedies. For others it was a powerful reminder of the fragility of human life, of the randomness of disaster, of how easily a child of theirs might have been in the place of Nicholas Corwin.

Nina Barker, the experienced, middle-aged staff nurse who was in charge at the emergency room, could not speak about Nicky's death without choking up, even months afterward, because it brought back the pain of losing her own child, eleven years earlier.

"It had a devastating effect upon all of us," said Peter Friend, executive vice-president of Highland Park Hospital. "The north shore is such a protected environment that the events of May twentieth seemed almost surrealistic. I walked into the emergency room and felt that what I saw couldn't be happening. There were nurses and paramedics sobbing, and everyone in shock."

Dr. Phillip Rosett was the emergency-room surgeon on call that morning. He had been about to leave his office in Skokie when the message came from Highland Park Hospital that he was needed there urgently. He was told only that there had been a shooting in Winnetka, and that several of the wounded were being taken to Highland Park.

Immediately he got into his car and headed north along the Edens Expressway, making the twelve-mile journey at considerable speed and telephoning two of his colleagues as he drove. Dr. Edward J. Margulies and Dr. Avram R. Kraft were partners, general surgeons like himself, and by good fortune both were in their Highland Park office when he rang. Minutes later all three of them rushed into the emergency room.

Two of the Hubbard Woods children had just been brought in: Peter Munro, who had been shot through the abdomen, and Nicholas Corwin. Peter was conscious, telling the medical staff in an astonished tone, "This lady came into the school and shot me—for nothing!" He was seriously wounded and it was essential to get him into surgery, but his chances of recovery seemed good. Nicky Corwin's case appeared to be hopeless.

None of the Highland Park surgeons knew that Winnetka's police chief had already pronounced him dead. But even knowing, they would still have felt compelled to try to save him. The urge was so powerful, the mental equation with their own children so immediate, their human need to restore this lost life so strong. Dr. Margulies thought of his own twelve-year-old son, a slightly-built child not much bigger than Nicky, and of his private nightmares of the kind that haunt every caring parent, that something terrible might happen to him, like being run over by a car.

"I looked at Nicky and felt defeated," he said. "But I thought that if we tried, maybe we could do something. And that is probably what motivated Dr. Rosett."

Phillip Rosett had three children of his own, aged six, four, and two, and inevitably he too thought of them. When he arrived at the hospital, the emergency-room staff was trying to resuscitate Nicky by external heart massage.

"It was not being effective," he recalled. "So I opened his chest in order to compress the heart from the inside. It is a trauma maneuver which generally does not work, but the alternative is to do nothing. This child looked dead but it was worth the chance to try to bring him back. If he had been my child I would have wanted everything possible done. And that's why I did it."

Dr. Kraft stood at Nicky's bedside, watching anxiously.

There was not the faintest response from the child. Sadly, Dr. Rosett stopped his resuscitation attempts. With Dr. Margulies he was to spend the next four hours performing lifesaving surgery on Peter Munro, more intricate than either of them had foreseen; then he would go home exhausted and, finding that his children had seen their daddy on the TV news and were eager to talk about it, feel the need to tell them about some of the events in which he had been involved, and to promise that no such harm could ever come to them, that they were safe, that they need not be afraid.

It would have been usual for a senior surgeon such as Avram Kraft to have walked away from Nicky Corwin's bedside, leaving the emergency-room staff to clean up. "But for reasons I do not begin to understand, I could not do this, and I told Dr. Rosett that I would take care of the child," he said. "Some people look dead when they die. This child looked as though he was sleeping. His innocence and his injury made a very powerful impact on me, and all kinds of feelings were surging through me which, even now, I cannot begin to put into words. I felt a need to do something for him, and all I could do was to close his chest wound.

"After I had done that, I picked him up as if to hug him while a nurse took the soiled sheet away from beneath him so that when his parents came he would look all right. I felt this need for physical contact because I had nothing else to give him, and I said a silent little prayer as I closed his eyes. There is a phrase in the Hebrew which we say when a person dies: May his memory be for a blessing. It went through my mind as I held this child.

"I wanted to meet his parents, but never did. By the time they got to the hospital another shooting victim had been brought in and I too was needed in the operating room."

EIGHT

Before the parents of this generation of Hubbard Woods children were born, and half a century ahead of its time, Winnetka's public-school system established its own team of therapists and psychiatric consultants. The underlying philosophy, that of nurturing the whole child rather than its intellect alone, was revolutionary when it was introduced here in the twenties by Carleton Washburne, a distinguished educator in the John Dewey tradition, who was then the village's superintendent of schools. Even after the concept became widespread, the extent to which it was developed in Winnetka's schools continued to be extraordinary. Children with learning disabilities or physical handicaps were given individual attention by specialists for as long as they needed it and for as much time as it took, always integrating them into the school system rather than treating them as different.

As an extension of this, by the 1980s therapeutic services for all age groups had become an accepted and flourishing industry along the north shore. Even Winnetka's village police force had its staff social worker, whose job involved finding empathetic solutions to problems which are not always considered police business in the inner cities: an Alzheimer patient found wandering, a potential suicide victim who should not be left alone, a husband or wife suddenly bereaved by a street accident.

On the morning of May 20, 1988, it was therefore natural, immediately after the injured children had been taken away in ambulances, for the school administration and the police to call in their therapists. There was an instinctive recognition that the emotional scars were likely to be extensive, even permanent, unless the healing process was begun right away. Donald Monroe asked his secretary to get an urgent message to Dr. Mary Giffin, the school's consultant child psychiatrist, and also to call the village clergy, most of whom were fortuitously gathered in a downstairs room at Winnetka Bible Church. Harry Dillard, the school district's head of pupil services, called in the trauma team of psychiatrists, psychologists, and social workers from Evanston Hospital. Herbert Timm summoned the police social worker.

Within an hour dozens of therapists had shown up. Afterward, some would feel their presence to be redundant, and yet as the morning went by the tension heightened, especially among the gathering crowd of parents outside the school, all of them desperate for reassurance about their children, angry at being told that they must wait outdoors, and taking out their anger on the reporters and photographers who were also rapidly growing in number, jostling for the best vantage points and vociferously insisting on being closer to the crime scene. Word of the shooting had spread fast, the first news flashes having interrupted a local radio entertainment program to which, it would seem, half Winnetka was listening. And that half immediately telephoned the rest. Soon it was evident that therapists and clergy were needed not only in the school but to help calm and console the crowd outside.

Elan Adler, the Winnetka police social worker, was one of the first of the mental-health specialists on the scene. She had been in the nearby village of Northbrook, consulting a psychiatrist about one of her current cases, when the pager in her handbag beeped. She broke off to telephone Winnetka's police station, and couldn't quite believe what she was told.

"A shooting? That's strange," she commented to the doctor as she hurriedly prepared to leave. On the eight-mile drive back to Winnetka, frustrated by delays at almost every traffic light, she thought this must be a case of domestic violence and wondered whom she could call upon to help her deal with it. It did not occur to her, until she walked into the chaotic scene at Hubbard Woods School, that anybody might have been wounded.

Timm assigned her the task of coordinating all the incoming mental-health experts to ensure that everyone who had been severely traumatized would receive attention. He put his arm around her shoulders as he explained this, and she was touched by the gesture. She thought of it as one of camaraderie and support, too intent upon the immediate crisis to appreciate Timm's personal concern for her. She was in the eighth month of her first pregnancy, and had reacted to the horror of the scene by putting her hands protectively across her stomach. It was a subconscious gesture which she would catch herself repeating in the remaining weeks before her son's birth, as though conveying the message to this unborn child: Just stay there and you will be safe.

"Are you all right?" Ron Colpaert, Winnetka's fire chief, asked anxiously.

He was standing near her, watching the wounded children being carried into ambulances. Mistaking her gesture, he added: "Please don't go into labor, Elan, because we can't get you to the hospital. All the ambulances are in use."

Police Sergeant Patty McConnell felt the same concern when she returned to the school minutes later, having vainly searched the streets for the woman Amy Moses had described. During that search she remembered chasing a stolen car in this neighborhood eight years earlier. Panicking, the driver had taken a wrong turn onto a dead-end street near Hubbard Woods School and in trying to reverse his car had crashed it by a driveway, then had run off into the woods. Thinking that the woman they were now looking for might have done the same, she suggested that Detective Bob Kerner should get out of their police car and search the woods on foot. She continued back to the school with Amy Moses. One of the first colleagues she saw there was Elan Adler, who had just arrived.

Patty, a young mother herself, had the immediate reaction: Elan should not be here. This is too traumatic for her. And yet we're going to need her. Badly.

Breathlessly, she briefed Elan: "This is the story. We have four children shot and one child dead. We have children in the classroom where this happened who are very scared. Some of the parents of the wounded children are already here and need attention. The mother of the dead child has just arrived. And here I have Amy Moses, the teacher who saw the whole thing, and she is a mess. She needs to talk to someone, but don't let her go home because I need her help."

Amy was standing there, glassy-eyed, staring, in shock. Later Patty admitted: "I was really worried about her. She was our only adult witness, and she was emotionally racked."

She watched tensely as Elan approached Linda Corwin to inquire whether Rabbi Schreibman would be able to stay with her, whether there was anything else anyone could do. This was Elan's training as a crisis-intervention worker, to start with the people most deeply affected. She appeared to be her usual calm, sympathetic self, totally involved with the other person's crisis. Only after her baby was born did she have her own strong emotional reaction, realizing in light of the Hubbard Woods tragedy how vulnerable children can be, how powerless their parents to protect them. "But so long as mine was in my belly I knew he was safe. So I was able to get on with the job as though it was all I had to worry about."

After reassuring herself about Linda Corwin, she turned to help Amy. Patty McConnell had gone into the principal's office, where her chief was in a discussion with Don Monroe and Dick Streedain. On a desk there Patty saw a spiral notebook with a red cover and a drawing on the front page, a child's representation of a woman's head with a crown, captioned: "This is a princess." She picked it up and began writing her notes, beginning with Amy Moses's account of the shooting. She had rushed to the school carrying only her purse, portable radio, and gun, and lacking her own notebook, used this one for the rest of the day.

It would soon be lunchtime and Monroe wanted to know from the police if it would be all right for the children to go home as usual. Those in the morning kindergarten session were always released for the day at 11:30 A.M. and badly needed to be comforted by their mothers. Some of them had been deeply affected by the sight of the wounded child who had staggered out of Room

7 into their classroom. Teachers and social workers felt strongly that the psychic damage to these children would be compounded if they were kept indoors much longer. Throughout the school, children were plaintively asking why they couldn't go home. And outside were anxious parents clamoring to be let in.

Herb Timm was adamant.

"No, you cannot let these kids out," he said. "I don't know where this woman is. She could be hiding in the neighborhood, waiting to shoot again. You can't let the parents in, either. This building is a major crime scene, and there are about three hundred and fifty people running around here already. As soon as it's safe to let the kids out I'll tell you. Then I want them to leave a few at a time, in an orderly fashion."

Again the school administration was obliged to defer to the police. Monroe told teachers that the children must remain in their classrooms until the middle of the afternoon. Unaware of how this decision came about, some of the teachers and mental-health specialists were critical.

"I really think he is wrong," Elan Adler remarked to a school social worker.

"So do I," she responded.

As it turned out, the children were best served, emotionally as much as physically, by being kept in school. Before the horror became a memory and the memory even more threatening than the reality, they needed this time together to talk about their fears and grief, to have the consolation of a shared experience, and to be reassured that school was still a safe place. Before they left that Friday, it was essential that they should feel positive about coming back on Monday morning.

Behind the locked doors of their classrooms, teachers tried to soothe the children by playing games with them and reading stories. There was a lot of quiet heroism among these women. Some of them had already risked their lives to protect children. Now they were calm and reassuring, even fearing as they did that the episode in Room 7 might be the beginning of a terrorist attack directed at the entire community. In this unusual school system they had already been given the freedom to follow their own instincts as educators, based upon the administration's respect for their empathy and intelligence. Faced with an emergency for which there were no rules, they justified the trust.

"The teachers were incredible," said Camille Picchietti who rushed to help at the school as soon as she heard of the shooting. She was a part-time special-education teacher, off duty that morning but with no question in her mind about where she belonged in this crisis.

"One teacher asked if I would read to her class while she went outside to catch her breath. She shook for a few minutes, composed herself, then went straight back into the classroom."

Even so, few teachers felt able to talk to the children about what had happened in Room 7 but tried to divert their attention to other topics. That was why the presence of the mental-health specialists became important.

Dr. Mary Giffin often described herself as "a rubbing your nose in the facts kind of psychiatrist." White-haired and grandmotherly, she had spent the last thirty years as medical director of the Irene Josselyn Clinic of the North Shore Mental Health Association, working with emotionally disturbed children. For twenty of those years she had been a professional consultant to the Hubbard Woods School, which was just around the corner from her house on Hamptondale Road. When she came to the north shore from Minnesota, she had decided to live in Winnetka because it impressed her as being quiet and safe, and to buy a house on this particular dead-end street because a quirk of its design was a constant reassurance to her about the village's sense of values. There were two huge old trees which must have been in the way of the original plan for Hamptondale Road, but rather than fell them, the contractors had narrowed and curved the street to accommodate them. And so instead of becoming subservient to the design of this short block, the trees dominated it, a minor hazard for unsuspecting motorists but a sturdy reminder to villagers that Winnetka's priorities were in the right place. Dr. Giffin often thought of this when walking her two dogs, secure in the knowledge that she was part of this caring community.

Her approach to healing troubled minds was just as down-to-earth. When she was called into Hubbard Woods School on the morning of May 20 she immediately determined, over the protests of teachers, that all the children from kindergarten on up should be told exactly what had happened in Room 7.

"Otherwise they will imagine the details," she argued. "Children's fantasies can be much more frightening than the reality, so it's always better to give them the facts."

She had been with a patient at her clinic in Northfield when Donald Monroe's secretary called. Normally she never allowed a consultation to be interrupted, but this call seemed so urgent that her secretary relayed it immediately. Dr. Giffin excused herself, and was at the school in fifteen minutes. The last ambulance had just left and those in charge were trying to collect themselves to determine the next priorities.

"The situation was so overwhelming and immense," Donald Monroe recalled afterward. "While we were trying to assimilate what had happened, we were struggling in our minds as to how we could relate to this incident, how we could bring some control, how we could make this a safe and secure place, what resources we would need, how we would conduct the rest of the school day, how we would distribute all the work that needed to be done."

Mary Giffin's first priority was to spend a few minutes alone with Dick Streedain. He was in shock, devastated by the death of Nicky Corwin and by the experience of carrying Lindsay Fisher to the ambulance, drenched in the blood that was draining away her life. Streedain knew all the children at Hubbard Woods, more than three hundred of them, and regarded every one as special. At this time it seemed likely that some of the wounded ones might also die.

Gently Dr. Giffin told him that he must give this news to the children, class by class; that she would go with him, and that they should begin right away. He moved to put on his jacket, wanting to spare the children the sight of those terrible stains on his shirt, but she dissuaded him. Again she stressed that it was essential for them to comprehend the reality, to feel involved in this violation of their school, to be encouraged in an open discussion of how they felt about it.

Afterward, when they understood the reasoning, parents were glad their children had been told the truth, and that it was Dick Streedain who told them. "He reminds me of people I knew in college in the sixties and seventies: sensitive, humanistic, and liberal," one mother said. "When I was in grade school my principal was someone to be feared. Dick was thought of with great affection throughout the school, and if anyone had to give bad news he was the one to have done it."

Streedain was a tall, slender man of forty-four, gentle and unassuming, with sandy-colored hair which would never sit right but fell in wisps and curls across his forehead. He had a warm and ready smile which was missing that day; instead, there were tears in his eyes.

It took two and three-quarter hours for him and Mary Giffin to make their tour of the classrooms. After a while somebody suggested lunch, and his instinctive reaction was, "Oh, no, the kids will throw up!" Then he realized that he was talking about the queasiness in his own stomach, and was happily surprised when the manager of the local McDonald's, a Hubbard Woods parent, sent in hamburgers, chicken, and French fries, and the children fell upon them.

He began his talk to the youngest ones by reminding them of a favorite picture story by Judith Viorst. Drawing up a child's chair to bring himself to their level, he told them: "Something very bad has happened. You all know about Alexander and the terrible, horrible, no good, very bad day he had. Well, this is much worse than anything that happened to Alexander. This morning a lady came into the school with a gun and shot some of the children in Mrs. Deuble's class. Nicky Corwin is dead. . . ."

Until then the shooting had been a kind of fantasy to those who had not seen it, like a drama played on television. A six-year-old girl in Robert Trossman's class made the comparison: "Robert was in the hallway when this lady came and shot him right through his shirt. He had blood on his back and tummy. I've seen people shot before but only on TV."

The news of Nicky's death made the drama real for children who had not seen any of the shooting. Repeatedly they asked Streedain if he was certain Nicky had died, if there wasn't some way of bringing him back, who was the bad lady who killed him, was she still in the school, what kind of a gun did she have, and what was she wearing. They needed to know not only the facts but the details.

"They had different kinds of defenses," Dr. Giffin remembered. "Some children cried, some wanted to talk more about it, some laughed hysterically, some were panicky, some went to the sink and played with water, some had things to say about Nicky. Those in his class talked about how he had just passed his bicycle-safety test, what a good soccer player he was, how he had written a story which some of the other children were getting typed."

Several other adults were already in the room with these second-grade children. One was Jan Wood, director of Christian education at Christ Episcopal Church, Winnetka, who had responded to the call for clergy helpers. A young mother herself, she already had a warm relationship with some children in the class through their church membership. One of them greeted her by asking: "What are you doing here? Why can't my mommy come in?"

"I walked into that room wondering how I was going to handle it," she said. "But because of the way the children were encouraged to talk, it became an incredible experience. At first they had some confusion about what had happened. Many of them kept saying, 'I thought she was just carrying a toy gun, but it was *real* and she had two of them!' They were still having difficulty believing that she had actually shot some of their friends.

"Most of them did not know that Nicky had died until the principal told them. They had been sitting around, playing, eating lunch, wondering why they couldn't see their mothers, when Dick Streedain and Mary Giffin walked in. They both sat on child's chairs and had the children sit around them, with themselves as part of the circle.

"Dick said to them: 'I have some very, very sad news. The doctors were not able to save Nicky. He probably died before he was taken to the hospital, and I don't think it hurt. We shall all miss him very much. But he has not really gone from us because we shall always think of him. All the other children who were shot are in the hospital. We don't yet know how they are, but they are getting the best attention.'

"Dick cried and they cried. He did not pull any punches or treat them like babies. But he was very gentle with them."

One little boy's immediate reaction seemed inappropriate. He started running around, pointing a finger like a gun and yelling, as though playing cops and robbers. Then he burst into tears. He was one of Nicky's close friends, and it emerged through his sobs that he had been expecting Nicky to sleep over at his house that night. Now his friend was dead, this child was overwhelmed by the thought that somehow he must try to take his place, and be the best at soccer and art and all the other things Nicky had excelled at.

Some of the other children tried to comfort him. "You don't have to be like Nicky," they said. "He loved you the way you are."

"It was a real gift to watch," Jan Wood commented. "As they talked about Nicky's death they came up with the idea that they could finish the storybook that he had begun, that this little boy could take on the direction of the book, and that they could give it to Nicky's parents. Putting this book together was a class effort, but Nicky had written the actual story. They went through all the emotions of feeling their own grief, to helping Nicky's friend understand that he didn't have to be like Nicky in order to be special, to ways in which they could memorialize Nicky and show their concern to his family. There was a real sense among them that he had not gone. Here were these little kids wrestling with these enormous concepts and coming up with their own solutions. It was amazing."

After Dick Streedain and Mary Giffin had moved on to another classroom, the children broke up into little groups, played for a while, helped themselves to the popcorn someone had sent in, munched on it contentedly, then reverted to their memories of the shooting.

"They were dipping in and out of the tragedy," Jan Wood said. "I think they understood death like we all do, and were as overwhelmed by it. They understood that they would never see Nicky again, and that death is final, and then they would begin to process this, to say, 'That's it, he is never coming back.' And they would grieve all over again."

Eventually the children kept their promise about finishing Nicky's book, and about giving it to his parents. It is the story of a group of fanciful animal characters, written and illustrated with the imagination and charm of an unusually talented child.

The story has its villain, a character named Dirty Dan, who deliberately shoots two of the animals while they are playing tag.

Everyone is very sad at their funerals. But then Dirty Dan dies, and the remaining animals rejoice. "And after that nothing bad ever happened to them," Nicky wrote. "They lived happily ever after."

His story seemed hauntingly prophetic. Not just because of the senseless shooting of innocent creatures at play. Or even the tragic funeral, in reality his own. But the name of the villain, Dirty Dan. Laurie Dann. The coincidence was uncanny.

NINE

SOON AFTER the shooting a police line was drawn around the school. Yards of yellow tape were wound from tree to tree, encircling the building like string around a package. CRIME SCENE. DO NOT CROSS it read. For months afterward that exclusionary yellow tape, isolating the school from the surrounding neighborhood, was one of the strongest memories many people retained of Hubbard Woods School that day. The children could see it from their classroom windows, and were bewildered. Waiting across the street, their parents were frustrated by this line they were forbidden to cross. By noon about two hundred of them had gathered, some angrily demanding, "Give us our children!" Rumors were spreading that more than one child might have been killed, and some parents were getting distraught.

Dr. Ronald Rozensky, a clinical psychologist and senior member of the Evanston Hospital crisis-intervention team, said that whenever he recalled the events of May 20, he had a visual memory of elbowing his way through this anguished crowd to the other side of the yellow tape barrier. That, and of being met by the school superintendent and principal in their bloody shirts, standing in the school's crowded hallway near a terra-cotta statue of two happy children, with all the turmoil of police and teachers going on around them. More than anything else he saw that day, it was the juxtaposition of yellow tape and that innocent terra-cotta statue which stayed in his mind.

"What can we do to help?" he asked, and was struck by the fact that instead of answering the question, the school officials began asking him for direction.

The team's leader, Dr. Ira Sloan, director of Evanston Hospital's department of psychiatry, walked into an even more poignant scene. In response to his hospital's emergency call, he had canceled the rest of his day's appointments, taken his own car, and headed north along the lake road toward Winnetka. He did not know where in the village to find Hubbard Woods School, yet some instinct guided him there, without a single detour or wrong turning. He arrived shortly after Dr. Rozensky and other members of their team, and was immediately taken to Room 7. There was no reason for him to enter that classroom—all the children had been removed—and he had a sudden strong aversion to seeing the scene of the crime. But the police were eager to show him and he did not want to seem uncaring.

Afterward he regretted going into the room because he could not get the image out of his mind. It kept coming back to him like a bad dream in Technicolor, this memory of children's torn clothing lying in bloody puddles across the floor and all those little orange chairs of molded plastic spattered with more of their blood. As a psychiatrist, Ira Sloan was skilled in helping people heal from the effects of trauma. But once he entered Room 7 he became personally involved in the Hubbard Woods shooting, and was unable to resolve his own feelings about it for many months, not until long after he had finished helping everyone else.

"It was such a dramatic image, the kind that goes through all your defenses and leaves a lot of emotion," he said.

That day his priority was to guide the school officials through the next few hours. Some of his team members went out into the crowd of anguished parents; some were assigned to the other schools in Winnetka, where bewildered children were being kept behind locked doors and not yet told the reason why. A message had already gone to the Chicago restaurant where, on their class trip through the city's ethnic neighborhoods, the fourth and fifth graders were having lunch. Their teachers were told not to take the children back to Hubbard Woods, but to Washburne Junior High School in another part of Winnetka. It was essential for mental-health specialists to meet these older children as they arrived, especially since one of them was Michael Corwin, Nicky's brother.

At Hubbard Woods School there remained the problems of keeping the children calm, the parents reassured, and the two groups apart until the police determined that the streets were safe for them to go home together. Streedain and Monroe prepared to go outside, beyond the yellow tape, to explain what was happening. Both men seemed to have lost cognizance of how they looked, and had to be reminded to change their bloody shirts for the clean ones which a school-board member had thoughtfully delivered.

"A crisis-intervention specialist needs to give directives," Dr. Sloan explained. "People in crisis use up so much energy trying to stay calm and to control their emotions that they often forget to take care of basic needs, like having something to eat before they pass out from exhaustion. Rather like a ventriloquist, you need to stand next to them and make minimal suggestions to do things they would normally think of themselves. The parents would have been even more panic-stricken if they had seen the bloodstains on Dick Streedain's shirt, and I suggested that he should change it before going out and talking to them. But it was as though he kept forgetting."

After they had been at the school, for a few hours, even some of the members of Dr. Sloan's team became so stressed that they, too, needed reminders. Jeffrey Berkson, a senior social worker from Evanston Hospital, recalled being confronted by a woman colleague in the late afternoon.

"She told me, 'You have to eat something.' I just looked at her and said, 'What do you mean? I'm too busy.'

"'You have to,' she said. 'You don't look so good.' And she stuffed a cheeseburger at me. There was a big box of food from McDonald's but I had not even thought about eating."

No one on the Evanston Hospital team had ever dealt with a disaster of this magnitude. Most of its members were social workers experienced in handling domestic crises, troubled teen-agers, sudden bereavements, and potential suicides. But as one carload of them drove up to Hubbard Woods School, Berkson heard a Winnetka policeman tell a colleague, "Let these people through. They belong to the Evanston Hospital trauma team."

"I had never heard us described in that phrase before," Berkson commented. "But the name existed from that moment, and has stuck ever since." Within an hour of the shooting there were about twenty of the hospital's crisis workers at the school, those who were normally on call as well as senior members of the Department of Psychiatry.

Before leaving Evanston Hospital, Dr. Rozensky and some of his colleagues had stopped to talk to the paramedics who had brought badly injured children to the emergency room.

"None of the paramedics was allowed to leave the hospital until we had been debriefed," John Fay remembered. "It was the first time I had ever met with a counselor, but before getting back in the ambulance and returning to the scene it was a great relief to be allowed to say how I felt about taking those terribly wounded little girls to the emergency room, and how I wondered whether I had done the right thing by not hooking up an IV. Ron Rozensky was very comforting and encouraged us to talk about our feelings. One of the hardest things about being in uniform is that you are not supposed to hurt in front of other people; you are supposed to be taking control."

The Evanston specialists understood this dilemma. Fifteen years earlier Dr. Sloan had modeled his crisis-intervention team in such a way that when the Hubbard Woods tragedy happened, it was automatically recognized that the team's work would need to go beyond the boundaries of the school, to the police, para-medics, doctors, nurses, teachers: everyone who had been emo-tionally involved. There is a widespread perception that professionals become so inured to violence and death that they are able to put an ugly experience behind them at the end of a working day. Ira Sloan and his colleagues already knew that these people might need therapeutic counseling for months to come.

Even the clergy had a hard time dealing with the tragedy. For the Reverend Richard Augspurger, director of Winnetka's in-terfaith counseling center, Institute for Living, it triggered the memory of his mother's violent death twenty-four years earlier.

She had been killed in an automobile accident when he was a student teacher. He had no recollection of the three-hour drive to his parents' home, except that he made it, so angry and tearful that to this day he did not know how or why he arrived safely. Now he experienced the same feelings. "I was shaky, angry, sad, and then I went to the school and did what I wished my own pastor had done back then. I tried to help people."

Seeing that the children were being taken care of, most of the clergy moved among the crowd of anxious parents, seeking out their own parishioners and talking to whoever else needed comfort. Village President Clarine Hall carried away a warm memory of Father Thomas Ventura of Saints Faith, Hope and Charity Catholic Church gathering a circle of teachers, aides, and others in the school hall and leading them, with linked hands, in prayer.

"I joined in," she said. "The quiet strength of the clergy helped us all that day."

Father Ventura felt less confident about his function at the school. "I did not know exactly what they wanted me to do or why I was there," he related. "Like everyone else, I was in a state of shock that anything like this could happen. Talking with parents outside the school I saw a lot of frustration. They felt besieged, gathered together like a lot of covered wagons with the Indians all around."

All of the clergy were uncomfortably aware of the yellow tape which they could cross and parents couldn't. Some of them ran messages between the street and the classrooms. "Andy, please find out if my little girl is all right," a woman parishioner called out to the Reverend Andrew Dietsche of Christ Episcopal Church. He did, and she was, but it had been a close call. The child's best friend was seriously injured.

The Reverend David Goodman of Winnetka Bible Church was impressed that, despite their anxiety, parents obediently stayed behind the yellow tape. "It was very traumatic for them," he said. "They felt their children were being held hostage in the school."

Herded into the little park across the street, some parents were becoming increasingly hostile to the reporters and photographers, demanding that they leave. Winnetkans were not used to being in the news; much of their investment in living here was to be protected from the intrusions of the outside world. Now, without even asking whether they minded, the media had descended upon their village, setting up television cameras outside their neighborhood school as though they owned the place. Some had the nerve to push microphones in front of people's faces and to ask how they felt about the school being violated. Surely it was the police's job to keep unwelcome elements out of the area. Yet here was Herbert Timm in a role they had never seen him in before, let alone envisaged for their police chief, taking command of the situation in a highly professional manner, resisting their demands to be let into the school, telling them in a quietly authoritative tone that the reporters had a right to be here, and that although he would ask them to be respectful he would not order them out. Some parents thought this was insupportable, and vociferously told him so.

"You don't know what you're doing!" they yelled.

Others insisted: "We demand that you prevent the press from talking to the parents of these kids."

Afterward Timm commented: "These are people who are used to getting their way. There was a lot of anger out there."

Donald Monroe came to his rescue. "Let me assure you we shall do everything we can," he told parents. Timm smiled to himself, knowing that the media was here to stay. But he appreciated the school superintendent's intervention.

Pastor Goodman had his own conflicting feelings about the reporters and cameramen. "They were doing their job, but they can't help shaping an event simply by being there. None of us was ready to deal with this. I knew right away that this event would shake us up for a long time afterward. But we did not expect to be front-page news across the United States. The media did not behave badly, but their sheer presence changed things. I understand the dynamic because all of a sudden, in the midst of the tragedy, there was a temptation to seize this opportunity in your own best interests, for publicity for your church. If like me you are not used to the media, you find yourself almost rehearsing what you will say if a reporter asks. That is why I avoided the cameras when I walked out of the school, because I was uncomfortable with my motives and felt this ambivalence."

Others who were allowed on the school side of the yellow tape included three parents who were physicians, all of whom showed up voluntarily. They asked the same question as the Evanston therapists.

"What can we do to help?"

"I'm not sure, but I'm glad you're here," Don Monroe replied as he ushered them in. He was thinking there might be children in shock.

Dr. Abby Adams, an attending pediatrician at Evanston Hospital, found herself a job of enormous value. By keeping in telephone contact with the head of the pediatric intensive-care unit, who knew her well, she was able to relay information about the wounded children to the school staff. At that time the four children who had been taken to Evanston were still in surgery, but their chances of survival seemed hopeful. "I used whatever phone I could find free, and called about every hour," she said. Jeffrey Berkson passed on the news to the crowd outside. These regular bulletins helped parents to feel less excluded, and prevented worse rumors from spreading. One pervasive story shared among the crowd was that the criminal was a black baby-sitter who had run amok. It was unthinkable that she might be one of their own kind.

Meantime, children in the school who knew Dr. Adams were asking her questions she could not answer: Will the bad lady go to jail? Is she locked up already? Where is my mom? When can I see her?

Through all this she kept remembering how she had been at the school only the previous day at 10:30 A.M., the same time as the shooting, in the next classroom to Room 7. About twice a week, as her work allowed, she was in the habit of dropping in to observe the mixed second- and third-grade class in which her daughter Hannah was enrolled. "I would watch for a few minutes, then leave. The children were so used to visitors that they never paid any attention. That was what was so wonderful about the way this school was run. It was like observing the class through a one-way mirror, without even your own child noticing you."

Having done this so often herself, Abby Adams fully understood why Laurie Dann was not questioned when she walked into Room 7, and why the children were not disconcerted by her presence. Some of them were now telling the therapists that even when Laurie drew a gun they mistook her for an Officer Friendly, one of the police visitors who made periodic visits to local schools to talk about street safety.

100

What troubled Dr. Adams was the question: What if she herself had been in the school on the twentieth, instead of at the same time on the nineteenth? Could she have saved Nicky Corwin? Could she have done more than the paramedics were able to do for the other children? In her heart she knew the negative response, but the questions would plague her for months. Even recognizing the outcome to be hopeless, she knew she too would have insisted on taking Nicky to a hospital after the police chief had pronounced him dead; she too would have made heroic attempts to revive him.

"If I had been there I would have tried with Nicky, even knowing he had no heartbeat," she said. "I deal with the death of children all the time, and it is never easy. But in most of the cases I see the parents have time to get used to the idea, and to say good-bye. I cannot imagine anything more terrible than the unexpected and violent death of a child. And Nicky was a child who had a special glow about him."

When she had finished at the school, Abby Adams went home and tried to put on a cheerful face for her youngest child's second birthday. He had been promised a treat and was waiting to be entertained. At the same time she tried to comfort Hannah, who had been frightened by hearing the gunfire from her classroom, and by the panic she had seen in the hallways.

"We had my son's birthday party the next day," she said. "He was too young to know what was happening, and it was good for the other children to have something to celebrate."

The other group operating from the school, the police, was having a very hard time. Even with the portable phones they had brought in, there was not enough telephone equipment. The school switchboard was jammed by incoming calls from reporters, from parents, even from villagers curious to know what was going on. There was a transatlantic call from a parent who, on a business trip to London, had heard of the shooting with remarkable speed. There were calls from newspapers as far away as Germany and Australia. There were fathers telephoning from their Chicago offices, insisting that their wives be let into the classrooms. Repeatedly saying no to them became so distressing to one school secretary that she collapsed in tears.

The principal's office was a confusion of people coming and

going. Police, teachers, social workers, clergy. His own officers kept asking Herbert Timm for direction. "Chief, what shall we do about this? How do you want us to organize that?" There was an urgent need to call in more police from the surrounding villages, and to set up roadblocks to hold back the influx of unauthorized cars. Desperate for news of their children, parents were leaving Volvos and Jaguars blocking the streets, some with their engines running.

In the middle of this chaos Timm kept reminding himself that this was a murder case and that clues must not be obliterated by all these people running around. At one point somebody came up to him and said, "I am working with the FBI. Would you like me to call them?"

"Call anybody," Timm responded. "Call the marines if you like."

Outwardly he was calm, organized, and in command. But the stress was beginning to show around his eyes, and there were cramps in his stomach. He had seen plenty of violent crime in his earlier experience as a Chicago police officer, but there had not been a murder in Winnetka since 1957, long before his time here as police chief. That murder was so shocking that more than thirty years later people still talked about it: the random shooting of a police patrolman by a deranged hitchhiker who pulled out a gun when told to move on. The hitchhiker then shot himself. Both men died instantly, depriving the village police of the satisfaction of a trial. A memorial photograph of Officer Robert E. Burke, young, promising, and dutiful, hung in the main lobby of the police department, a constant reminder to Herbert Timm and his staff that even in Winnetka there are risks to being a policeman.

He knew that this new crime might not be so easy to solve, and that the demands for justice would be more vociferous. Winnetkans had a phrase for it—"Children are our most prized possessions"—as though their offspring belonged on the same list as their architect-designed homes and custom-made furnishings. That wasn't true, of course; it was the choice of words that jarred, yet they carried the accurate implication that Winnetka children were valued differently from youngsters in Chicago housing projects, who were at constant risk of being randomly shot. The me-

dia's massive descent upon Winnetka and its passing interest in
the projects validated the judgment. The message was that if this
could happen in Winnetka, it could happen anywhere, and from
the number of press people here this message would undoubtedly
go around the world. Timm knew the consequences for his department if this investigation was bungled.

As he stood by the school entrance, worrying about which
priority to tackle next, Fire Chief Ron Colpaert remarked that his
men at the house fire on Forest Glen Drive had learned that a
baby-sitter named Laurie was somehow involved. Now she could
not be found.

"Maybe the two incidents are related," he suggested.

Timm doubted it. He had almost forgotten the fire.

"I thought the fire department was just trying to get into the
act," he said later.

Police Officer Richard Carlson, the first policeman to reach
the scene, was the one who wrapped that memorable yellow tape
around the school. When he had almost finished winding it
around trees and street signs, a message came through on his police radio from Detective Floyd Mohr of Glencoe. Mohr had put
out the emergency traffic signal for everyone else to get off the
air because he wanted to broadcast some information of great importance. He sounded breathless and excited.

"I believe I know the name of the offender," he said. "I
believe her name is Laurie Dann, otherwise Laurie Wasserman,
otherwise Laurie Porter, and she lives in Glencoe."

He described two automobiles, either of which she might be
driving. One was a blue Honda, the other a white sedan, also
Japanese, with the license plate NW 000.

"I was trying to write that on my note pad while I was walking around the school putting up the tape," Carlson stated. "As
I was finishing, Patrolman Craig Tisdale came up to me and said,
'Talk to this guy over here.' He was a workman, working on the
outside of one of the houses in the area. He told me he had seen
a small white car roar past him and into Hamptondale, and that
it had not come out."

Hamptondale Road was the short dead-end street near the
school where Dr. Mary Giffin lived, the street that curved around

two huge trees in such a way that no driver could navigate it in a hurry. As soon as Carlson began to walk down it he saw fresh skid marks leading to a sapling which had recently been knocked down. A little farther on, half hidden in a private driveway, its engine still running, was a white Toyota Cressida with the Illinois license plate NW 000. Whoever had abandoned it had tried to make a fast turn in the driveway, hitting a boulder which immobilized the car. Carlson took a cursory look inside it and saw a quantity of ammunition, incendiary devices, and the ingredients of homemade napalm. Ducking behind a tree he radioed police headquarters for help.

Later, when the sequence of events became clearer, he realized that it must have been his direction of the funeral traffic which prevented Laurie Dann from making her getaway onto Tower Road. Unexpectedly held back by Carlson instead of by the traffic light, she panicked, turned back down Gordon Terrace, then into Hamptondale Road, expecting this to be another way out of Winnetka. But there she met the bend in the street and the dead end and the boulder which would force her to run into the woods where Detective Bob Kerner had already been searching for her.

TEN

DETECTIVE FLOYD Mohr knew the white Toyota well. He also knew Laurie's own car, the blue Honda. Often when he drove along Sheridan Road, Glencoe, on radio patrol, he would see them parked in the driveway of her parents' home, and it always struck him that they did not fit into the local landscape.

"You just know if a car belongs or not," he observed. "Most people on Sheridan Road would have a Cadillac, a Mercedes, a few Porsches. The Wassermans lived differently."

Sheridan Road starts south of Evanston and meanders along the shore of Lake Michigan through Wilmette, Kenilworth, Winnetka, Glencoe, Highland Park, and Lake Forest. There are subtle changes in the ethnic composition of these villages as the road runs north, from the comfortable cosmopolitan style of Evanston through the WASPishness of Kenilworth and Winnetka, to the heavily Jewish neighborhoods of Glencoe and Highland Park, where the Danns and the Wassermans had established themselves. As a Glencoe resident expressed it: "Most Jews would rather live in Winnetka, but they are more comfortable in Glencoe and Highland Park."

In all these lakeshore villages, Sheridan Road is the best address, implying a generous slice of waterfront property, which the Wassermans, who lived on the west side of the street, didn't have. Neither did they own an architectural gem like one of the Frank Lloyd Wright houses that people from Chicago drive up on weekends to photograph, or simply stare at. Though substantial, the Wassermans' fieldstone ranch was smaller than its neighbors, had no architectural merit, and a yard that was bleakly landscaped. It was as though Norman and Edith Wasserman were content to have arrived in this prestigious place, with no mind or taste for any of the trimmings. The cars parked on their driveway belonged to their undistinguished house rather than to the distinguished neighborhood. The well-kept Toyota Cressida would have fit into an old-money village like Winnetka, where ostentation is frowned upon. But not on Sheridan Road, Glencoe, parked alongside a six-year-old Honda Accord with an interior like a rat's nest. The combination wasn't right, and with the sharp insight of a policeman, Floyd Mohr noted this and fretted over its meaning.

Over the past two years he had had several meetings with Laurie, and every one of them bothered him. She struck him as lonely, lost, and defenseless, yet something about her made him feel uncomfortable—he could never quite tell what. She claimed to have been a crime victim more times than the law of averages allowed, reporting burglaries and assaults to which there were no other witnesses. Every story she told could have been true, but the way she told it raised unanswerable questions.

Mohr's first contact with Laurie followed a reported burglary at the Wassermans' home on April 25, 1986. She had lived there intermittently after separating from Russell six months earlier, and was often alone in the house. In his middle fifties, her father had semi-retired from his accountancy business and, with her mother, spent a lot of time in Boca Raton, Florida, where they owned a condominium. Russell Dann was still living at the marital home on Hastings Avenue, Highland Park, and Laurie had access to it while a divorce was being negotiated. According to her report to the Glencoe police, she left her parents' home at 10:45 A.M. to do some errands, and returned at 12:55 P.M. to find the place ransacked. The front door was ajar and the television set from her parents' bedroom was sitting on the front step. In all three bedrooms the contents of drawers were scattered across the floor; a video tape recorder and a few items of Laurie's jewelry were said to be missing. She claimed that fifty dollars in bills had been taken from an envelope, and that a plastic water-cooler bottle filled with one thousand dollars' worth of quarters had been emptied. The worst mess was in her bedroom. Among the strewn clothing was her white-leather wedding-photo album with Laurie's bridal pictures scattered around, some of them ripped in pieces.

The first Glencoe policeman on the scene was John Fay (the officer who, two years later, in his role as a paramedic, would take Lindsay Fisher to the hospital). Fay felt sympathetic to Laurie but was uncomfortable with her story. There were no signs of forced entry and he could not understand why a burglar would take the time to tear up photographs, yet fail to remove a TV set he had carried as far as the doorstep.

"That's my husband, Russell," Laurie told him, pointing to one of the wedding pictures. She gave him the impression that she was happily married.

He guessed that the damage had been done by someone she knew, a person she had argued with, whose identity she did not want to reveal.

"She was very timid, quiet, and confused," he said. "I thought she was hurting."

Because of the inconsistencies in Laurie's police report, Detective Floyd Mohr was called in. He found her to be "a very calm, peaceful little girl who seemed believable." But he too doubted her story. What he saw in the Wasserman house was not evidence of the way burglars usually operate. Most of the obviously valuable items had not been touched. It also struck him that if a thief wanted to take four thousand quarters out of a plastic container, he would slash it open with a knife rather than slowly shake out the money, a few coins at a time.

Laurie was more frank with Mohr about her relations with her husband, hinting that he might have been the intruder who defaced her wedding pictures. Mohr then interviewed Russell Dann, who gave permission for a police search of his Highland Park house. This revealed nothing. Russell told him that Laurie had emotional problems throughout their marriage, and suggested that she had invented the burglary to draw attention to herself and to get back at him. Mohr telephoned Norman Wasserman in Florida, who appeared to believe his daughter's account and wanted to be assured that she was all right. That seemed to be as far as the police could go. The case was left open.

Two weeks later Russell reported to the Highland Park police, who shared the information with their colleagues in Glencoe, that Laurie had bought a gun. Months hence, with a hindsight he lacked at the time, Floyd Mohr would speculate that she might have staged the burglary not only to cast suspicion on Russell but also to justify arming herself. It seemed all wrong to him for this fragile ninety-seven-pound girl to own a handgun that was heavier and more powerful than the weapon he carried in the line of duty, a Smith and Wesson .357 Magnum, the very gun which two years later she would discard in a boys' bathroom at Hubbard Woods School because she could not make it work, a gun which could have blown dozens of children to pieces.

Russell's story was almost as strange as hers had been. He said that a friend at his country club happened to be in the Marksman Gun Shop in Glenview at the same time as Laurie, and saw her make the purchase. This seemed an unlikely coincidence but Russell's report checked out. The Marksman was six miles from Glencoe, the nearest gun shop in the area, and its records showed that on May 10, 1986, Laurie had bought the .357 and one hundred rounds of ammunition, at a total cost of $344.01. She told a salesman that her home had been robbed, and that she needed a gun for self-protection. There was nothing illegal about her purchase. In the state of Illinois any adult who has a FOID card (Firearm Owner's Identification) may buy a gun. Application for a card simply requires proof of state residence, along with a notarized statement that the applicant has never been convicted of a crime, is not under indictment or a fugitive from justice, is not drug addicted, and has never been committed to a mental institution. Laurie answered a truthful "no" to all these questions, and after a routine police check her application was approved. The fact that she had been treated by a psychiatrist was not an issue. Having learned this from Russell, Mohr called Dr. Robert Greendale at his office in Highland Park.

"Doctor, in your opinion, could she be homicidal or suicidal?" he asked.

The psychiatrist thought not. "But he would not give me any hint of her condition," Mohr said. "He said the only way I could get that confidential information was with her approval. Now I look back I think she may have fooled him. She fooled a lot of people.

"It bothered me that she had a gun. I worried about it being misused or accidentally discharged. I was not raised with guns. If I were not a police officer I would never own one. I called her on the phone and said, 'Laurie, I don't think you should have that gun. I don't think guns are safe. Say you are burglarized, most likely the intruder would grab it from you. Then you could really get hurt.'

"She said she had a valid FOID card which gave her the right to own a gun. I checked with the guy at the gun shop, who said he had told her about an indoor range in Waukegan where she could practice. I tried to find out whether she had been there, but they didn't keep records.

"I called Norman Wasserman again, and told him that his daughter had a gun. He was kind of surprised, but felt she might need it for self-protection after the burglary. On one of his visits to Glencoe I saw the two of them at the house. Laurie kept saying that Russell was trying to make her look crazy, and her father agreed. He said that everything was fine with his daughter before Russell came along.

"Over the next few months I had eight or ten conversations with Laurie, trying to persuade her to put her gun away. And I had several more meetings with her father. Her mother was always in the background. Norman Wasserman was very protective of his daughter, agreeing with her that she needed a gun. But I'm sure he did not own one himself. He said he hated guns."

Russell Dann reacted by asking the Highland Park police to keep a close watch on his Hastings Avenue house and on the homes of his parents, his sister, Susie Taylor, and his brother, Scott Dann, all in the same village. He admitted that Laurie had never harmed anyone, but said he thought her capable of irrational behavior.

The police promised to do so, but did not seem seriously concerned. This was the kind of tale they heard all too often: marital allegations that he did this to her, and she threatened that to him. Divorce negotiations are complex along the north shore because the financial stakes are so high, and village police officers are often called into fractured households to hear charges of mistreatment, not because the complainants fear for their safety but because each partner is documenting evidence for a lawsuit against the other. In the private estimation of the police, such calls belong with the demands to drive home a drunken executive or to remove a raccoon from the attic. But they have to be answered. Laurie's report of a burglary seemed of a piece with the rest of them, this unlikely tale of an intruder who seemed to have entered the house with a latchkey, intent upon ruining her wedding pictures.

It became even less believable to the Glencoe police when their Highland Park colleagues revealed that seventeen days before reporting the burglary at her parents' home, Laurie had called them to her Hastings Avenue house where, she alleged, Russell had kicked her in the stomach, slapped her in the face, twisted her legs, and verbally abused her. She had no visible marks of assault and declined to sign a complaint against him. He denied her charges, and the Highland Park police noted that such complaints were "an ongoing problem" in the Dann household.

Russell Dann, however, feared for his life. Once he knew that Laurie owned a gun, he moved out of the Hastings Avenue house and rented a small townhouse in a condominium complex near the Highland Park shopping district. His sister signed the lease, hoping this would prevent Laurie from discovering his address. Nevertheless, Russell reported seeing Laurie outside his building early one morning, wearing an outfit with a revealing halter top. By that time he had a girlfriend, and she had begun to receive anonymous, threatening phone calls at her Chicago office. A few weeks later, in the early hours of September 30, 1986, Russell called the Highland Park police and told a story that struck them as too strange to be believed.

He said that at about 3:00 A.M. he awoke, screaming, in crippling pain. He staggered to the bathroom, groggily wondering whether he was having a heart attack, turned on a light, and saw a small stab wound on the left side of his chest. Back in his bedroom, fumbling for the telephone, he looked around. On the floor by the headboard there was an ice pick he had never seen before.

110

Immediately he thought of Laurie and the suicide threat she made during a recent quarrel. "Russ, if I go, you are going with me. And don't tell me that isn't true love." Recently he had missed his spare house keys, with no recollection of losing them.

"Oh, shit," he said.

Gasping for breath, and in shock, he called the police. Shortly after the officers and paramedics arrived he was at odds with them. At thirty, Russell was excitable and talkative, with the assertiveness of a man who knows exactly where he belongs in north shore society. That is what came across to the police, more strongly than a critical need for medical treatment. Russell was in excellent physical condition from hours regularly spent on the tennis courts of his country club, and although his wound was an inch deep, it was barely visible externally. Right now he seemed more concerned with accusing his ex-wife of trying to kill him. He was also scared, and fear made him argumentative.

As he recalled the conversation: "When I began talking to the police it was with the utmost respect. But then they started asking me questions like was I seeing someone, had I been drinking, was I doing drugs. They wanted me to sign things. I had a punctured lung, I could barely walk, and these guys were acting like the Keystone Kops. So I said to them, 'Guys, get the fuck out of my house,' and I called my brother to come and help me."

This did not endear him to the Highland Park police. Nor them to him. He felt he knew their prejudice. "It's this whole socioeconomic thing. These police see me with my four-hundred-thousand-dollar house and my thirty-thousand-dollar car with a phone in it, and when I try to tell them my wife tried to kill me, they think it's just a case of two north shore rich kids who can't get their act together."

Scott Dann arrived before the police left, and confirmed that his brother always slept so heavily that it might take an earthquake to wake him. Nevertheless, Russell's story did not seem credible. He was alleging that his attacker had entered by the front door, gone across the living room and up a flight of stairs, stabbed him, and left by the same route without being seen or heard. Moreover, according to Russell, this person had left an incredible number of clues in the living room: a brown ski mask, an aerosol can of mace, a glass cutter, a flashlight, gloves and a pair of women's sneakers. Russell insisted that none of these items was his, nor were they there when he went to bed at midnight. He thought the sneakers were Laurie's.

Scott drove his brother to the emergency room at Highland Park Hospital, where the attending physician, Dr. Mark Jalakas, thought Russell's story too bizarre to be true. Although the stab wound was small, it was deep enough to have punctured a lung, and potentially dangerous. Around it were some scratches and abrasions which looked like hesitation marks. Dr. Jalakas reasoned that if these had been made by an assailant, Russell would surely have wakened in time to see his attacker. Noting that he was right-handed, the doctor stated in his report that the wound could have been self-inflicted. This struck him as the only plausible explanation.

The police accepted it, and there is no record of their checking on Laurie's whereabouts until several hours after Russell was stabbed. Then she vehemently denied any part in the incident. Before ordering the police off his premises, Russell had handed over to them the keys to his Hastings Avenue house, where Laurie still stayed from time to time, but they did not enter it until the next evening, after Russell was released from the hospital. Then he and Scott insisted on taking the police there.

Laurie was not in the house. The bedroom she used was a mess, with an unmade bed and assorted items scattered around it. Among them was her FOID card and a paper bag. Russell drew the detectives' attention to the bag, as though he already knew what it contained. At least, that's how his gesture struck them. Inside the bag was a recent receipt from Eckart's hardware store in Winnetka. Ignoring the police warning to leave the searching to them, Russell and Scott rummaged around and found another bag containing the wrapper for an ice pick, with an Eckart's sale tag.

"What's the matter, don't they send you guys to cop school?" Russell demanded. "Look what we found in the other bag. See, we're doing your job for you."

Forever after there would be a dispute between the police and the Dann brothers about how the receipt and the sale tag got into Laurie's room. Did Russell find them or plant them? Nothing could ever be proved because the detectives had erred in letting the brothers go through the house ahead of them. Police inquiries at Eckart's produced two salesmen, aged twenty-nine and thirty, who recalled a casually dressed young woman with long brown hair, the same color and style as Laurie's, coming into the store to buy a glass cutter eight days before Russell was stabbed. They remembered her vividly—indeed, she had been the subject of a spirited conversation between them after she left because of the absence of a bra under her pink shirt, and the sinuous movement of her breasts. They could not describe her features, having focused their attention below her chin, but one of them thought she might have been the same woman who purchased an ice pick from him several days earlier.

All this was reported to Detective Floyd Mohr, who added it to his file of circumstantial evidence on Laurie Dann, none of it strong enough for police action.

"I became obsessed with the case, and often discussed it with my supervisor," he said. "Something was not right about it. In fact, nothing was right. How many times would you happen to have a friend in a gun store at the same time as your wife is buying a weapon, or be stabbed in the night and not see the attacker? And yet it is possible. I can sleep through thunder and lightning, although I'm sure I'd wake up the instant somebody stabbed me. Then there was the story of the burglary with no entry marks. Why would a real burglar want to rip wedding pictures? These were questions I kept asking myself: Is she crazy or is he? Is she trying to make him look crazy, or is he doing it to her? I went back and forth, back and forth, like a ball in a tennis game, and could not come up with the answers."

Russell Dann had questions, too. "What was the motivation for me to stab myself? And if I was trying, would I miss my heart by half an inch? And if I wanted to frame Laurie, why wouldn't I say I saw her in my bedroom with the ice pick? It would have been so easy, my word against hers, the same as it is now. Think of what the police believe happened, and think of how I could have pulled it off. I buy an ice pick and go home and wound myself with it. Then I arrange for the receipt to be found in Laurie's room. Think of me going to all that trouble when all I need to say is 'I saw her do it.' But I didn't say that because I have always told the truth."

113

Russell's overt contempt for the village police and their earlier involvement in his unraveling marriage had lost him his credibility. There was also what he called this socioeconomic thing, and it worked both ways.

"I am in the same age group as Russell and Laurie, but I could not relate to them," Floyd Mohr admitted. "In their income bracket people happily pay twenty thousand dollars to join a country club. I came from a small New York town and went to a state college. It was a different social background, another world."

After he was stabbed Russell moved out of the townhouse into his brother's home. For the next twenty months, until the night of the Hubbard Woods shooting, he never got into his car without looking around it first, never drove anywhere without frequently glancing in the rearview mirror, never sat in a lighted room without the curtains drawn, never let people know where he was living, never felt safe.

ELEVEN

THE STATE'S attorney for Lake County ruled that there was not enough evidence to prosecute Laurie Dann for stabbing her husband. It was all too circumstantial. Highland Park's police chief agreed. There was no proof that Laurie was the woman who bought the ice pick at Eckart's; even if there had been, there was no proof that it was the ice pick used on Russell. It was hard to imagine how she could have obtained a key to his home unless he gave it to her, or, if she really did try to murder him, how Russell failed to see her the instant he was stabbed. In the neighboring village of Glencoe, hearing about the case at second hand, Detective Floyd Mohr saw no reason to question this judgment. Laurie looked so frail and vulnerable that he thought of her as more depressed than dangerous, thrown off balance by an imminent divorce which would leave an enormous void in her life.

After the stabbing report, he had several more conversations with Laurie and her father, reiterating his concern about her ownership of a gun. Eventually they promised him that Laurie would deposit the .357 Magnum and its ammunition in a safe at the

Harris Bank in Glencoe. Mohr pestered them to show him the bank receipt, but was refused. He could go no further. If Laurie had been indicted she would have had to relinquish her gun. But Mohr was just as skeptical of Russell's story as his Highland Park colleagues had been. He did not warm to Laurie, she wasn't his kind, but he never thought of her as a potential murderer. It was always her suicide he feared.

North shore policemen are a gentler breed than most, but even among them Floyd Mohr was unusually sensitive. He was a quiet man in his early thirties, tall and athletic, who had studied agronomy in college. After moving from his hometown of Peeks-kill, New York, to be near his brother in Illinois, he soon discov-ered there wasn't much financial future in working for a north shore park district. So he answered an advertisement for a job in Glencoe's Public Safety Department, attracted by the idea of combining the jobs of policeman, firefighter, and paramedic. Ini-tially, the ambulance work appealed to him most, but to his own surprise he showed a natural aptitude for police detection, and this became his specialty. He put a lot of time into his cases, sometimes taking them too much to heart for his own comfort. His involvement with Laurie was to last more than two years, causing him more stress than all the other cases in his experience put together: the man who bludgeoned his father to death, the sexual assaults on children, a variety of gory accidents and sui-cides. Whenever he thought he had done with Laurie, she would come back into his life, at the heart of a new tale which stretched his credulity and left her blameless.

Shortly after Russell's stabbing, the anonymous telephone calls began. Some came to his father, Armand Dann, some to his brother, but most to his sister and her husband. In tracing a call back to the Hastings Avenue house and getting Laurie arrested, the Taylors hoped to make the Highland Park police take a harder look at the cause of Russell's chest wound. Now Laurie would have to be fingerprinted, and with luck her prints would match those on the ice pick which had stabbed Russell.

To protect himself from further charges from Laurie, Russell had hired a Highland Park attorney, Richard Kessler, who was a contemporary of his and a friend of the Taylors. Kessler readily understood the police's problem with his client. He explained: "Russell is aggressive, tense, highly competitive, and always comes across that way. The impression I got from the Highland Park police was that he was an asshole and a liar who was trying to blame Laurie for an injury he had done to himself. As I got to know him and to understand Laurie's vindictiveness toward him, I became convinced that she had indeed stabbed him. Did I have that conviction when I was called to the case? No. Can I understand why the police department, having been told to fuck off, decided he was responsible? Absolutely."

Kessler was unable to vindicate Russell. There were none of Laurie's fingerprints on the ice pick, only Russell's, and not enough evidence to prove that she was in the Hastings Avenue house when the anonymous telephone calls were made. So the record of her arrest was expunged. Mohr added this information to his file on Laurie, uncertain what to make of it.

On April 21, 1987, seven months after Russell's stabbing, Laurie alleged that he had assaulted her. By now she was less than a week away from her divorce, looking utterly miserable about the prospect of a future alone. Her story of being attacked at her parents' home bore an uncanny resemblance to Russell's, in that she too claimed to have been stabbed by a piece of kitchen equipment while she was alone late one night. Unlike her husband, she could identify her attacker. She alleged that Russell broke in by cutting the screen on the porch door, and she showed the police an eight-inch slit by the doorknob as proof. Her description of the encounter was bizarre.

She said she had spent the evening at home with a friend, a thirty-three-year-old single man who lived nearby. They watched television movies together until 11:15 P.M. when he left. The friend confirmed this, stating that although he had dated Laurie several times, his relationship with her was platonic. "Nothing hot and heavy," as he put it. Laurie did not lock the front door after him. He said she rarely locked it, and noted that it had been open when he arrived at 7:00 P.M. She told him she had a cold, so was about to take a bath and go to bed.

Later that night Laurie summoned the police and related that when she came out of the bathroom, scantily dressed, she saw Russell in her father's den rummaging through desk drawers. She said he told her he was looking for her engagement ring, an antique that had belonged to his family. The police officer noted in his report that nothing in the desk seemed to have been disturbed; in fact, it was tightly closed, with a radio on top, the cord running in front of several drawers to a wall plug and still in place.

Laurie alleged that Russell threw her on the bed in her parents' room, ripped off her clothes, and forcibly inserted a steak knife into her vagina. She said he told her he wanted to see her dead, or else a paraplegic so she would suffer. She described trying to fight him off and, in the effort, grabbing hair from his head and pubic area. According to her report, he screamed and fled. The police officer noted some hairs in the bed, as well as a small bloodstain on the sheets. Laurie explained the absence of fingerprints on the desk by stating that Russell was wearing long rubber gloves. She was taken to Highland Park Hospital and examined shortly before 3:00 A.M. by the emergency-room physician, Dr. R. S. Brodhead, who could not find any injury or symptoms of trauma.

"She was alert and oriented," he said later. "There was no laceration of the vagina, and it was apparent that what she alleged had not happened. She may have been the victim of some kind of attack, but it was not rape." He urged her to go for a follow-up interview at the Department of Social Services.

"It was a routine recommendation," he explained. "For her to tell that story, I felt she must have a problem, possibly emotional. It was a touchy situation and I am not a confrontational kind of physician. I told her in an almost apologetic way that I did not find evidence of the assault she described. It is not uncommon for women to allege rape when it hasn't actually happened, sometimes because there may have been an indiscretion they feel guilty about. But throughout our talk Laurie Dann was calm and did not waver in her story. She was convinced that what she said happened did happen."

Laurie spent the rest of that night at a girlfriend's home. Floyd Mohr interviewed her the following day, and she repeated her story, with more graphic detail. She said that Russell attacked her after she refused to tell him where she kept her engagement ring, at first holding the knife to her throat and threatening, "If you don't give me what I want, I'll make it look like a suicide and no one will believe you, not even the cops. They think you're crazy."

Then, she said, he put the knife inside her and told her that if she did not sign the divorce papers, "I'll cut you all the way up, bitch."

Dubious of her tale, Mohr asked Laurie if she would take a lie-detector test, and she agreed. Three days later she repeated her story to a polygraph expert so convincingly that after a three-hour interview with her he noted: "I found Mrs. Dann to be a very timid, introverted, naïve, and a very frightened individual. . . . Examination of her charts did not indicate any deception. It is my opinion that she is telling the truth in this matter."

Russell denied Laurie's charges, describing her as "a pathological liar." He insisted that he was at home asleep at the time of the alleged attack. Now he too was required to take a polygraph test. He did so under protest, fidgeting throughout the interview and urging the polygraph expert to hurry up because he had friends waiting to take him to dinner. Afterward he complained: "I was told it would take fifteen minutes and they kept me for over two hours."

Russell's restless behavior was assumed to indicate guilt, and he failed the test. The polygrapher reported that "he engaged in purposeful acts to distort the test," and commented: "It is my experience that when a person does that it is to avoid the result."

Floyd Mohr was baffled. In the meantime, he and a woman officer had taken Laurie to a rape-crisis center in Evanston, where she had a second physical examination.

"They saw a very tiny laceration in the vaginal wall, but could not say when it occurred or what caused it," Mohr stated. "We had only Laurie's word for what happened and I could not believe her story, any more than I could believe that she stabbed Russell without waking him up. I could not imagine her being held down and struggling against a knife without being badly cut. Also she did not behave like any of the rape victims I had ever dealt with. She showed no symptoms of trauma. But the woman officer who was with me believed she had been raped. Part of this was Laurie's manner. She seemed such a meek little girl.

"After that I took her to Des Plaines for felony review before a state attorney. He listened to the case in detail and felt the evidence was not there to make an arrest. A few days later Laurie's parents came back from Florida and were upset that Russell had not been arrested. They were convinced that he had been doing all these things to their daughter, so I met them at Nancy Sidote's office in Skokie. She's the state's attorney for our area of Cook County and has power to overrule in a case like this. I went over all the details: the alleged burglary, the alleged stabbing, the alleged sexual assault. After looking at all the evidence, Nancy Sidote would not approve of an arrest either. But she gave us time to get more evidence.

"Laurie was very timid and kept saying, 'Why is Russell doing this to me? When is he going to let me alone?' And I kept coming back to the question: Is she making all this up or is he? I did not believe her story about being attacked with a knife, but now I had a well-respected polygrapher saying that she was telling the truth. However, that polygraph report would not be admissible as evidence, so if Russell really did attack her, we had to prove it some other way."

Mohr then had Russell served with a peculiar kind of search warrant. It ordered the seizure of "25 pubic hairs from the genital area and 25 head hairs (5 from right side, 5 from left side, 5 from top, 5 from back, 5 from front), the total 50 hair samples to be hand pulled by nurse personnel at Evanston Hospital emergency room, and placed in an Illinois Department of State Police sexual assault evidence kit."

Russell went reluctantly to the hospital "humiliated, scared, and enraged," according to Richard Kessler who accompanied him. Floyd Mohr was there to collect the evidence, his unexpected presence irritating the two of them because of the way in which he was covering up his own discomfort, watching television in a hospital waiting room, apparently engrossed in Oliver North's testimony at the Iran-Contra hearings.

Essentially the hospital tests showed that while the hair Laurie claimed to have grabbed was morphologically similar to Russell's, it could not be positively identified as his. The case remained open, and the Wassermans went back to Florida.

"They were worried about their daughter's safety and they did not have a burglar alarm," Mohr recalled. "We put in a portable one, which was connected to the police radio alarm system.

It had a button for Laurie to press, like a garage-door opener. I put out a bulletin to my police colleagues in Glencoe, saying that there was an alarm at Three-four-six Sheridan Road and that Laurie had a gun. I wanted that known because I was afraid of someone getting hurt.

"On May twelfth, 1987, at three-forty-five A.M. the alarm went off. The police responded and Laurie told them that she had wakened and smelled kerosene. On a desk table there was a candle stuck in a glass jar which had a kerosene type of fuel in it, like a homemade incendiary device. A window screen had been cut and bent in from the outside, in such a way that a person could reach through the opening to the table. Laurie insisted Russell had done this. He denied it. Again she was the only witness. It was another strange story, a continuation of the Ping-Pong game with accusations going back and forth. We sent the glass to the lab. They said it could have been a fire bomb but they found no fingerprints."

Laurie told Mohr that she thought Russell was being vindictive about the divorce settlement, which gave her $125,000 from the sale of the Hastings Avenue house, plus $1,250 a month for the next three years. She claimed to be afraid of her ex-husband and of the harm he might do to her. At 8:00 A.M. that morning Russell was stopped by the police on his way to work. It was easy to pick him out in the Highland Park traffic: the lone driver of an Audi with a distinctive Illinois license plate: RUS 19. Two police officers frisked his body and searched his car for flammable material, but found nothing incriminating. Again Russell's irritation showed. Asked to contact Glencoe's detective bureau later that morning, he replied that he would do so at his convenience. He said he was on his way to an important business seminar, ironically, a course on stress management. Angrily he drove off.

Again Floyd Mohr telephoned the news to Norman Wasserman in Boca Raton; he again flew back to be with his daughter. Mohr described him as "a very quiet man, not at all overbearing," and on this visit he asked Wasserman about Laurie's emotional condition.

"He told me she was seeing Dr. Phillip Epstein, a Chicago psychiatrist who was treating her for obsessive-compulsive disorder and for a chemical imbalance. He said that everything was fine with his daughter before she married Russell, and that even after the divorce Russell was still trying to make her look crazy.

"I spoke with Dr. Epstein and explained that a lot of things had happened between Laurie and her ex-husband, accusations of assaults which could not be proved. I told him that she owned a three-fifty-seven Smith and Wesson, model nineteen, blue-steel revolver, and I asked him the same question I had asked Dr. Greenwood: 'In your opinion, could she be homicidal or suicidal?' He said: 'No, I have no reason to believe that. I am treating her for a chemical imbalance. For me to give you any more information she would have to sign a waiver.'

"I asked Laurie to sign a waiver, but she refused. She said: 'You have no need to know my private life, or to talk to my psychiatrist about me.'

"Throughout my dealings with her she was strange. Things about her bothered me. Her mood swings, her manner. Things I sensed but did not actually see. That's why I kept bringing up about the gun. I don't know why I did it so much, but I just did not like her having it. I had an intuition that if it stayed in her possession something terrible would happen, but I had no idea what."

Soon after the divorce, the baby-sitting incidents began. Before and during her marriage Laurie had worked briefly at office jobs and as a country-club waitress, but never for more than a few weeks at a time, and rarely to her employers' satisfaction. She had no professional skills; despite four years in college she had not qualified for a degree. Baby-sitting helped to fill the gap in her life after her marriage failed, and the work was easy to get. She put a handwritten advertisement on the notice boards of the Glencoe public library and of a village grocery store, describing herself as a twenty-eight-year-old graduate student who lived in the neighborhood and drove her own car. To Glencoe mothers the description sounded almost too good to be true. Several of them called her, and none of them asked searching questions, not when they heard her Sheridan Road address. It established her as one of them.

Laurie looked like a student. She wore almost no makeup, a simple hairstyle, and casual clothes. "She was small, plain, shy, almost childlike, but you could see that if she were dressed up and made up she could look stunning," commented a Glencoe mother who hired her.

Floyd Mohr thought of Laurie as "typical north shore." While Russell was one of those driven young people assured of corporate success, she fell into another local category: a young adult supported by wealthy parents, short on ambition and a sense of direction, dropping in and out of jobs and college with no aim in view. Although some young mothers may have suspected this of her, they thought her a prize as a baby-sitter: a nice Jewish girl capably doing a job for which Glencoe teenagers had little enthusiasm. As a parent who employed her put it: "Before age thirteen, kids want three dollars an hour for doing nothing. After thirteen they hit the bar mitzvah circuit, go out partying, and don't want to baby-sit anymore. It's the curse of an affluent area."

Most of Laurie's employers trusted her; some even felt they had found a treasure. Occasionally, something about her made them feel uncomfortable, an impression that like Peter Pan's Wendy she wasn't quite connected to the world she lived in, but these reservations were mitigated by the fact that, also like Wendy, she was caring and comfortable with little children. In sharp contrast to this, a few parents found her behavior odd, even deranged, and made disturbing reports to the Glencoe police.

The first complaint came to Floyd Mohr's attention eighteen days after Laurie's allegation that Russell attacked her with a knife, and less than two weeks after the two of them were divorced. Laurie was hired for an evening by a Glencoe mother who had heard glowing reports about her from a friend.

"Keep this one under your hat," the friend had told her as she passed on Laurie's telephone number. "She's twenty-eight years old, working at Glenbrook Hospital, going to graduate school at Northwestern, getting her MBA. She's a real find, so don't spread her name around."

On that recommendation, Laurie was hired to look after two little girls while their parents went to a party. The parents left her sitting at a table happily playing a game with their daughters and returned at midnight to find the children asleep in bed and Laurie watching television.

"How did it go?" the mother asked.

"Fine," Laurie replied. "But I have to tell you that during the evening a man knocked at your door and asked to use the telephone. He said he was a neighbor who was locked out of his house, so I let him in."

The parents exchanged nervous glances. They weren't on close terms with their neighbors, and never answered the door themselves after dark. It struck them that Laurie had very poor judgment. After she left they searched the house, fearful that the mysterious caller might have done some damage or even be hiding somewhere. The next morning, a Saturday, the husband went to get out his car for an early game of golf and found both of the garage-door openers missing from a kitchen drawer. Worried about the prospect of yet another burglary, his wife drove to the Wasserman home. Norman Wasserman said that his daughter was taking a shower and left his visitor sitting in her car on the driveway. Laurie appeared a few minutes later, her hair hanging damply around her shoulders.

The mother explained: "We need to get some information from you about the man you let in last night so we can make a report to the police. Some things are missing. How long was he in the house?"

"I don't know." Laurie's face was expressionless.

"What do you mean, you don't know?"

"I let him in at the deck door. He used the kitchen phone while I went upstairs to check the children."

"You left him alone in the kitchen? For how long?" Silence. "Would it have been five or ten minutes?"

"Yes, about that long."

"What did he look like? How old was he?"

"I don't know, just a kid."

"A high school kid? Like sixteen or eighteen years old?"

"That's right."

"What color hair did he have?" Silence. "Brown?"

"Yes, brown hair."

"Did you let him out?"

"No, he left while I was upstairs."

Even more disturbed, the mother left. Only months later did it occur to her that Laurie's visitor might not have existed. In the meantime, she kept finding strange damage to her furnishings,

124

which must have been done that night: cuts in the leather of a new armchair, a seat-cushion slit, one slash in the dining-room rug and another in the living-room carpet, two cuts in the burlap wall covering of the living room and one on the dining room's floral wallpaper; every cut from two to four inches long, as fine and straight as if made by a razor blade held against a ruler, all of them precisely vertical or horizontal, some at right angles to one another, yet so discreetly placed that it was weeks before she found every one of them. They looked almost ritualistic.

"Perhaps your children did it," the police suggested.

She knew that wasn't true. Several weeks later she saw Detective Floyd Mohr at the village's Fourth of July celebrations, and asked if he had any news for her.

"I just want to know whether some stranger came into my house," she insisted.

"All I can tell you is that there have been some funny things going on between Laurie and her ex-husband," he replied. "I can't say any more because I'm still working on the case."

Toward the end of the summer, late one Sunday evening, she received an anonymous phone call. In a gravelly voice a woman said, "You are so stupid," and hung up. Over the next few weeks there were between twenty and thirty silent hang-up calls, many of them in the middle of the night. She reported them to the Glencoe police, mentioning the earlier incident with Laurie. Soon the calls stopped.

None of this made sense to her until May 20 of the following year when a morning television program was interrupted by a news flash about the Hubbard Woods shooting. A few bulletins later Nicky Corwin's murderer was named. Immediately the woman called her friend, the one who had recommended Laurie Dann to her.

"Please meet me in the village," she pleaded. "I must talk to someone."

They met at a small hot-dog restaurant and sat there for some time, nervously watching the television news. An announcer described Laurie Dann as heavyset with red hair. They wondered to one another whether this really was the fragile brunette they had both hired and, knowing in their hearts that it was, shared the terror of what might have happened to their children.

* * *

In September 1987, within five months of the furniture-slashing incident, two other Glencoe couples who employed Laurie as a baby-sitter complained to the police. Both of them missed quantities of food after leaving her alone with their children. In one instance a neighbor reported seeing her furtively glance around before struggling to carry a large plastic bag to her car. Later, her employers for that evening, Bruce and Dolores Benton, found much of the meat and fish in their deep freeze was missing. Twenty packets of rice had also inexplicably disappeared. The Bentons estimated the loss at between four hundred and five hundred dollars.

"I approached the police and they said that Laurie was known to them, but that if we sued, the best we could get was restitution, and that would cost us money," Benton stated. "I also called Laurie's father. He said he was certain she had never taken anything, and that he had not seen any of the food in his house. But he was not going to call me a liar, and if we could settle this amicably . . ."

They did. Norman Wasserman reportedly paid the Bentons four hundred dollars, and they agreed not to sign a formal complaint.

"Laurie understood how the system worked, and knew how to beat it," Bruce Benton observed. "Although I am an employer, my employees know more about how to get money out of unemployment than I do. And the comparison holds."

Another Glencoe couple, Dr. Kenneth Beckman and his wife, Pam, wanted to prosecute Laurie after some frozen food and a new pair of women's shoes were stolen from their house within a week of the Benton theft. They had a witness, their five-year-old son, who said he crept downstairs from his bedroom and saw her filling up a box with food. The police felt that the unsupported testimony of such a young child was not sufficient for a prosecution, and no legal action was taken. Frustrated, Pam Benton took down Laurie's notice from the Glencoe library's bulletin board, the same advertisement she herself had answered. Soon a new notice appeared with the warning: "Do not take this down. Stay away."

"I was really angry," she said. "The items she stole from us were so weird that I felt very disturbed about her, and I did not want her sitting for anyone else. I talked to the people at the library, who told me that Laurie had come in there and done something strange in a bathroom, but they would not say what. I told them she stole, and I tore up her notice. Then I went to the local grocery store and took down her notice there. As fast as I did this, new notices would appear. She must have been out almost every day putting them up."

Floyd Mohr questioned both Laurie and her father for hours about the baby-sitting incidents. Both denied all the accusations. Mohr stated: "Norman Wasserman kept saying to me, 'Why would she want to do this? She loves kids. Why do you keep bothering her? You can't prove anything.' And I couldn't. If I could have, I would have arrested her."

TWELVE

Bruce benton was right. Laurie knew how to beat the system. Whenever the suspicion was on her, she shifted it to somebody else, usually Russell. However crazed her behavior might seem, she could make him out to be crazier. Whenever the police began to suspect her of criminal activities, she became a victim.

In the fall of 1987, when the Glencoe police were trying to discover the truth behind the baby-sitting stories, Norman Wasserman stopped by Floyd Mohr's office with some anonymous letters he said Laurie had received. They had a local postmark and were unevenly typed with such gross misspellings that the errors seemed to be deliberate, as though the writer were pretending to be someone else. One message read:

> I told you I would warn you only once
> you are eiother stuiobborn or just plaion dumb
> it is your funeral i mean choice

Another spelled out in capital letters:

I WANT MY RING BACKI YOUN SPOILED
BIYCH   BIUT MIOST
OF ALL I WANT IT ALL AND I ALWAYS GET
WHAT I WANT

And another:

i can always break   you physically and emotion
ally   ICAN MAKE MINCE MEAT OUT OF
YOYU

Mohr said that Wasserman told him: "Laurie thinks Russell is trying to get even. She is terrified that something will happen to her." Wasserman gave the police a photograph which he said was enclosed in one of the letters. It showed Russell embracing a young woman in a garden.

A few days later, on October 2, Laurie made another strange allegation about her ex-husband: that he had sexually assaulted her in a parking lot. It was a huge open lot serving several multi-storied office buildings on Skokie Boulevard, Northbrook, a heavily trafficked six-lane highway which runs west of the north shore villages. One of these buildings housed the corporate offices of Dann Brothers, the family insurance business of which Russell was an executive. The next building contained a health club where Laurie sometimes exercised. That Friday afternoon, Russell left his office between 4:30 and 5:00 P.M., got into his car, looked anxiously around as usual, and was alarmed to see Laurie's Honda parked close to his in the lot, with her sitting in it. Convinced that she was waiting to trail him home, he picked up his car phone and called the police. They came and told Laurie to move on because she was parked in a fire lane. According to Russell, she drove away.

Laurie had a different story. Later that evening she went to the Northbrook police station and alleged that Russell had walked over to her in the parking lot and pushed her back into her car so that her head struck the door. As she was sprawled across the front seat, she said, he threatened her with a weapon (which she neither named nor saw) while he partially undressed her and masturbated in her face. Then, she said, he went back to his car and telephoned the police to complain about her being there.

As evidence, she produced a piece of toilet tissue stained with what appeared to be semen, stating that she tore it from a roll which she happened to have in her car and used it to wipe her face. A roll of toilet paper was an odd item for a motorist to be carrying around, although almost anything might have been unearthed from the chaos of Laurie's belongings. "There was so much junk in that car, it looked like she had been living in it," a Northbrook police officer remarked.

Laurie insisted there had been a witness, a man who came out of the building that housed the health club and who responded to her shouts of distress immediately after Russell left. She said he saw the state of her face before she wiped it, but left without giving his name. Several times over the next month a Northbrook police officer tried to make an appointment with her to accompany him on a tour of the offices in the building where Laurie said the man worked. But she was always unavailable.

Russell angrily denied the charge. Again he had unanswerable questions. "If I did this obscene act, would I have immediately called the police about Laurie being in the parking lot? And when they came to move her out of the fire lane, why didn't she tell them that I had just assaulted her, instead of waiting several hours before making a complaint?"

Scott Dann's outrage was more graphic. "Imagine, it is around five P.M. on a Friday afternoon, the busiest time along this highway. And right here, in full view of our employees leaving work, all of them walking across this open space to pick up their cars, Russell is supposed to have taken his pants down. As for the sperm Laurie produced several hours later, that isn't hard to do. Any reasonably attractive woman can get laid."

Although the Northbrook police went through the motions of investigating Laurie's complaint, none of the officers believed her story. "We thought she was wacky," one said. But recognizing that wacky people can be assaulted, he questioned her in detail. Two things struck him. "When she talked about being attacked she used the correct legal terminology, with phrases straight out of the Criminal Code. It was as though she had memorized the words of the statute, and knew exactly what her legal rights were. Victims don't usually talk like that. But when she described what her ex-husband was supposed to have said and done to her, she used some very vulgar expressions, not what you would expect from a young lady as quiet and well mannered as she seemed to be. Most women are so embarrassed about repeating obscene language to the police that we often have to ask them to write it down. She came right out with it, and that was unusual. I had a feeling that she may have been sexually attacked in childhood, and that nobody believed her. They're the ones who get messed up the worst."

Laurie's written statement contained the same discrepancies. It began in her firm round hand, which was almost as neat as printing, factually describing how she was about to walk across the parking lot to go to the health club when "my ex-husband Mr. Russell Dann pushed me into the car. He had a coat he was taking off. He took the coat and put it over my face and held tightly over my mouth. He told me he had a weapon and would hurt me if I didn't oblige. He removed the coat and told me he wanted me out of his territory."

Suddenly the handwriting changed, deteriorating into a misspelled scrawl. Apparently quoting Russell it continued: "But as long as your hear and in a cute leotart why not watch me masterbate in your face and listen to me talk dirty If you would talk dirty I wad come faster. . . ." And more in this vein, with the handwriting increasingly illegible and unpunctuated as the details became more salacious. This account did not seem to fit the quiet, frightened-looking woman who had written it. Furthermore, there was a subtle shift in the narrative, coincident with the change in the handwriting. Laurie started out by accusing Russell of masturbating in her face, but ended by describing an act of oral sex that appeared to be consensual.

The Northbrook officer telephoned the Wassermans and asked them to come to the police station. They arrived promptly, Laurie's father doing most of the talking. "He was very nice and he tried to be helpful, but I don't think he knew what to make of her story any more than I did," the officer said.

The police report was filed and, for a while, forgotten. It was remembered almost eight months later, after the Hubbard Woods shooting, and added to the gathering pile of evidence about Laurie Dann. By then the police were too involved in the major issue to notice this seemingly minor discrepancy, which may in fact have been a vital clue to her personality. That night at Northbrook police station there seemed to be two Laurie Danns, one who was traumatized from being forced into a demeaning sex act, another who savored and changed the details in such a way that she might have been recalling an event from another time and place.

Later, in Glencoe, Floyd Mohr discussed the parking-lot case with Laurie and her father, with the usual unsatisfactory results. "He was still defensive of his daughter," Mohr commented. "But I think he knew something was wrong with Laurie and did not know what to do about it, or how to handle it."

Mohr never saw Laurie again. A few weeks later he heard that she had moved to Madison, 130 miles away, to study at the University of Wisconsin. He felt relieved. Right now his energies were concentrated on a difficult case he was close to resolving, the apprehension of a man who had sexually assaulted young boys, and this was causing him enough anxiety because he kept thinking of his own two small children and of the dangers they might encounter as they grew older. At the same time he could not forget Laurie Dann. Whenever he drove by the Wassermans' house he would glance in the driveway, compelled to check whether her blue Honda was there.

Even after he missed seeing it for months he continued to worry about her, and would have worried much more if he had known that five and a half weeks after the incident in the parking lot, she went back to the Glenview gun shop and bought a .32 Smith and Wesson revolver. Seven weeks after that purchase, on December 29, 1987, she bought her third gun, a .22 automatic Beretta. There was no requirement for these transactions to be reported to the police. While Floyd Mohr continued to fret about Laurie's ownership of the .357 Magnum, she had begun to assemble a small arsenal of guns without his even suspecting it.

On May 7, 1988, six months after his last encounter with her, Mohr was in the dispatch center of the Glencoe police station idly looking at a blank computer screen. "All of a sudden, out of nowhere, up popped a message from a state's attorney in Arizona asking police departments across the country for any information they might have on Laurie Wasserman, alias Laurie Dann. It said she was being investigated for criminal activity, and it could easily have been missed, but I happened to be standing right there. It was like God wanted me to see it.

"I ripped the message off the printer and called Arizona right away. I was given the name of an FBI agent in the state who was investigating Laurie for telephone and letter threats to a doctor in Tucson whom she had known years ago in college. Apparently the threats were so serious that the doctor was afraid she would harm his family and ruin his career. I made copies of everything I had on Laurie Dann and sent the agent the complete package by registered mail. He said they wanted to prosecute her, if only the doctor would sign a complaint. He had me meet with an FBI agent in Chicago and I told this man all I knew about Laurie, and about her having a gun. That was about May tenth. I learned that Laurie was still living in Wisconsin, but I drove by the Wassermans' house in case she was there. I even rang the doorbell just for the heck of it. I kept remembering all the crazy incidents I had investigated, and I began to think to myself that maybe Russell was telling the truth."

This new view of the ice-pick incident became part of a May 13 FBI memorandum which went out to police and security officers in the Madison area, listing Laurie as a suspect who might be armed and dangerous. It stated that her threatening telephone calls to the Arizona physician had been traced to pay phones near The Towers, a college apartment building in Madison where she had been living. And it added: "Suspect has been known to attack former husband with an ice pick, and is also registered to carry a .357."

The net was closing in on her, but Laurie eluded it. On the advice of his attorney, the Tucson doctor dropped his charges, although he had been harassed by Laurie for some time. Almost two years earlier she had telephoned him to say that she had a small daughter whom he had fathered, and that she needed child support. She and the doctor had been lovers as fellow students at the University of Arizona, but had not seen one another for almost six years. After he refused to believe her story about the child, an anonymous woman complained to the New York hospital where he was then an intern, alleging that he had raped her in the emergency room. He felt sure this was Laurie, trying to ruin his career.

Now, almost two years later in Tucson, she was harassing him again. An anonymous complaint had been sent to the administration of his present hospital, again alleging attempted rape. At the same time he received several threatening telephone calls which were traced to Madison, Wisconsin. Since this involved interstate traffic it became a case for the FBI, whose local agent was anxious to get Laurie indicted. But fearful of the embarrassing publicity of a court action, the doctor withdrew his complaint. He knew of no one else being threatened by Laurie, and did not want to be the only plaintiff. If he had pressed charges she would have been arrested, and Winnetka spared its day of terror. But he was living his own nightmare. Even after he requested an unlisted telephone number, the anonymous calls to his home continued. His wife picked up one of them, and heard the now familiar voice say: "You don't have to change your telephone number. This won't stop me from killing you. So you can take your little baby and throw it in the garbage can."

The doctor might have acted differently if he had known that Laurie was harassing others; that Susie and Jeff Taylor had again gone to the Glencoe police about her renewed telephone threats to kill their children. While he remained ignorant of this, they were being reassured that the FBI would soon arrest Laurie in Madison, even after the doctor had decided against signing a complaint.

"This was consistent with the lack of communication between police authorities which we had seen on this case from the start," Jeff Taylor grumbled. "In fact the FBI lost track of Laurie in Madison, and none of us had any idea that she was back in Glencoe."

Laurie was last seen in Madison early on Monday, May 16. The next day a woman who fit her description called at the Ravinia School in Highland Park to check on the hours of assembly and dismissal. Without much doubt Laurie was also the woman who visited the nearby Jewish day-care center, pretending an interest in enrolling her nonexistent children, and stealing the card-index file which would have told her that Susie and Jeff Taylor still had a child there.

She then surprised Marian Rushe by an unexpected call at her Winnetka home, avoiding an explanation for her radically changed appearance and long absence by talking about a forthcoming honeymoon in the Virgin Islands with a fiancé who did not exist. Woven into this narrative was a recurrent anecdote about a missing engagement ring, an heirloom from the family of the man she loved. Russell had once given her such a ring, and Laurie had told another kind of story about this to Floyd Mohr. The missing ring had become symbolic of the lost marriage, and to make it all seem right again she had created the image of Laurie Porter: the innocent, easygoing young woman Marian Rushe had come to know and trust, the woman Laurie Wasserman had hoped to be, back at the time when she was engaged to Russell Dann and expected to live happily ever after.

The house on Sheridan Road was empty when Laurie returned to it from Madison. By now her parents had enough insight into her disturbed state of mind to cut short their spring stay in Florida, and to hurry back to Glencoe on May 18, the day after her arrival. They are unlikely to have known about the FBI investigation, about the anonymous phone calls and death threats, about the extent of her bizarre behavior in Madison, certainly not about her systematic plan to destroy dozens of people whom she perceived had hurt her. Shortly after arriving home, Edith Wasserman, in all innocence, worked with her daughter in the kitchen making Rice Krispie cookies, which Laurie would later lace with arsenic and offer to unsuspecting acquaintances.

The Wassermans must have been dismayed at Laurie's sudden return, and were trying to make the best of it. They knew it meant she had cut short her treatments with Dr. John Greist, the Madison psychiatrist whom Norman Wasserman had contacted before arranging his daughter's move there. At thirty years old she was only a token student at the university. It was Dr. Greist, a leading specialist in the treatment of obsessive-compulsive disorders, she had gone to see. Norman Wasserman had asked him to help his daughter, and had arranged for her to live in a student apartment near the campus so that she could consult with him regularly.

Greist was treating Laurie for manic depression as well as obsessive-compulsive disorder. The four months in which he saw her, from November 1987 to March 1988, were too short a time for him to probe the depth of her complex problems, although he had recently become concerned enough about her deteriorating mental state to recommend voluntary commitment to a psychiatric institution. She ignored the recommendation, and had not kept her appointments with him for more than a month. When she returned to the north shore, she was in à manic phase, losing her last shreds of control.

This was the condition in which she was seen by an Evanston bus driver, carelessly dressed and ritualistically pacing up and down late on a night when she seemed to have nowhere to go and no need for sleep. The next time anyone saw her was shortly after 8:30 the following morning, looking alert and reasonably tidy, chatting to some children in the playground of Hubbard Woods School. Significantly, the much-washed T-shirt she was wearing with her shorts bore the emblem of the medical school which the Tucson doctor had attended, and was probably a relic of her romance with him. A teacher wondered who she was, but saw nothing strange enough about her to inquire.

At that same time Floyd Mohr arrived at the Glencoe police department. He was not on duty there until 3:00 P.M. but he had a noon meeting of juvenile officers to attend in Des Plaines, and had come in early to prepare for it. This conscientious decision would soon cause his path and Laurie's to cross for the last time. But with no hint that she was anywhere in the neighborhood, he got on with his paperwork while she drove from the school to the Rushe home, taking with her a plate of the poisoned Rice Krispie cookies and the arsenic she would slip into the children's milk.

THIRTEEN

FLOYD MOHR was working at his desk when the Winnetka fire call came in. Glencoe's fire department, housed in the same building as the police, was standing by for its colleagues in the next village during Larry Carney's funeral.

"I knew our guys would have to go so I decided to follow in my squad car in case they needed help," Mohr recalled. "The call was for a house in Winnetka which had a basement fire in which some people may have been trapped. When we got there I hooked the hose to the fire hydrant, then stayed next to the engine while our people went inside. Every few minutes I helped them change air packs so they could go back in. When they had almost finished I heard about the shooting at Hubbard Woods School on my police radio. I thought someone must have been fooling around with a BB gun and I called out to the Winnetka officer who was directing traffic: 'Craig, did they say it was a shooting?'"

Craig Tisdale, who had been dispatched from the funeral to the fire scene, indicated that it was serious. Mohr dashed back to his unmarked car and headed for the school. On the brief drive there he heard a radio description of the perpetrator: a heavily built young woman with reddish hair, wearing light shorts and a yellow T-shirt with a medical-school emblem. It did not sound like anyone he knew.

"There was chaos at the front of the school, but at the back it was peaceful," Mohr said. "I circled the building and saw two women sitting in the rear playground. They seemed to have no idea that anything had happened. I told them I was a police officer and that they must leave at once because there had been a shooting."

They did not seem to believe him. "What?" they asked incredulously.

Mohr, who was wearing plain clothes, showed his police badge. "Get the hell out of here," he ordered.

"I was mad at them, and they thought I was crazy," he said later. "Then they saw the ambulance, and ran into the school." He drove on, searching the village for a young woman who fit the police description.

On one of Winnetka's quiet streets he thought he had found her. There was a car with two women in it, one young, the other middle-aged. The younger one seemed to have the physical characteristics he was looking for. Mohr radioed for help. Seconds later three police cars drew up. The women were ordered to throw their ignition key on the street and put their hands out of the windows while police surrounded their car, pointing shotguns. They looked terrified. Affronted, too. Even though Mohr addressed the older woman as ma'am, this was not the Winnetka way of doing things.

Soon an unmarked police car pulled up, driven by Sergeant Patty McConnell with Amy Moses in the back seat. Amy looked at the beleaguered women and shook her head.

"Floyd, it's not her! It's not her!" Patty yelled, and drove off.

Mohr recalled: "We put away our guns and tried to apologize to these people, but it took them some time to calm down. They were so badly shaken."

At that moment another police car arrived, driven by Lieutenant Joseph Sumner, Herbert Timm's immediate deputy in the Winnetka police force. As its director of operations, he had remained in charge at the station while his chief went to Larry Carney's funeral. When the emergency call came in from Hubbard Woods School, he hurried out to his car, and on the drive there heard Mohr's radio message, so made a detour. Now as he picked up the car keys and apologetically returned them, he had the presence of mind to instruct one of his officers to stay with the two women until they had composed themselves well enough to drive off safely. With thirty-two years of police experience behind him, Joe Sumner never missed a detail.

At the school he joined his chief, who had arrived there from the funeral a few minutes earlier. He took a quick look at the bloodied scene in Room 7 where Nicky Corwin's body lay under a blanket and paramedics were tending the injured children, and immediately made radio calls for Winnetka's off-duty police to be brought in, for evidence technicians to be sent to the school, and for crime experts to be requested from the state police. In crises of this kind small towns can call upon the state police for help, and Sumner particularly wanted two of its experts. "My brother William and his partner," he explained. "All they do is evidence processing. I asked for them by name because I wanted the best we could get." He also issued a call for all plainclothes detectives to report to the school.

Answering the call, Floyd Mohr got his first glimpse of Room 7. He was so shocked by the sight of wounded children and of the great pools of blood that he could barely concentrate on what Joe Sumner was saying; at the same time he was picking up snatches of conversation between Herb Timm and fire chief Ron Colpaert who were standing close by. They were talking about a missing baby-sitter at the house where the fire had been, and saying that Mrs. Rushe had spoken of her as Laurie. Immediately Mohr thought of Laurie Dann, and of her bizarre baby-sitting experiences in Glencoe.

"I was gathering information, yet I couldn't concentrate," Mohr recalled. "I was asking myself whether this could be her. The description didn't match, but I had to find out. I dashed out of the school and into my car with my heart pumping. The car was blocked in and I was sitting on my horn trying to get through the traffic; finally I drove around it on a sidewalk. When I got back to the fire scene there was still smoke coming from the house, but the flames had been put out. There were a lot of people around, and I screamed out that I was a police officer, and that I needed to talk to the lady whose house this was."

He had learned from the firemen that there was a strong suspicion of arson. They had noted pour patterns of gasoline on the basement stairs, but had not found the missing sitter.

"I was hoping it wasn't the Laurie I knew," Mohr said. "But I had to have an answer to the question, no matter who was in my way. I saw this woman on the lawn, standing against a tree, being treated by paramedics for cuts and burns. I went up to her and said, 'I'm Detective Mohr. I'm from Glencoe and I have to talk to you now. Let's go into your house.' She was trying to tell me that the house was on fire, and for the moment I had forgotten that. I just wanted to get her away from people, so she led me to a neighbor's house." There a conversation took place which Mohr would never forget.

"I heard you could not find your baby-sitter," he said. "What was her name?"

"Laurie," Marian Rushe told him.

"What was her last name?" She hesitated for an instant so he repeated the question. "What was her last name?" He was almost shouting in his impatience. He didn't realize that she had narrowly escaped death, and was in shock.

"It's Porter," she told him. "She lives in Glencoe."

The surname was wrong, and at first Mohr felt relieved, then realized he didn't know any other Lauries in Glencoe. "Do you know her phone number?" he asked.

Again he broke in on her hesitation. "Is it 835-1263?"

She looked astounded. "How do you know?"

"What kind of car does she drive? Is it a blue Honda with an Illinois license plate XHV 351?"

Even more surprised, she asked again: "How do you know?" Then she added, "But today she was driving a white—"

"Toyota?"

"Yes, Toyota."

"Was the plate number NW 000?"

"Yes, I think so."

All those numbers of Laurie's were so deeply imprinted on Mohr's memory that, stressed as he was, he recalled them without an effort.

"Ma'am, just stay here," he told Marian Rushe as he hurried outdoors. He was thinking so much faster than he could run that it was as though his mind and body were in different dimensions. If Laurie Dann had been crazy enough to try to kill this family by setting fire to their house, it must have been she who had gone straight to Hubbard Woods School and shot the children. And she was still out there, somewhere in the neighborhood, with a gun. He thought of the many times he had tried to get that gun away from her, of the arguments that she and her father had given him, of the negative responses of two psychiatrists to his urgent question: Could she be homicidal or suicidal? He remembered his own gut feeling that so long as she had a gun something terrible might happen. Remembered also the only Laurie he had ever known, a mere five feet three and ninety-seven pounds, whom he had not even believed capable of stabbing Russell, much as she was hurt by his rejection of her. Now he was confronted by the image of a woman whom he and her doctors had never known. And he suddenly felt angry at them, at her, at the legal system that allowed her to have a gun, and at himself for failing to see what all the others had missed.

He was shaking as he picked up his police radio. He had to let his colleagues at the school know immediately, but there was still the discrepancy between Amy Moses's description of a heavy-set woman with reddish hair and the slender brunette he had last seen six months ago. Both were Laurie Dann, of that he was almost sure, but it was as if the murderous Laurie was a newly created monster who had swallowed up the petite and pretty girl he remembered.

From outside the Rushe house Mohr put out the radio message which would stop all the police in Winnetka in their tracks: "I believe I know the name of the offender. I believe her name is Laurie Dann, otherwise Laurie Wasserman, otherwise Laurie Porter. . . ."

He got in his car and headed back to the school. On the way there he heard the police radio message Officer Richard Carlson was putting out from his crouched position behind a tree on Hamptondale Road. Carlson had just found the abandoned white Toyota, NW 000, with its cargo of ammunition and incendiary devices, and was taking cover until other police could join him.

Bypassing the school, Floyd Mohr drove straight to Hamptondale Road. He recognized the Toyota immediately, saw the bullet casings on the seat and floor, and no longer had any doubt who the driver, the arsonist, and the killer had been.

It was about 11:00 A.M., less than an hour after the shooting, and this was an important break in the case. Police mug shots of Laurie, taken eighteen months earlier when the Highland Park police arrested her for telephone harassment, were rushed to the school and shown around. She had been photographed in a white turtleneck sweater and red windbreaker, college-style clothes, and in profile her unsmiling face had a childlike quality. Amy Moses recognized it at once.

"It was a big thing to have her identified so quickly, and if Floyd Mohr had not been there it would have taken much longer," commented Patty McConnell. "Up to then we were looking for an unknown person. Now we had a photo, a name, an address, and a description of her cars. We also knew something about her criminal history."

By now police from surrounding neighborhoods were pouring into Winnetka, and in this small world of north shore villages the first of several officers to reach Carlson by the wrecked Toyota was one of his high school classmates, Phil Brunell from Kenilworth. Then Mohr and others arrived, followed by Joe Sumner, who took charge. Since the wrecked car was stuck at the entrance to a Hamptondale Road driveway, they began by checking the large house on the property. Sumner radioed the police station to telephone the occupants. Three maids were there, only one of whom spoke English, and it took a while to persuade them to come outside while a police dog was sent in to hunt for a possible intruder.

As soon as it became clear that Laurie wasn't there, the police fanned out into the strip of woodland between Hamptondale and Kent roads, the area where Bob Kerner had searched and missed her earlier, while she was still trying to escape in her car. At the back of 6 Kent Road, Richard Carlson and his partner thought they were on Laurie's track. There was a broken window in the French doors and a garden spade nearby, which she had apparently used to smash it, but the doors had not been forced

142

open. Inside the house a dog was barking fiercely; obviously it had frightened Laurie away. Carlson was checking the grounds when a police colleague radioed: "A woman from Two Kent Road says there's a strange woman in her house with a gun." Immediately every officer in the area stopped searching, and ran there.

Number 2 was a handsome white house with a shallow front yard and a semicircular driveway. At the left of the building was a high wall with a stone archway leading to the kitchen entrance, and sitting on a chair against the wall was a heavyset elderly man who seemed unable to speak or move, with a nurse beside him. The victim of an earlier stroke, Vincent Wolfe lived here with his daughter and had been enjoying the spring sunshine when Laurie had run right past him toward the kitchen door.

Now, almost half an hour later, police were trampling across the garden, some of them shouting: "We've got to get this man away from here!"

While the nurse took refuge in a parked car, Floyd Mohr and Bob Kerner picked up the aluminum garden chair with its helpless occupant and, covered by the pointed guns of their police colleagues, ran with it to the garage.

After that, events moved so quickly that an hour or two elapsed before anyone remembered that the old gentleman was still there, and went to rescue him.

FOURTEEN

IT WAS not only her parents' Toyota which Laurie had to abandon after it struck a rock in her hurry to get away. She needed to do something about the incriminating bloodstains on her shorts. As Amy Moses had noted, she was not wearing underwear. In the back of the car she still had the blue plastic garbage bag which had caused so much mirth with the Rushe children when she tried to wear it as a disguise at the Ravinia School. Now, after stripping off her shorts, she tied the bag around her waist like a sarong, reloaded her two remaining guns, and sprinted into the woods between Hamptondale and Kent roads. It was too small an area for her to hide in successfully, and her only alternative was to take refuge in one of the large houses backing on to it. Without her car she had already lost the chance to escape, but she was not thinking that far ahead, only of the immediate power of her guns tucked into the garbage bag which was flapping around her legs. She could use them to force people to shelter her. Despite all this bravado she was scared away from the first house by a barking dog, and made herself more vulnerable by running on to another.

There she was luckier. The helpless old man sitting by the wall was no threat, and the kitchen door was unlocked.

"My car has broken down and I need to use a phone," she called out to him as she ran toward the kitchen door.

His daughter, Ruth Andrew, was standing by the sink chatting with her twenty-year-old son, Philip. Earlier that morning she had attended Larry Carney's funeral mass—not that she had been a close friend but two of her children had gone to parochial school with two of his. "I thought it would be a nice thing to do," she said. Turning into Kent Road on the way home, she had heard sirens for the fire at the Rushe house and, like Clarine Hall, assumed they were being sounded by Carney's colleagues as they escorted the procession to the cemetery.

Phil, a twenty-year-old student at the University of Illinois at Urbana-Champaign, had come home for the college vacation two days earlier. He had great plans for the summer, one part-time job working for Congressman John Porter and another in the state's attorney's office, plus lots of swimming. He was excited about his summer jobs because he hoped for a career in politics, and swimming was his favorite recreation. He was captain of his college swimming team, a lean and muscular six feet four, in superb physical condition; otherwise he might not have survived the danger he was about to face. But he had no sense of it as he leaned against the kitchen counter, chatting easily with his mother. She was in a reflective mood from the church service she had just attended, still thinking of the unpredictability of life, and of Larry Carney's untimely death. She had set his mass card down among the last of the breakfast dishes, and her thoughts from the funeral drifted into the conversation she was now having with her son.

They were talking about Phil's career ambitions, wondering whether it was still a handicap for an election candidate to be a Roman Catholic, or whether the Kennedys had changed all that. Only the previous day Ruth Andrew had shown him the latest copy of *Newsweek*, marking the twentieth anniversary of Robert Kennedy's assassination. The memory of that tragedy was still vivid to her because on the afternoon of June 5, 1968, she had waited with hundreds of others in a little Mexican-American town near Pasadena, California, to catch a glimpse of Kennedy, only hours before he was assassinated.

"I had no business being in such a crowd because I had two little kids with me, and you in my arms," she had reminisced to her son. "But Bobby was there and I was cheering him."

It was uncanny, she would think later, that they should be talking about Phil's future, and about death by gunfire, at that moment when Laurie Dann walked in.

Nothing ever seemed to faze Ruth Andrew. She had successfully reared seven bright, handsome, loving children by detaching herself from all the worrisome little details of family life, and concentrating on essentials. The fact that a young woman dressed in a garbage bag had just entered her kitchen without knocking was not, in her view, anything to get alarmed about.

"I thought she was some goofball who knew one of my kids," she explained. "Any moment I expected her to open up the plastic bag and show a pair of shorts with a slogan like 'Welcome Home, Phil' or 'Happy Summer.' She had been running and was sweating. Running around this town is a big deal. All the kids do it."

Ruth summed her up quickly, and continued working at the sink. "She was not very pretty. Her face was fat, and she had shortish red-brown hair which looked as though someone had given it a wet perm. She kept smoothing it back and biting her lower lip. She was not wearing a bra and her T-shirt was sticking to her flesh, showing large nipples. It was kind of gross. She had beady eyes and kept staring forward. Most people have a softness about their eyes, but she had a very piercing look. And she seemed excited and confused."

Phil noticed something else, the handle of a gun tucked into the garbage bag. He too thought this girl was having fun, and assumed it to be a water pistol, which would explain why she had wrapped herself in plastic.

Even when Laurie walked between the two of them, pulled out a second gun, held both weapons in front of her, and announced, "You are my hostages," they did not take her seriously.

"Who are you?" Phil asked.

So he doesn't know her either, Ruth thought, and began to feel uneasy.

Laurie gave the explanation which came readily to her, and which had always brought her sympathy. She said she had been raped. She had been out in her car when a man had assaulted her; she shot him in the struggle, then ran all the way from River Forest. Or perhaps it was Forest Park. She was confused about the names, neither of which belonged in Winnetka, and must have been thinking of Forest Glen Drive, the street where she had fire-bombed the Rushe house. She said she had used the gun, which she kept in her glove compartment for self-protection, and was afraid the police were out looking for her.

Ruth tried to soothe her. "But you did it in self-defense," she said. "The police will understand."

"How would it look," Laurie argued, "for a north shore girl to kill a man after he had raped her?" She gave the impression that she had known her attacker. "It might be better to kill myself," she said.

"You don't know that he's dead," Ruth reasoned.

The more Laurie talked, the more discrepancies appeared in her story. A young woman might keep a revolver in her car, but not two of them. And surely the car would have been her best means of escape, so why had she abandoned it? If she had been raped, why was she so afraid of the police? Yet the garbage bag looked like evidence of rape; so did her breathless, excited state. Ruth had never seen a rape victim before, and did not know what to expect. Ever practical, she went upstairs and returned with a pair of yellow calf-length pants belonging to one of her teenage daughters.

Turning her back to the two of them, Laurie pulled on the pants, holding up the garbage bag with her elbows. She accomplished this awkward maneuver by warily setting both guns on the counter. Phil quickly picked up one of them, the .22 Beretta, took out the magazine, and put it in his pocket. Then he reached for the .32 revolver but she snatched it first.

He had observed, while she was telling her rape story, that the guns were real and that she was lying. Phil had learned quite a lot about automatic weapons from his older brother Daniel who was training to be a police officer at Cook County Police Academy. In the few seconds that the .32 lay on the counter, he noticed that, like the Beretta, it was fully loaded. There were two possible explanations: Either this woman had not actually fired a shot, or else she had reloaded one or both revolvers before leaving the scene. He could not imagine what was behind her lie, but felt impelled to get the second gun away from her.

Curiously enough, Phil had helped Dan practice defensive tactics only the previous evening, with Dan acting as the law-enforcement officer and he as the criminal who had to be disarmed. As they wrestled Phil had joked: "I'm tired of playing the crook. Can't I be the cop for once?" They were having fun reenacting the boyhood game of cops and robbers, only this time there was a trick to it: With the gun pressed against his back, its lever cocked, the policeman had to know how to knock it out of the criminal's hand before he pulled the trigger. Phil never did get his turn to try this, and had argued to his brother: "If I was the crook, I wouldn't hold my gun right up against you like that. I would stand back to shoot."

He was now in that position in the kitchen, a few feet away from Laurie, and he could see why it was so vulnerable. "When this woman picked up the gun from the counter, I was not close enough to jump her, but close enough to risk being shot."

Buying time, he bombarded her with questions. Where did she live? What did she do? She answered most of them truthfully, stating that she had been married but was now living with her parents in Glencoe. She was currently at the University of Wisconsin—then came the fiction—studying journalism. It was the same kind of easy lie that she had told Emily Fletcher almost six weeks earlier, that Sunday morning when she begged a ride from Winnetka to Wilmette and talked about committing suicide. Her behavior was suicidal right now, or else psychotic; otherwise, why would a person hiding from the police reveal so much about her identity?

"You'll have quite a story to write when you get back to journalism school," Ruth Andrew remarked.

A similar thought was running through her son's mind. He felt excited at the prospect of entertaining his friends with this tale about being held up by a woman wearing a garbage bag. It was such a strange episode. He wasn't afraid of her; as he later observed, "When you are in great shape and have just been offered two fantastic jobs, you feel invulnerable." But he was trying to find a way to get the other gun from her. "If she had not been armed, there was very little she could have done, even to my mother. She could have ruined her day, that's all. It was the guns that made her threatening."

Phil asked Laurie if she would like to use the kitchen phone to call her parents. Surely they would come and get her, he thought. She seemed relieved to make the contact, and dialed a number while nervously clutching her remaining gun. Again, this wasn't the behavior of a fugitive. In a brief conversation they heard her say she had done something terrible and that the police were looking for her: "Mother, it's bad."

Phil took the phone from her and told Edith Wasserman that her daughter had been raped, had shot her attacker, and was very scared. Would she please come right away and pick her up? He was incredulous at the response. As he remembered it, "She said she had no way of getting to Winnetka because her daughter had taken her car. I asked why she couldn't call a cab, and I don't remember her answer. If there was no cab she could have asked a neighbor, or the police. But it was clear that we could not expect her. The last thing she said to me was 'See she gets home safely.' It was hardly the response I would expect from a mother whose daughter has just been raped."

After Phil put down the telephone, his father, Raymond Andrew, walked into the kitchen. As soon as the older man had taken in the situation, he started arguing with Laurie about handing over the gun. She insisted that she felt more comfortable holding on to it, and he became angry. This was his house, he said, and he wasn't having guns toted around in it. Laurie ignored the statement, and he repeated it more emphatically. They were getting nowhere. There was a frying pan in the drainer by the kitchen sink, and it crossed Ruth's mind to end the argument by hitting the intruder over the head. Then she thought: If I miss, this woman may shoot Ray and Phil. Laurie was already holding the gun in a firing position with her finger on the trigger. Ruth decided to try persuasion.

"My daughters will be coming home from school soon, and if there are police outside they will follow them in," she told Laurie. It wasn't true. Catherine and Patricia would not leave New Trier High School until she picked them up at 1:00 P.M. but she was looking for an excuse to get out of the house and call for help. Phil tried another tactic. He persuaded Laurie to make a second call to her home. Again, she seemed glad to make the contact and they heard her say: "Tell Dad I'm sorry." Then Ray Andrew grabbed the phone from her.

"Can't you get a neighbor to drive you?" he asked Edith Wasserman. "If your daughter has shot this man, she is going to need bond money. Don't you have a lawyer?"

Like Phil, he soon realized that this mother was unwilling, or perhaps too scared, to help. "She has a gun and you have to explain to her that she must give it up," he insisted. "We are all in danger."

Laurie took the phone, walking around a corner of the kitchen by the pantry so she could talk more privately. While she was preoccupied Phil looked across to his mother and jerked his head toward the hallway. Ruth had already moved in that direction to get out of the line of fire. Unseen by Laurie, she went quietly up the backstairs, across an upstairs corridor, down the main stairway, and out the front door.

She walked down the driveway and onto Kent Road, a street so short and quiet that she could easily see both ends of it. Looking right, toward the dead end, she saw a man crouched beside a German shepherd dog, utterly still as though listening intently. She had a strong sense of there being people in the woods behind him.

"It was an eerie feeling," she said. "It was very quiet and there was just this man with the dog, not moving. I looked the other way and there were three or four policemen directing traffic at the corner, which was unusual, and a lot of cars going along Hibbard Street."

As she would find out later, most of them were driven by panic-stricken mothers who had heard the first news bulletin about a shooting at their children's school. Knowing nothing of this, she was glad to see policemen and hurried toward them.

"What happened?" a neighbor called out, referring to the traffic.

"I don't know," Ruth answered. "But please call Sacred Heart School and tell them not to let Michael home at lunchtime." He was her youngest child, aged twelve, and she was worried about him walking into whatever might be happening in her kitchen.

At the corner of Kent Road and Hibbard Street she put a hand firmly on the arm of one of the policemen.

"There's a woman in my kitchen with a gun, and my husband and son are in there with her," she told him.

"That must be her!" he responded. "What was she wearing?"

Ruth told him. He said something into his radio, and immediately police officers came running from all directions.

"Warn them to be careful of my father and his nurse," she urged him. "They're sitting outside the house."

She did not see Detectives Floyd Mohr and Bob Kerner carry her father to the garage because the police made her stay at the corner. After a while an ambulance turned into Kent Road and stopped some distance short of her house. She was not allowed to go near it, but she felt certain it had come for Phil, that he had been shot, and that he was dead.

Laurie's second phone call to her mother lasted seven minutes, one minute longer than the first. She put the telephone down at 11:15 A.M. and immediately resumed pointing her revolver at Phil and his father. She seemed more frightened than threatening, as though she wanted Phil to stay with her and didn't know how else to insist. Both men continued urging her to hand over this remaining gun; if she would do so, Phil promised to go with her to the police. He saw her as a terrified young woman to whom something rather more than rape had happened, but he did not feel in personal danger. It was hard to take her seriously as she alternated between pretending he was her hostage, and wanting her mother to take her home. His only fear was that she might pull the trigger in panic. He still had her .22 Beretta; not that it was of any use without the bullets, but it made for a certain equality between them.

"If you don't put that gun down we're not staying around here," his father told Laurie, moving toward the hallway. "It's too dangerous."

She did not try to stop him, and he left by the front door, assuming Phil would follow. Laurie raised her gun, ordering Phil to stay. He repeated his promise to go to the police with her. They had both edged around the kitchen so that she was now in a position to look through the window and he was not. She glanced outside, saw several police officers warily closing in on the house, and, in that moment of panic and madness, pulled the trigger and shot Phil in the chest.

The pain was searing. He could barely breathe, his throat was choked, and there was a tightness around his heart. He was incredulous that she had done this to him, but although bleeding heavily into his T-shirt he still had the finely honed reflexes of an athlete. It would amaze him later, how instinctively he knew what to do without even thinking about it. He dived into the large pantry, slammed the door behind him, and flattened himself against a side wall while he reloaded the Beretta with the magazine he had pocketed. Expecting Laurie to shoot through the door, he stayed there for several minutes, out of range, listening carefully.

There was no sound from the kitchen. Intending to shoot his way out, he cautiously opened the pantry door and looked around. It was a large kitchen with various counters and corners, but she did not seem to be hiding there. His strength was being sapped with every breath, and he was willing himself not to collapse. It was like coming up to the last lap in a swimming race, the same burning sensation in the lungs when endurance begins to fail, the same concentration of will to keep going. If he could cross the room and get outside the back door he would be safe, and as free to relax as when he wearily hoisted himself out of a pool after a one-mile swim.

With the gun cocked in front of him, he backed out of the kitchen. He was holding it in his left hand and clutching his chest with his right as he stumbled into the yard. "I can't believe she shot me," he gasped.

At first the police did not realize he was wounded, mistook his gesture, and assumed he was threatening them with the revolver. For all they knew he was an accomplice of Laurie's, ready to shoot. Their guns were still pointed at him when he collapsed. As he fell, Laurie's Beretta slipped out of his hand. Detective Bob Kerner ran forward and kicked it out of reach. An officer who was also a paramedic removed Phil's T-shirt and put a gauze pack on the open wound. Lying on his back on the driveway, Phil tried to tell him that Laurie was still in the house with five live rounds in her revolver. He wanted to help the police as much as possible but was barely able to speak, and they were backing away from him, out of Laurie's range. In the background his father was yelling, "We need an ambulance! My son has been shot! Somebody get an ambulance, for God's sake!"

Phil retained a vivid memory of the next half hour, and it was as though all the endurance tests he had undergone in championship swimming had prepared him to survive it. His lungs were deflating with every breath, and he was concentrating on making the breaths last, extending the period between each intake of air, the way he had learned in hypoxic training. This time he was struggling to stay alive, and he held on to the image of being in sight of the flag and forcing himself to keep going until he could reach it. He recognized that he might die if he lost consciousness before he was taken into surgery, and told himself that he must not let that happen. "I can't die now," he thought. "It's too beautiful a day to die."

Lying there waiting for an ambulance, he had nothing else to stare at but the blinding blueness above him. This was one of those rare May mornings when the last splendors of spring and the promise of summer coalesce into a skyscape so cloudlessly intense that it is like a glimpse of eternity. The burning in his chest and the feeling of suffocation were almost unbearable, like the remembered pain of pushing himself to stay in the lead when he had swum past the point of exhaustion. It was a revelation to him that the brink of death and the edge of victory should feel like the same place, and he was surprisingly unafraid.

He could feel the strength of the sun on his bare flesh, and was struck by the irony of being wounded and getting a tan at the same time. His injuries were much worse than he imagined; a man a little less fit or a few years older would not have survived them. A single high-velocity bullet had bounced around inside his chest, puncturing both lungs, tearing his stomach and pancreas, and shredding his esophagus. Grazing the cardiac membrane, it had missed his heart by a millimeter.

When an ambulance came, the Andrew house was surrounded by police officers with their guns aimed toward it. Although they were standing back they looked like easy targets for a person firing from an upstairs window. Phil was the most vulnerable of all, and the paramedics were reluctant to risk their lives by going onto the driveway to get him. The ambulance driver had pulled into a spot higher up Kent Road, out of range, and was reluctant to come closer.

Lieutenant Joe Sumner recalled the scene: "Mr. Andrew was standing by the circular driveway in front of his house. He was extremely agitated, demanding that we get his son out of there. The young man was still breathing, you could see that, but no one could get up to him without risking being shot. I had to physically restrain Mr. Andrew by holding his arm."

Detective Floyd Mohr could not bear to watch this any longer. If nobody took the risk, another of Laurie's victims would die. Phil was already turning blue from lack of oxygen. Mohr had to try and save him.

"I wasn't thinking of danger because what I did was totally stupid," he said later. "The ambulance was parked near the end of the street. I ran there and tried to persuade the paramedics to bring it to the house, but they did not want to take the risk, and I don't blame them. So I told them to lie on the floor of the ambulance, and had the driver work the gas and brake pedals with his hands while I steered from the passenger seat with my gun out of the driver's window."

Sumner and his men pointed long-range guns at the house while Mohr made his perilous journey. As soon as he pulled up on the driveway three armed policemen ran forward and helped him carry Phil to the ambulance. At that moment a shot rang out in the stillness. Everyone tensed.

"Who fired that?" Sumner shouted into his radio. There was silence, followed by smiles of relief. One of the officers had been standing behind a car with his shotgun propped against it. As he shifted position to keep Mohr and the others covered, his weapon had caught in the rain gutter on the car roof, triggering a shot into the air. It could not have happened at a worse moment.

Mohr was so tense that all his senses were heightened. "I was scared and I was holding this young man in my arms, wanting to play God and cure him. I was sure he was going to die, didn't doubt it, and although I had never seen him before, everything about him made an impact on me. I could smell his body, his sweat, his blood, his shampoo. For a long time afterward I could still smell his blood in my sleep. I had heard about things like that, but didn't think they could happen to me."

At the edge of the danger zone he let the paramedics take over, and returned to his police colleagues by the house.

Philip Andrew knew exactly where he was going. At the end of Kent Road the ambulance turned right onto Hibbard Street, then left on Tower Road. That meant Highland Park Hospital. Evanston Hospital, the larger of the two, was in the opposite direction, its resources already stretched by four severely wounded children needing extensive surgery. Highland Park could still cope with another emergency, although its staff was dealing with a fifth child, and with the death of Nicholas Corwin. Phil felt every turn in the road on the journey there: north on Hibbard, west on Tower, then several miles north on the expressway and a short turn east to the hospital. He was aware of the fluorescent lights in the emergency room and the faces of people leaning over him. Once the chest tubes were inserted he was able to breathe more easily. Then X rays were taken, and hearing a nurse ask for a lead vest, he tried to crack a joke about wishing he had been wearing one when he was shot.

"I wanted them to know I was okay," he explained. "And I told them I was a swimmer. That was important to me because I wanted to swim again. There were so many things going through my head, from my girlfriend to swimming. They weren't just flashing by. I knew exactly what was going on, and I was trying to be helpful."

He was in surgery for six hours. As he was being wheeled to an operating room he saw a familiar face, that of his parish priest, Father Raftery. He thought he was being offered the last rites and didn't particularly want them because he was confident of survival. Actually it was the anointing of the sick, and Father Raftery accomplished it in record time.

Thomas Raftery, a man no longer young, had been moving from one dramatic scene to another. He had gone from saying Larry Carney's funeral mass to the bloodshed at Hubbard Woods, to the hospital for Philip Andrew. His next call would be to his own parochial school, so close to the Hubbard Woods School that there had been a panic about whether it might be next on Laurie's list; then he would go back to Hubbard Woods to see how else he might help. In the evening there was to be a confirmation at Sacred Heart. He made a mental note to telephone Bishop Wilton Gregory and ask whether, in light of today's events, he wanted to postpone the service.

Before he could do this, the bishop called him. No, he did not want to change plans. He changed his sermon instead. The coming Sunday would be Pentecost, and at the confirmation, the bishop made the parallel between the bereft and confused state of Christ's disciples before the first Pentecost, and the feelings of Winnetkans at the end of this terrible day. There was a bigger congregation than usual at the service. People felt a need to pray.

FIFTEEN

THERE WAS enormous relief when word reached Hubbard Woods School that the killer had been found. Police Chief Herbert Timm made the announcement to the hundreds of media people and parents gathered in the little park east of the school. It was early afternoon by now, and dozens of fathers had joined the anxious crowd. They had come off the Chicago train expecting to take their children home, and were irked at being kept waiting. Timm summed up the events of the past two and a half hours, adding: "We are reasonably sure that Laurie Dann is in the house at Two Kent Road."

This sent most of the reporters scurrying to the Andrew house. The parents remained, their anxiety turning to belligerence.

"What do you mean, you're reasonably sure?" a father demanded. "Aren't you positive?" There was an edge to his voice, implying that the police had been remiss. Timm was allowing for the slender chance that Laurie had run out of the Andrew house after shooting Philip, somehow evading his men while they were positioning themselves around the building. If so, she would not get far, not with so many police around.

Herb Timm and his deputy Joe Sumner were coping with three major crime scenes in a small area: arson at the Rushe house, the shootings at Hubbard Woods School, and Laurie holed up in the Andrews' home on Kent Road. With its staff at thirty-five, Winnetka's police force could not possibly cope with all this; even with all the reinforcements from surrounding villages there continued to be critical staffing problems. No matter how many extra portable telephones were brought in, there were never enough in whichever place they were suddenly needed. And since many of the media people also had cellular phones and microwave transmitters, the local frequencies were soon overloaded. At one point a National Broadcasting Company helicopter hovered low enough for its camera crew to take aerial photographs, and knocked out all the police radios and phones in the area. It took a call to the Federal Aviation Administration to get the helicopter out of range; in the meantime, there was a ten-minute halt in police communications which seemed like hours.

"They took some beautiful pictures, but they made a big problem worse," Timm commented.

Right now, outside the school, he had to deal with the media on another level, and this was new to him. Timm had spent most of his life, and most of his police career, on Chicago's north shore where crime was rarely more serious than burglary or drug abuse; where press relations meant an occasional chat with a young reporter from the local weekly newspaper. He had become Winnetka's police chief at the unusually young age of thirty-three, almost twelve years ago, and saw police work as a form of public service, having been drawn to it in the Kennedy era when there was a lot of idealism about serving one's country. A dedicated Roman Catholic, Timm had never lost this purity of purpose. With it went an ingenuous charm, the alert, scrubbed look of an altar boy grown older. He was one of those men who even on a day as stressful as this still managed to look tidy: always the immaculate white shirt, the well-tailored suit, the thinning fair hair evenly brushed back. As his police colleagues often remarked, Herb Timm had class.

Inwardly he was a worrier, and he worried now about dealing with the press. In many ways the media was an irritation and a burden at a time like this. He needed to concentrate his energies on organizing police work at the three crime scenes, and Hubbard Woods was still the most vulnerable. "We had three to four hundred people running around," he recalled. "In the midst of all the confusion we had to try to stabilize the school environment and isolate the witnesses, most of whom were children eight years old. We also had to stabilize a community which was coming apart at the seams. I was worried about the massive influx of people to the area. It was essential to set up roadblocks, and that alone took us one and a half hours."

What he didn't need right now were the insistent requests: Chief, is there anything new on the injured children? Can you give us an update on the Kent Road situation? Chief, I have a deadline in half an hour. Can you add anything to your previous statement?

He answered the questions fully and accurately, which gained him instant recognition among reporters as a friendly and reliable source. He in turn developed a respect for them.

"For the most part they did not get in my way," he remarked. "Some asked some very pertinent questions which helped my thinking. They got the information out to people along the north shore, which was very helpful to us. One Milwaukee reporter gave us some useful information about Laurie Dann's recent activities in Madison. And you wouldn't believe the communication equipment they have. They are real pros."

A few of the pros overstepped the mark by thrusting cameras and microphones in the faces of bewildered children when they were eventually let out of school. "Did Laurie Dann ever babysit for you?" one youngster was asked. But most reporters cooperated with Timm's request to stay behind the police barriers and to respect the privacy of those who had been badly traumatized. "I think the media people handled themselves admirably," Village President Clarine Hall commented.

Early in his career when he was a Chicago policeman, Timm had seen plenty of violent crime, but this was his first direct encounter with major news organizations. He had been mistrustful of reporters until he took an intensive course in media relations at the FBI Academy in Virginia, and learned that they were as skilled at their work as he was, and that if he wanted their cooperation he had better respect that. He remembered the advice as he walked out of Hubbard Woods School to the biggest crowd of reporters and cameramen he had ever faced. Remembered also was an incident in the FBI Academy when a police colleague had been called upon to practice giving a press conference. "He was from Tennessee, older than I was, a real good old boy. He had his hair combed over his bald patch, but when he went to the men's room before class the hand dryer blew it the wrong way, and he didn't check the mirror. So he went into the 'press conference' looking like that. He tried to be tough, but everyone was laughing. One of the first rules we learned was to collect ourselves before addressing the media."

As police chief of a village where nothing really bad happened, he had never expected to find himself in that situation. But the advice came back to him as he straightened his hair and the jacket of his neat gray suit, neither of which needed straightening, before walking across from the school to the herd of reporters and photographers in the little park. He held several of these impromptu press conferences in the next few hours, describing the latest developments in a voice deliberately loud enough for the parents to hear. Their questions hit him hardest. "What do you mean, you're reasonably sure? Aren't you positive?" Reporters didn't talk to him like that.

School Superintendent Donald Monroe worked with Timm, bringing out to the reporters those people they wanted to interview—the school principal, the psychologists—in return for a promise that they would not try to enter the school or talk to children. He reassured parents: "Your children are all right. If they had been hurt you would have already been informed. But at this point we think it is best for them to remain in school. We have mental-health professionals in the building, and the children are sharing what has happened with them."

None of the parents liked this decision and a few of them argued, but most showed faith in Monroe's judgment. The presence of clergy and social workers moving back and forth between them and their children inspired confidence. It also allowed them to talk about their concerns. One set of parents confided to the Reverend Marcia Heeter of Winnetka Presbyterian Church that they were afraid to go home when their child was released from school. They had known Laurie Dann as a baby-sitter, and feared she might come after them with her gun. They recognized this fear to be farfetched, but it was there, and they did not want to communicate it to their already frightened child.

Monroe, looking surprisingly calm in his borrowed shirt, carried away from one of his encounters in the little park the lasting memory of "a sleazy-looking man with a forty-inch belly held in check by a thirty-inch alligator belt handing me an envelope to give to Amy Moses, offering ten thousand dollars for her story." Later Monroe mailed it back, without comment, to the supermarket scandal sheet the man represented.

By early afternoon it was judged safe for the eighteen remaining children from Room 7 to go home. They were to leave before the others, a few at a time by the back doors, avoiding the press across the street. But first their parents were brought into the school and taken to an empty room. There some of the mental-health professionals described what their children had seen, and the delayed reactions parents might expect: nightmares, fears of darkness and of sleeping alone, temporary regression to infantile behavior. Handled sensitively, these symptoms could be the beginning of healing, parents were told.

The school authorities were about to let the first set of parents pick up the first child when Herb Timm stopped them. He had been conferring with Nancy Sidote, the state's attorney for the area, who had recently arrived on the scene. They both felt strongly that the children who witnessed the shooting must be interviewed by the police before any other adults talked to them. If this was put off until tomorrow the children's recollections could become colored by parental influences and admonitions, and the police might hear a subtly different story.

This was the last straw for some parents. Herb Timm had to physically restrain one father, an acquaintance of his, who demanded to go to his child. Timm tried to explain that the interviews would be done very sensitively by a woman police officer, but none of them wanted to hear this. Sergeant Patty McConnell was standing close by, nervously wondering how she would handle the situation. As a mother herself, she understood the parents' anger. "They were tearful, furious, and vehement about wanting to be with their children," she related. "I understood where they were coming from. They needed physical reassurance that their children were okay. I'm sure they expected the worst, as I did. And their anger toward us came out of their own fear."

Patty's maternal feelings were very close to the surface at that moment. Eight months earlier she had given birth to her first child, and was inwardly worrying when this nightmare of a day would end, and whether her baby-sitter could continue to look after Kristin until it did. Normally Patty would have been off duty by the early afternoon in time to take over the parenting chores from her husband, Matthew, a patrolman in the Wilmette police department, who was scheduled to work the late shift. She had telephoned him around noon, and learned that he had just been called in to work because of the Winnetka emergency. On his way there, he intended to drop off the baby at the sitter's house. While Patty had every confidence in this arrangement, she too felt anxious about her child.

Unaware of her empathy and of her interviewing skills, the parents would not be placated. Patty did not look very professional in her blue jeans and sweatshirt, clutching a child's red notebook, her soft brown hair loose about her shoulders. Nancy Sidote, an older woman with a commanding presence, faced the parents and stated firmly: "This is Sergeant McConnell. She must talk to your children. And this must happen before you see them."

That left Donald Monroe with the task of explaining to the parents: "Please understand that this is a crime scene as well as a school. If we were just acting like a school you would have been reunited with your children already. But the police need to gather evidence, and we have to compromise."

Patty had Amy Moses with her, which was essential. She was unknown to these eighteen children, and the last strange woman who had walked into their classroom had shot to kill. As they walked down the corridor together Patty remembered the gun in her waistband.

"I can't go into that room with this," she whispered to Herb Timm, handing him her revolver. She was so accustomed to the feel of it against her body that she had forgotten its existence. She and Amy held on to one another, equally apprehensive, as they walked into the classroom.

They found the children calmly sitting in a group with a teacher, as though waiting for story time. They were pleased to see Amy, who explained: "This is Patty McConnell and she is a policewoman. You know I went with her to try to catch the woman who shot some of your friends. Now she wants to know if there is anything you can tell her."

Patty would have liked more time to phrase her questions. She was so afraid of adding to the children's trauma by saying the wrong thing. She wasn't sure whether they knew that Nicky Corwin was dead and was worried about mentioning him until it became clear that Dick Streedain and Mary Giffin had already told them.

"May we tell you about Nicky?" they asked her.

There were tears in her eyes as she listened to their recollections. "He was so nice to everyone. . . . He was a classroom helper. . . . He was good at sports. . . . Even when he won at soccer he would be kind to the ones who had lost. . . . He was the smartest boy in class. And the nicest."

When they had finished, Patty asked them, very gently, if they could tell her what happened when the bad lady came into the room. She needed to know whether they could add anything to the account Amy had given. If there were to be a murder trial, these children would have to testify, and she was thinking how hard it would be for them, yet how bravely they would do it.

In the three hours since the shooting, they had done a lot of talking about it, and by now their individual versions of the event had blended into a collective memory. That was a pity, Patty thought; someone should have interviewed them sooner. Their recollections were much the same as Amy's, except for their conviction that Laurie had left by a different door from the one she remembered. But it had been essential to have their confirmation of her account.

Half an hour later she told the parents: "I have talked to your children. They are fine and calm and anxious to be with you."

They hurried past her, barely acknowledging her presence. As soon as they were out of sight Herb Timm quietly handed back her gun.

The chief's next assignment for her was to go to the fire station and interview Marian Rushe and her children. He teamed her up with Sergeant Michael O'Connell of the Glenview police department, an old friend of hers who had just arrived. This was O'Connell's day off, and he had been relaxing at home when he heard the radio news. He hurried to his office, arriving in time to receive Patty's telephone request: "If any of you can come and give us a hand we would appreciate it." He knew it must be a major crisis for other police departments to be called in, and he immediately thought of his sixteen-year-old daughter at Northbrook High School, and of the possibility that a killer might go there too.

When he got to Winnetka he, like Ira Sloan, was not prepared for the horror of Room 7. "It was shocking," he said. "Normally in a north shore grade school you would see a clean classroom with pictures of smiling faces. Here there was blood on the floor, ripped clothing, syringe caps that the paramedics had used, bullet holes in the wall. From a police officer's viewpoint, you can deal with that. But not as a parent. Normally the worst thing that comes out of a classroom is a flunking grade. Here it was a deceased child. Even to look at that room made me very uncomfortable."

He was glad of the diversion, this assignment to go with Patty to the firehouse. She had walked out onto the street ahead of him to take a moment's break from the tension.

"Give me a cigarette," she said as he joined her. "Just one."

She had not smoked for six months and thought she had broken the habit. Now she puffed away gratefully as she juggled the car through a mass of awkwardly parked vehicles, the worst traffic jam ever seen in Winnetka. Normally it was only a few easy blocks to the fire station, in the same building as the village police headquarters, but today the drive was an obstacle course. Marian Rushe and her children had been taken there until somebody from the police department had time to talk to them. They found her waiting in the day room, having refused hospital treatment for her burns because she had not wanted to leave Patrick and Carl. They were now running around boisterously, unaware of the danger they had survived. Patrick, the six-year-old, was able to give a clear account of their outing with Laurie; about how she had taken them to a little park and offered them funny-tasting milk from a Mickey Mouse cup.

As he listened, Mike O'Connell was making notes of things the police must do: Locate the park. Get officers to search the grounds. Get Teletype messages to other police agencies to check schools and parks along the north shore. Get the milk from the refrigerator at the Rushe home and check it for poison.

"This thing is mushrooming," he said to Patty. "We already have half a dozen evidence technicians at the school. How many more are we going to need?"

Marian's concerns were focused on Laurie.

"How could she? And why?" she kept asking. "I thought she had changed a lot, but I never thought she was crazy. She was always so wonderful with the children."

The house on Sheridan Road, Glencoe, where Laurie lived with her
parents, Norman and Edith Wasserman (*Stephen Longmire*)

Hubbard Woods School, Winnetka (*Stephen Longmire*)

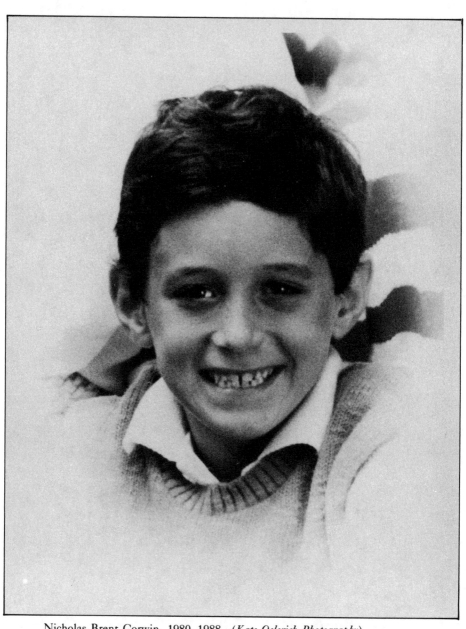

Nicholas Brent Corwin, 1980–1988 (*Kate Oelerich Photography*)

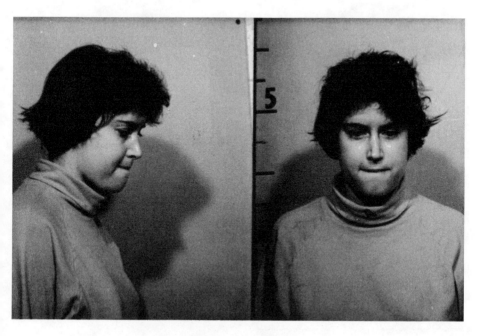

The last known photos of Laurie Dann: police mug shots taken in March 1988 when she was arrested for shoplifting in Madison, Wisconsin

ABOVE LEFT: Winnetka Police Chief Herbert Timm (*Phototronics, Inc., Winnetka*)
ABOVE RIGHT: Lieutenant Joseph Sumner, director of police operations, Winnetka (*Phototronics, Inc., Winnetka*)

LEFT: Sergeant Patricia McConnell, supervisor in charge of police investigations, Winnetka (*Phototronics, Inc., Winnetka*)

Richard Streedain, principal of Hubbard Woods School, reading to parents from a list of the injured children. His shirt is bloodstained from carrying one of them to an ambulance. (*Copyright © Chicago Tribune Company, all rights reserved, used with permission*)

BELOW: Amy Moses, the Hubbard Woods substitute teacher who defied Laurie Dann, describing the scene to reporters (*Copyright © Chicago Tribune Company, all rights reserved, used with permission*)

Norman Wasserman (*right*), with a dog leash attached to his belt, being led by Detective Floyd Mohr to the Andrew house, where Laurie had taken refuge (*Copyright © Chicago Tribune Company, all rights reserved, used with permission*)

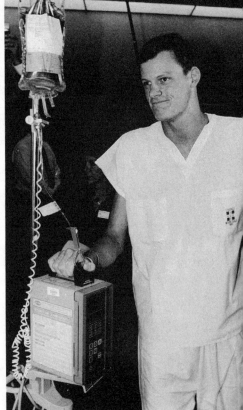

Philip Andrew, Laurie Dann's last victim, giving a press conference at Highland Park Hospital while still recovering from his wounds (*AP/Wide World Photos*)

Anxious parents supporting one another while waiting outside Hubbard Woods School for news of their children (*AP/Wide World Photos*)

The Hubbard Woods shopping district, Winnetka (*Stephen Longmire*)

The Andrew house on Kent Road, Winnetka, as Laurie would have seen it
when she approached from the woods (*Stephen Longmire*)

SIXTEEN

Timm had already made sure that public schools up and down the north shore had been warned to keep children indoors until he was absolutely sure that the streets were safe. There were not enough police to protect all these buildings, so doors were locked and tables pushed against windows as a barricade against the unknown enemy. Some children were told the reason why, others were left to imagine, and a few were lied to: At one school a story was put out that pesticide had been sprayed in the area, temporarily contaminating the atmosphere. Predictably, the children who were least traumatized in the months ahead were those who were told the truth in the beginning.

It was still uncertain whether Laurie Dann had acted alone or as part of a plot, whether it was she or an accomplice who had tried to fire-bomb the Highland Park school and day-care center earlier that morning. If an accomplice, how many more might there be out there? And why did they want to kill children? From Highland Park in the north to Skokie in the southwest, both heavily Jewish communities, there was fearful speculation about

175

what the plot might be. Mimi Ryan, a teacher at Wilmette Junior High School, heard it from a student and was appalled.

"I was in the teachers' lounge in the lunch hour when a bulletin was passed around to all teachers about the shooting at Hubbard Woods School," she recalled. "Then the principal came and told us that everything was being locked up. We were not to tell the children what had happened, only that there had been an emergency and that there was some concern. It did not take me long to realize that this explanation wouldn't work. When I got into class some of the children had already gotten word about something terrible happening at Hubbard Woods, and there was a lot of talk among them. They were so worried, and began to ask me questions. One boy of eleven or twelve, I shall never forget him, said: 'I bet it's anti-Semitism. They are after the Jews. I just know they are after us.'

"I thought: 'My God, I can't let this go on.' This child was a wreck. And that precipitated my decision to tell the class the truth. There had been a rebirth of anti-Semitism in the area, but I had no idea the fear ran that deep. The children were horrified when I told them about Laurie Dann. I did not tell them that she might come to Wilmette. But I did tell them that the doors were locked for their own safety and that they would not be going out for the lunch recess. They seemed to relax after they knew why."

This was not an isolated incident, and Herbert Timm was right about the entire area coming apart at the seams. In all the north shore villages there had long been a comfortable and friendly accommodation between Christians and Jews, based on a mutual pride in their shared communities. They served on the same school boards, planned block parties and fund-raisers together, campaigned for many of the same causes, voted one another in and out of local office on merit. But there was an essential difference that colored the social fabric of north shore life: The WASPs settled here first, and had created villages like Winnetka and Kenilworth in their own image. Before the Jews worked their way up to the north shore by way of Chicago's blue-collar suburbs, Winnetka's early Episcopalian dead were already lying in a green pasture by the lake, a prime piece of real estate, more beautiful and orderly than an English country churchyard.

The Jews were obliged to build their temples farther north and west, and to create their own country clubs, it being implicit that they need not apply to those the Protestants had established. At one time membership applications to Winnetka's exclusive Indian Hill Club were handed out with the Christ Church pledge cards. While such overt prejudice was no longer acceptable, it still manifested itself in the kind of jokes which were privately told over martinis.

Outwardly, the distinctions had become blurred as some Jews acquired WASP names and some ceased to practice their religion. Nevertheless, the fear of the ghetto was still imprinted on their collective consciousness; many had grandparents who did not speak English, and others had lost loved ones in concentration camps. Beneath the self-assured life-style which money had bought them, they still carried their singular form of post-traumatic stress, an old wound so well hidden beneath scar tissue that it might never again have obtruded upon their thinking if Laurie Dann had not gone mad.

When the truth came out they had to deal with a different pain: the fact that the killer, as well as the killed, was one of their own. But early on this Friday afternoon all that was known was that with the unexpectedness and horror of the Holocaust, there seemed to be a plot to eliminate a new generation. Along the north shore this reaction was exclusively Jewish and deeply fearful. The rest saw it as a single, terrifying, meaningless event.

In Highland Park, a heavily Jewish community, there had been police around the Ravinia School all morning, ever since that strange woman had planted an incendiary device in the children's cardboard playhouse. From the time it happened, just before nine o'clock, until the 11:30 A.M. break, it was treated as an isolated incident, a disturbing prank for no known reason. But shortly before noon the principal came into the staff lunch room, his face deathly white, with the news that some children had been shot at Hubbard Woods School.

"I thought and he thought that this was some kind of attack on Jewish kids, and only a few minutes earlier we had just turned two hundred kids loose for lunch," said Paul Grant, the second-grade teacher who had given the alarm about the fire bomb.

177

"There are a couple of fast-food places close to the school where most of them eat, the White Hen Pantry and Shelton's. We took off immediately and told them to send all the children back to school. And we stood on all the nearby street corners, the whole staff, and hustled the children back into the building."

Outwardly calm, Grant was struggling with an unexpressed fear. Seen in this new light, the bizarre behavior of the woman in the red wig suddenly became explicable: It seemed to be part of a terrorist pattern, which meant she would not have been working alone. "They are going to come back and get the children they missed," he thought to himself.

After lunch the police brought in mug shots of six women. Grant identified the one of Laurie Dann, and learned that it was she who had done the shooting at Hubbard Woods. The news spread quickly, and soon parents were streaming into the school to pick up their children. "We signed out every child who had an adult to go home with. We wanted to get them home because Laurie Dann was still loose, and we thought they would be safer out of school. By two-thirty only three children in my class were left."

There was a similar panic at the Jewish day-care center that Laurie had set out to fire-bomb. At first teachers had not felt threatened by the woman who tried to walk into their building carrying a gasoline can. Now that they knew about Hubbard Woods they were frantic to send the children home before she returned to destroy them.

"We telephoned all the parents to ask them to come early," a teacher recalled. "It was a very emotional day. I hate to talk about it because this brings back memories I would rather forget."

Most of the schools in the area kept their children behind locked doors, with desks and tables barricaded against windows. There was a pervading sense of an unknown enemy outside, more powerful than all their combined strength. Except for the crowd outside Hubbard Woods School, well protected by police, the streets were as deserted as if the entire north shore had come under siege. People who went outdoors, unaware of what had happened, were struck by the eerie silence. One woman was so affected that she telephoned the Winnetka police station to express her feelings. "Something terrible has happened to our village," she said. As if they did not know.

Very few children avoided the trauma, no matter what north shore school they attended. Hubbard Woods had its mental-health professionals encouraging students to talk about the immediate horror. Principals at other schools gave imperfect explanations for the locked doors and the strained looks on the faces of teachers, leaving children to worry and speculate. That evening on the television news they heard a great deal about Laurie Dann, and she became so real to them that for a long time afterward their childish drawings were strikingly similar to those done by children at Hubbard Woods: a woman's face at a window, peering into a room where a child lay in bed alone. The woman came out of the darkness with a gun in her hand, sometimes two, and there was no escaping her. Eventually she would become incorporated into playground games: "Laurie Dann will get you if you don't watch out." But on this incongruously bright and beautiful May day all energies were concentrated on the children's physical safety. It was impossible to predict the aftermath.

Parents felt immediate panic. One Winnetka mother was sitting on the village green in charge of four small children at play when a neighbor came by and told her the news; immediately she hustled the children into her car, hurried home, and locked the doors. "It seemed to take so long to get them there, and I was so afraid because I did not know what the danger was, how near it was, or how soon something terrible might happen," she said. "We stayed indoors for days, the children and me, not wanting to go outside even after the danger had passed, because the house was the only place where I felt safe."

Rosemary Shugar, a skin-care specialist at a Winnetka beauty salon, heard the police sirens while she was working on a client. "They were so shrill and loud and they went on for about ten minutes, so I knew something terrible had happened."

As soon as she learned the reason she thought of her son, a first grader at Greeley School, one of the two other elementary schools in Winnetka. "I tore to Greeley like a bat out of hell," she recalled. "Some other parents had already arrived, and the principal was standing by the door telling them that the children would have to stay inside and that we would be telephoned later.

She said that the school did not yet know much about what was going on.

"I went back to the shop, and finished the girl I had been waxing. She had been so nice about it and had said, 'Oh, my God, just you go!,' and when I came back half an hour later she was still sitting there. There was another woman with foil on her hair, having it colored, and she was ripping the foil off. Someone rinsed her quickly and she took off for one of the schools. It was a crazy day. Some people kept their appointments and some did not show up—probably mothers of Hubbard Woods children. We were all trying to listen to the radio. By this time they knew the name of the killer but did not know where she was. I was afraid that she would come into the shop. I was afraid to go onto the street. I was afraid to get into my car. There were rumors that she had put time bombs in all the parks, and it felt as though nowhere was safe."

George Pence, a father who had been working from home that day, hurried to Greeley School at the same time as Rosemary Shugar. He returned without his child. "Jeanne, I cannot get Georgie out," he told his wife. "They have locked all the doors."

She had been waiting outside their house, so conscious of the street's stillness that she could hear her heart pounding. She wanted to run to the school and insist on seeing her son, but her husband restrained her.

"You're not going anywhere," he said. "The police are out looking for a woman of small stature with reddish hair—and you fit the description. Jeanne, they could shoot you!"

So they locked themselves in the house, and waited for the telephone to ring.

Shelley Galloway did not hear the sirens because she was shopping in the village hardware store. From there she went to Crow Island School, Winnetka's other elementary school, to pick up her children for the lunch break. Normally at 11:30 they would be sitting on the stone wall along with several others, waiting. Today the street was deserted. She was met at the school door by a teacher who walked her back to her car.

"Go straight home," the teacher said. "Something bad has happened at Hubbard Woods School."

"What is it?"

"I cannot tell you."

Immediately she reached home Shelley telephoned a friend who had a child at Hubbard Woods, asked the same question and got the same answer. "I cannot tell you."

"But I need to know," she insisted.

Her friend answered cautiously, spelling out the words she dared not say. "Some children have been S-H-O-T and one of them is D-E-A-D."

The story spread around the village and grew in the telling. By the time one Winnetka mother heard it, just before the telephone lines became too overloaded for any more calls, it had become: "There are a lot of fruitcakes loose, shooting children, and no one knows how many or where they are going."

One Glencoe mother was so fearful that she bundled her three small children into her car and headed for her husband's office in Chicago. She had reason to be terrified. Eight days earlier, shortly after 3:00 A.M., she had been wakened by an anonymous telephone call. "Your three girls are going to die," a woman announced, and hung up.

The threat was so specific and had been so much on her mind that it was the first thing she thought of on the morning of May 20 when a friend drove up to her house, her car radio blasting, screaming hysterically about the shooting at Hubbard Woods. The mother sent her cleaning woman home, gathered up her children, and drove like a person pursued down the expressway to the city. There was no doubt in her mind that Nicky Corwin's murderer had been her anonymous caller, and that her children were next on the hit list.

For most of the eighteen-mile journey the little girls slept peacefully in the back of the car. Their mother's attention was focused on the road and on the radio news. She was driving as fast as she dared, constantly checking her rearview mirror for a pursuer when she heard the news announcement Floyd Mohr had inspired: the identity of the killer.

"I almost stopped the car," she said. She could barely believe what she was hearing. Up to six months ago she had employed Laurie as a baby-sitter.

"She was very sweet, with an innocent-looking face," the mother recalled. "There was something a little spacy about her, as though she was not quite comfortable with herself, but she was so good with the children. She liked them, she played with them, and they liked her."

The last time Laurie came to the house she had behaved oddly, and was not hired again. "I had left her in charge of my three children plus another five-year-old. I came home in the late afternoon and walked into the family room, and it was like a cyclone had hit it. Laurie said the five-year-old had a temper tantrum and had thrown things. I went upstairs and found scribbles of purple crayon on a lower part of a bedroom wall, and an orange design higher up. The scribble could have been done by a child but the rest was beyond a child's reach. I asked Laurie about it and she said she did not know what happened. She was very calm, and helped to clean up. Afterward the two eldest children told me that she had made them watch a scary movie on TV and would not turn it off."

Before returning to the house on the evening of May 20, the mother and her husband checked at the police station, to make sure their family would be safe. "The next day Laurie's picture was all over the news," she recalled. "To see those photographs of her face and to know that she was in my house, alone with my children, while she was in possession of those weapons . . . it just killed me. And the guilt I feel that I did not pick up on her . . ."

Joan Allison heard about the shooting while she was shopping in a Wilmette's Jewel supermarket, two villages away from her home in Winnetka. What stuck in her mind was the checkout girl's exclamation, "It can happen here!," and her own sense of déjà vu. She had been a fourteen-year-old student in a Dallas high school when John Kennedy was assassinated in the city, and all the emotions of that day flooded back to her.

"In history class we had been discussing Adlai Stevenson's visit to Dallas the previous week. He had been picketed, and a demonstrator struck him on the head. This was Catholic school, which was unusual in Dallas, and we were talking about how conservative the city was. Shortly after that, during one of the afternoon classes, we heard about the shooting of President Kennedy. We were stunned and everyone started to cry. We felt doubly bad because it happened in Dallas. For a long time afterward there was a lot of unwanted attention focused on the city. Even when I went to college in Iowa, the fact that I had come from Dallas was like wearing a label. So I already knew that this could happen in Winnetka, that there might come a time when people would not want to admit they live in the village, even though it is so idyllic."

By 3:15 P.M. all the children had been signed out of Hubbard Woods School. None was allowed to leave without an adult known to the teachers, and all of them went straight home along streets that were still strangely quiet. Most of the media people had moved to the end of Kent Road, as close as they were allowed to the latest scene in the drama: the Andrew house, tensely surrounded by armed police, with Laurie and her remaining gun inside. At the school only teachers and social workers remained. Relieved of the tension of appearing braver than they felt, many of them hugged and wept.

"How shall we ever heal from this?" one teacher asked.

They talked back and forth for two hours, searching for answers. "We had gathered in Dick Streedain's office," Jeff Berkson, the Evanston Hospital social worker, remembered. "It's a square room with photographs of his own children, and a lot of wonderful drawings from children in the school. Dick had changed his shirt, and seemed to be feeling better. He was remarkably even, his thinking was good, and he was very anxious that we should have a continuing contact with the parents and children over the weekend. And that's when we began to plan bringing them all back to the school the next day, Saturday, so they could share their feelings and see school again as a safe place."

The psychiatrists, Dr. Ira Sloan and Dr. Mary Giffin, felt this to be crucial and began to make plans for the support staff they would need.

"We had a lot of discussion about this, and by the end of the afternoon I had a feeling that Dick had made an attachment to me, and specifically wanted me to be there," Berkson said. "It embarrassed me because the next day at the school assembly he introduced me as the person who had helped him the most. I am not sure what I did, except to be around."

Privately, he was worrying about his own son. There was no reason for concern and he knew it; by now thirteen-year-old Daniel would be safe at their home in Evanston. Yet he had an urgent and deeply human need to reassure himself of the fact, a need shared by every parent who was in any way involved with the Winnetka tragedy, even those who knew the reaction to be illogical.

In a quick phone call he discovered that his son had seen a shot of him on the television news. "He said he knew I would be there, and he was clearly proud that I was. We share clothes a lot—he is taller than I am—and I was wearing his blue Hawaiian shirt that day, so he spotted me immediately. He asked when I would be home.

"'Probably late,' I said."

Shortly before the group broke up a message came to the school that there would be an open meeting at Winnetka's Community House that evening. So far as anyone knew, it had been spontaneously arranged by parents to give villagers a forum to discuss the day's events.

"We had better be there," Don Monroe said.

Jeff Berkson recalled: "I did not think I wanted to go, but there is something strangely seductive about a crisis. You want to stay part of it." He decided to wait around, and see if he could do any more to help.

Others felt compelled to get away from the scene. "When I got home at six P.M., the first thing I wanted to do was to take off every piece of clothing and throw it away, right down to my shoes which were brand-new," a woman teacher said. "I knew I could never wear that outfit again without being reminded of the last time I had it on."

Linda Corwin spent much of that afternoon in a funeral parlor. Word reached her there that some of the media people had been asking for a statement, and with an extraordinary effort of will she wrote one. It was not what they expected. They were looking for an expression of her anger or her pain, her feelings about the societal ills which had allowed this horror to happen. But she wrote only of her son Nicky:

"A gifted athlete, a gifted artist, and a gifted student. A child that was full of love and humor. A child who made his parents weep with joy at his talent and his attractiveness. He brightened our lives with such a brilliant light that we cannot believe he is gone."

SEVENTEEN

In the early afternoon Joe Sumner had to move the police command post for the second time, from the convenience of an indoor location to the discomfort of a street corner. He was glad it wasn't raining. It was bad enough coping with the complaints of press people as he and his officers herded them farther back from the Andrew house and set up operations at the junction of Kent Road and Hibbard Street.

"But you just let Channel Seven through. Why are you blocking us?"

After Hubbard Woods School proved unsatisfactory he had set up a command post in the living room of a house at 12 Kent Road. The owners were away but gladly gave permission by telephone, including an invitation to the police to help themselves from the refrigerator. Extra telephone lines were quickly installed, but this ideal headquarters had to be abandoned after Laurie barricaded herself in the Andrew house, a few yards down the street. Her presence there put police officers going to and from the command post directly in her line of fire.

By midafternoon the area around the Andrew house looked as though it had been prepared for battle. Through the Northern Illinois Police Alarm System (NIPAS), a Special Weapons and Tactics team had been brought in, only it was not called a SWAT team because too many television serials had given the name an aggressive image, and that wasn't appropriate for the north shore. Instead it was described as an Emergency Services Team. Commander Gary P. Stryker, who headed EST, explained: "Our mission is to rescue people, not to shoot them." But the approach was similar.

The team was a new concept for the north shore, designed to serve the lakeside villages and those immediately west of them, augmenting local police departments in the rare instances when they might have to confront violence. The first EST training school had been held the previous October when twenty-nine officers drawn from the police forces of twelve communities were trained to deal with terrorists, snipers, barricaded suspects, and hostage situations. The team had gone into operation on May 1, only nineteen days before being summoned to Winnetka, and this was its first emergency call. Stryker, its leader, had served in the military police in Vietnam, and in almost two years of severe fighting had developed the sharply honed instincts of a survivor. Before EST was formed he had been in charge of a smaller SWAT team for Deerfield, a sprawling, modern community west of Glencoe, but in this peaceable social climate the worst case he had dealt with was that of a frail, elderly man with Alzheimer's disease threatening his invalid wife at gunpoint. It took only two of his men to kick open the couple's apartment door and rescue her. Capturing Laurie Dann would be another matter.

Normally EST members would have to be summoned from a wide area but on the morning of May 20 most of them were attending a staff meeting in Deerfield when the alarm call came in. Within fifteen minutes the first contingent was at the Andrew house, relieving the Winnetka police man by man. As they did so Sumner moved his officers to the outer perimeter of the scene, setting up additional roadblocks while Stryker's team surrounded the house, some of them taking up positions at the upstairs windows of neighboring homes. They looked like commandos, carrying submachine guns, handguns, and rifles with telescopic sights; dressed in black fatigues with ballistic helmets and bullet-proof vests. It might have been a movie scene, except that normally filmmakers came to Winnetka only when they wanted to portray an idyllic American village.

Stryker was not in a hurry to capture Laurie. First he needed to be absolutely sure she had not escaped, and that involved talking to the police officers who had surrounded the house from the time Philip Andrew was shot.

"It took two hours of inquiries until I was ninety-nine percent convinced she was still in there, and that no one else was with her," Stryker stated. "By then it was about two-thirty P.M. and there was no reason for us to try to make an entry at that time. We had to gather intelligence, find out about her habits, determine what the house looked like inside, what the floor plan was." To send even heavily armed men into an unknown building where there might be a sniper at the top of the stairs would be insanity. And he wanted to take Laurie alive. Like Timm, he was thinking of her accountability at a trial for the murder of Nicholas Corwin, and the attempted murder of five others.

He learned from Ray Andrew, Philip's father, that the only blueprint of the house was inside the building, in the den. Still agitated, Andrew was about to be taken by a Winnetka policeman to New Trier High School to pick up his daughters, and then on to Highland Park Hospital. Ruth Andrew had already been offered a ride there by a *Chicago Tribune* reporter. Stryker couldn't delay any of them, not with Philip in such serious condition. He telephoned the village hall in the hope that there might be a plan of the house on file, but drew a blank. Meantime someone remembered that Dan Andrew, Philip's brother, was a student in the police academy at Maywood, forty miles south.

"We called and told him to come at once," Stryker related. "It took him almost an hour to get to Winnetka but he was a great help. He knew his brother had been shot, but was pretty calm and had a very good idea of what we wanted to know."

Dan drew a floor plan from memory, pointing out the turns and bends in the hallways of his family's rambling old house. Built around the turn of the century with twenty-two rooms, a full basement, two staircases, and a lot of unexpected alcoves and closets, it was full of hiding places for a sniper. Stryker wanted to know the direction in which every door opened, and any furniture arrangements which might create obstacles. He feared that Laurie might have more weapons than a single handgun, and a house as complex as this one gave her enormous advantages. Remembering the chemicals which had been found in her abandoned car, he asked the police crime laboratory in Highland Park whether any of these could be combined to make an explosive. No, he was told, but they could make incendiary devices.

During the next few hours Stryker discovered the gaps in the new EST system. "The deal was that the town that called us would provide communications," he said. "We did not have our own radio system, and Winnetka did not have enough portable radios to give us. Their police had to go out and gather up enough from surrounding communities. These had batteries which would generally last three to four hours, but some had not been fully charged and we did not have fresh batteries. Sometimes we had to use runners to pass on messages. The media had so many crews there, broadcasting live, that the area was congested with microwaves, and that impeded our communications all day."

The media people weren't enjoying their situation either. At one point tempers became so frayed that a fistfight broke out between two cameramen jostling for position near the Andrew home, and police had to intervene. Larry Schreiner of Chicago's WGN Radio, one of the first reporters on the scene, was keenly aware of being resented by villagers who saw him broadcasting from street corners. Yet his frequent running commentaries on the situation were one of the chief sources of information for people along the north shore.

"The media was trying to do the best job it could, trying to inform, but it got very uncomfortable," he said. "People in Winnetka were offensive. Just the fact that you are not a local resident, that you are carrying a camera and a portable telephone, makes them hit out at you. Yes, some media people are real jerks, like the ones who walked up to little children outside the school. But most of us behaved responsibly. I feel that every report I did was tasteful, that I did not violate any standards. And yet some people were screaming obscenities at us. I cover a lot of crime, and I am treated better in the ghetto than in Winnetka."

Schreiner had one good experience in the course of his long day. "There was a man living on the corner, not far from the Andrew house. I asked if I might use his phone and he let me.

I asked him for a drink of water because it was hotter than a witch out there, and he gave me one. Most people were not that pleasant. Yet most of them got their information from my reports on WGN."

As crime stories go, he did not rate this one highly. It was the place where it happened which gave it importance.

"I keep score of the shootings in Chicago, and from a Friday afternoon to Monday morning there are often about thirty people shot, just within the city limits. At Altgeld Gardens, one of the worst places on the South Side, the police get so many, many shootings that even to have a child shot in a school is not unusual. The only reason people remember any particular incident is because they relate it to all the others."

Rick Rosenthal, WGN Television's newsman, was probably the only reporter to be warmly received by villagers. He had the dual advantage of living in Winnetka and of being instantly recognized as the man whose handsome face came into their living rooms with the Channel 9 nightly news. Parents in the crowd outside the school greeted him like an old friend and even offered him information.

Herb Timm joined Joe Sumner at the corner of Kent Road in midafternoon. He had been at the school until then and, remembering that he had eaten nothing in the eight hours since breakfast, wondered if he should stop for a quick snack. But the thought of food sickened him, and he hurried to join his deputy. Like a lot of other people that day, he was operating on adrenaline.

By now there was a considerable gathering at the command post: a state's attorney, the medical examiner for Cook County, some FBI agents, men from the Emergency Services Team, and a steady stream of police. Making decisions turned out to be simpler than implementing them. There was general agreement that listening devices should be used to determine Laurie's exact whereabouts. "They're known as spike mikes," Sumner explained. "You pound them into the foundations of a house, and they pick up the sound of someone walking around." But even when that someone was a criminal and a fugitive, under Illinois law the police could not eavesdrop without a court order.

190

Gary Stryker approached Nancy Sidote, the state's attorney, who was among the group at the command post. She recommended taking the quicker course of working through local FBI agents because they could get direct permission from Washington. That, too, presented problems.

"It took a long time to get the FBI technicians to Winnetka because they were working on a case southwest of the city, a good hour's drive to Chicago and another forty-five minutes to us," said Stryker. "It was a case involving bodies in a mob graveyard, and it took quite a while for them to get approval from Washington to leave that assignment."

In the meantime, he had the three people closest to Laurie brought to the scene. Norman and Edith Wasserman arrived together, bleak and tearful, she wearing slacks and a sweater, he in jeans and a short-sleeved sports shirt. Russell Dann was summoned from his office. He and the Wassermans were questioned about Laurie's habits and left to wait out their misery in separate rooms of the house at 12 Kent Road, which the police were now using as an adjunct to their street-corner command post. They had nothing to say to one another. They had parted in anger when the marriage broke up, and had not spoken since.

Stryker asked Norman Wasserman what time Laurie went to bed the previous evening. He and Timm were not yet in agreement about how long they should wait before going into the Andrew house to capture her. Timm felt the assault should be made in daylight because of the slim chance that she might escape after dark. Stryker wanted to wait until late enough into the night for her to have fallen asleep. He was worried that she might throw a fire bomb at his men if she saw them trying to storm the house. He learned from her father that Laurie had not gone to bed until at least 1:30 A.M. and had been up early the same morning. That was good news to him. After so little sleep and so much tension she would soon be exhausted. If he waited until 2:00 or 3:00 A.M. it should be much easier to capture her. He planned to relieve the men every two hours; it was tense work for them, and wearing such heavy equipment, they were all suffering from the heat.

Russell offered some disturbing information. He said that when Laurie was depressed she would hide in closets. Once when he had thought he was alone in the Hastings Avenue house he had discovered her crouched in a closet with a portable phone, listening in to his telephone conversations. He realized she must have been there for hours.

"We were worried she might be hiding because we saw no sign of her," Stryker said. "We did not even catch a glimpse of her through windows, and there are a lot of windows in that house. We thought of suicide, but couldn't assume it."

His men tried shouting at Laurie through bullhorns, and calling her on the Andrews' telephone. No response. Norman Wasserman wanted to go into the house to talk to her, but was firmly refused.

"We would never let a family member negotiate," Stryker said. "It is against all principles. You can't take the chance because you don't know how a relative will react. Any contact has to be made by an impartial third party."

Wasserman responded with a flash of anger. Unable to grasp the enormity of Laurie's actions, he could focus only on the immediate fate of his little girl, the damaged child he had protected all these years, alone and afraid in that house, surrounded by a posse of gunmen.

"You're treating her like a wild animal. Look at those guys with machine guns!" he exclaimed.

To the police Wasserman presented a problem and an opportunity. He was the one person who might be able to communicate with Laurie, but he could not be trusted to do it their way. They planned to escort him onto the driveway of the Andrew house and have him call to her through a bullhorn, begging her to give herself up. But not yet. They wanted to capture her alive and at the least risk to themselves, but were afraid of Wasserman breaking away and dashing into the building to protect her. He was already distraught about the possibility of her being shot by the police. As always, he seemed to be handling this crisis alone. There was never any suggestion that his wife might be able to influence their daughter.

Stretched out on a carpet, Russell Dann was following the story of his ex-wife's rampage on television news. He was leaning on one elbow in an almost indolent gesture, disguising his own feelings with this expression of bravado. In Highland Park his sister, Susie Taylor, her husband, Jeffrey, and their children were being given police protection while their house was searched for time bombs. For months Russell and she had lived in fear of a disaster like this, except that they saw themselves as the likeliest victims. Time after time they had tried to convince the police of Laurie's propensity for violence, and were not believed. Now it was hard to resist the temptation to say: "I told you so."

Russell did say something of that sort to Floyd Mohr who was also waiting around in the house at 12 Kent Road. Mohr responded with an abject apology, explaining that he had not realized Laurie's criminal potential until he had talked with an FBI agent in Arizona thirteen days earlier. He was sitting with his head in his hands, trying to hide his tears, overwhelmed by his inability to prevent all this bloodshed, blaming himself because he wasn't (as he put it) supercop. Russell felt a stab of compassion for him.

"Maybe you can learn something from this, be a better detective," he said, putting an arm around Floyd Mohr's shoulder. He meant it kindly but could not resist the condescension. He was hurting every bit as much as Mohr. It would be a long time before he could begin to describe his own feelings, and even then his thoughts would race ahead of the words.

"When you think about going from the highs of getting married to the lows of thinking your wife is crazy, to being treated as a criminal when you are a victim, to the experience of not coming across well in the press when you expect them to give you a fair deal . . . There were times when I was scared shitless of being arrested by the police for something I didn't do. And through all this I was being stalked by a crazy person. I got screwed by the police, by the press, and by her parents. No way could I live a normal life."

Then there were his regrets. "I loved Laurie. And I was the one who hurt her the worst by leaving her. She tried to kill me because, in her own distorted way, all she could remember was that hurt, and she wanted to get back at me. She was afraid of losing me. I asked her, after we were separated, why she behaved as she did. And she said, 'Russ, I am desperate.' What she was really doing was crying out for help."

He had not known how to answer that cry. "I tried everything I could think of, but I didn't know what mental illness was, and all the crazy things she did I took personally."

Now he was seeing the consequences, and it was heart-breaking. However this day might end, she was doomed. "Laurie had something like a slow cancer of the brain, and the woman who shot those children was not anyone I knew. I married another Laurie. How can I not mourn for her?"

EIGHTEEN

Richard kessler, the attorney whom Russell Dann hired to protect him from Laurie, had been her contemporary at Red Oak Junior High School in Highland Park. He remembered her as "a skinny girl with a big nose," so unremarkable that nothing else about her made an impression. By the time Russell met her, after she had left college, her nose had been surgically trimmed, her projecting ears flattened, and her lank brown hair softly styled. Now the features that struck people were her wide brown eyes and trim figure. Photographs of her taken around this time catch a vivacity so intense that her face seems to sparkle.

"She was gorgeous," Russell recalled.

During his subsequent dealings with the two of them Floyd Mohr would often wonder why they had been attracted to one another. What he saw during his long investigation was not enough to make a marriage. Russell had wanted a girl he could feel proud to be seen with, and Laurie had sought the security that came with money and an ambitious husband. Both had grown up on the north shore, the youngest children of successful Jewish parents; otherwise they had little in common. He was generous, gregarious, aggressive, and impulsive. She was withdrawn and uncommunicative, with no apparent aim or interest in life. He was a sports enthusiast; she was not.

They first met in a bar near his office when he was with a group of friends. He bumped into her again at his country club, and with the warm smile that came readily to him, he remarked that he had seen her somewhere before. It was an old gambit to which she had a ready response.

"That must have been my twin sister."

He thought the comment cute and asked her out for dinner. This led to an eighteen-month courtship which led to a Jewish country-club wedding. It was a lighthearted, zany affair, neither of them having much interest in the religious aspect of the ceremony. As newlyweds they were expected to enter the social circle of north shore yuppies which was already Russell's habitat, but after only a few weeks of marriage he began to see that she did not fit.

According to his brother, Scott, "Laurie was never popular with Russell's friends. She was a wet rag; not an entertaining, vibrant, enjoyable person to be with. My wife and I never got close to her. But most of the erratic behavior that Russell was subject to went on behind the scenes from all of us. It has always bothered me that he didn't see any of these things when he was dating her, and I can't speculate why he didn't."

Russell felt he could explain that. "I was a twenty-three-year-old kid. Not experienced, not a clue. I met this beautiful girl, we had fun together, it was time to get married, and so I did. Treated her like a princess. Then all of a sudden, when it was too late, I woke up. Before we were married Laurie could on occasion be a little snippy. But so are most girls I know. She was very quiet and reserved, but she said she used to date a lot."

From that he assumed she was like the other trendy north shore girls of his social circle; that the snippiness was the outward sign of an ambition and confidence to match his own. And her looks beguiled him. He kept a photograph album of all the beautiful girls he had dated, and she fitted right into it. In her quest for a well-to-do husband, Laurie's nose job paid off handsomely.

About two months after their marriage Russell noticed signs of her obsessive-compulsive disorder. She had a distressing need to walk back and forth counting her paces, to touch lampposts, to avoid cracks in the sidewalk, to open the car door and touch the cement with her foot whenever he pulled up at a stoplight. She couldn't bear to touch metal and would put on gloves to handle cutlery. She would try to ride a bicycle without holding the handlebars, and when asked the reason would say that if she did not do these ritualistic things she feared something terrible might happen to Russell. Or else make a frivolous comment which ignored the question.

Some of her strange behavior was apparent to others early in the marriage. Their first home together was Russell's condominium apartment, a duplex in a forty-eight-unit complex near his office in Northbrook, known as Cambridge Court. It was not a place which had any sense of permanence. People lived there during transitions in their lives, as Russell had done in his bachelor days, as he and Laurie were now doing while they looked for a house to buy.

Not long after she moved in, a fellow resident of the complex, crossing the courtyard after parking his car, saw her late one evening at an upstairs window, her nude body pressed against the pane, silhouetted against the bedroom light. While he walked in full view of her she continued to stand there exposing herself, and must surely have seen him look up, avert his gaze, and hurry on.

Russell knew nothing of this, and none of the people in his warm and close-knit family shared with him their concerns about Laurie. They pretended she was one of them, worrying to one another about her, hoping marriage would give her stability, and allowing him to think he had chosen well.

She seemed to get along with the other residents of Cambridge Court, some of whom found her easier than her husband. "He gave us a lot of trouble," according to Nic Schnettler, manager of the complex. "He was asking for the kind of services which you can have in your own home if you are an absolute perfectionist, but in a communal living situation you have to give up some of those rights. He didn't like doing that." When Laurie moved in, Schnettler found her to be more accommodating. But he thought her "very unusual."

He recalled: "We have a laundry room in each building, and she would go down there with a basket of clothes and wash them over and over and over. She was acting like she was super clean but her car was an ungodly mess. It was filled with junk. If anybody wanted to ride with her, she would have to throw things in the back seat to make room. But Russ was very fussy about his car."

Her husband's extreme neatness mirrored the life-style of her parents. Visitors to the Wasserman home commented on an appearance so immaculate that the place looked unoccupied, or occupied in such a way that the personalities of its owners left no mark. Russell's home was more stylish and contemporary, but the effect was almost as bland. Laurie gave most of his furnishings away when, after being married about six months, the two of them bought the house on Hastings Avenue. Her need to shed these relics of his bachelor days was understandable; in fact, it was customary for privileged north shore brides to "work with a decorator," establishing a marital home of character. But Laurie didn't do that, even though Russell would have been proud to pay the bill and to show off the results. Right up to the divorce the Hastings Avenue house was furnished barely, as though the bride had neither the skill nor the interest to make a home.

She had several short-term jobs before and during her marriage, but none of them lasted. Some were clerical, and at one time she was a country-club waitress. Her invented résumés sounded impressive, but before long her employers would tire of her, or she of them. Believing her tales of mistreatment, Russell sympathized with her until there were too many tales to be believable. At the same time he reassured her that she didn't have to work. "It would be hard to find anyone who treated her nicer than I did," he said.

He couldn't understand what she did with her days. Sometimes she would stay in bed until the afternoon and then sit around doing nothing, a symptom of profound depression which was unknown to him.

"I would leave for work at seven A.M., get home at six or seven," he recalled. "When I came in I would fold her clothes, get dinner, tidy up. Or we would go out to eat. At weekends we would go dancing. But I didn't have a wife, I had a daughter. I tried to help her constructively, I tried being totally supportive,

I tried looking the other way, I tried getting mad at her. You name it, I tried it."

He had been welcomed into Norman Wasserman's household, which was more frugal on demonstrated affection than any he had known. Smaller, too. Laurie's only sibling, her elder brother, Mark, had already married and moved to Texas. She spoke of him fondly, saying that he had been wise to get away from all this, whatever all this was, and that she missed him. It was not a family in which feelings were easily shared. Wasserman had been the hardworking son of a widow; had taken care of his mother, his wife, and now his daughter. He appeared to love these women, and showed his love by organizing their lives and by providing luxuries which had not been part of his childhood. Evidently he thought he was making things easier for them. Even when Laurie had a husband he found it hard to let go.

While the marriage lasted, Russell was on good terms with him. They played tennis and golf together, were Russ and Norm to one another. But as Laurie's emotional state worsened, each began to blame the other, Russell insisting that Norman Wasserman had been too controlling with his daughter. "Norm always did for Laurie," he complained. "Took her out to dinner, bought her clothes, managed things for her." According to Russell, his own father, Armand Dann, was told by Wasserman: "When I gave my daughter to your son she was perfectly normal, and now she is all screwed up."

Laurie began to see a psychiatrist, but gave up a few months later. After a while the doctor wrote to Laurie, urging her to return to therapy. His letter (which Russell showed to Norman Wasserman) expressed the opinion that her problems were severe, and did not relate to her marriage but went back to early childhood. Eventually Laurie started seeing him again, but Russell observed no change in her condition. In his opinion, "This psychiatrist was a very nice man but he did not have a clue what was wrong with her because she was not honest with him. She could lie very convincingly." When Russell could take no more, he called on her parents to tell them the marriage was over. His attempt to cover his discomfort was ingenuous.

"I took them taffy apples," he said. "I told them there was a problem, that I had tried everything I knew and nothing was working. And I asked their help. Threw up my arms and told them I was open to suggestions."

This was the only time he saw any involvement by her mother. "She said they knew about the problem, that it was not that bad, and with a little help it would get better."

Russell felt the marriage to be past mending. He was searching for a kind way to separate from Laurie, and wanted to be sure that her parents would be there to comfort her when the parting came. When he left their house, he understood that they would do this. He delayed the separation because he didn't want to spoil Laurie's twenty-eighth birthday, on October 18, 1985, although it was destined to be spoiled.

"I got her a nice warm-up suit, pink, I think it was, and some flowers. She cried. I had already told her, 'Laurie, I cannot go on like this,' and she had asked for a month to get herself together. In that time she really did try. But it was like she was being pulled by this dark force."

At the end of that month her parents were in Florida. Russell called them to relate that the separation was imminent, feeling confident that they would return to Glencoe to be with their daughter. They commuted back and forth often enough. As usual, her father answered the phone. In Russell's recollection Wasserman received the news almost casually, saying that he would be home in a week or two.

"Okay, Laurie, hang in there," his son-in-law heard him say.

"After he had promised!" Russell exclaimed. "I put the phone down, and Laurie melted in my arms. I called my best friend's wife to come and stay with her. Then I called Norm back, and I said, 'Norm, you are a son of a bitch. I cannot believe you!' And I hung up."

They had not spoken since. And here the three of them were, two and a half years later, waiting out the end of the drama in separate rooms of a strange house, each of them engulfed in a misery too personal to be shared, silently holding the others responsible for a disaster none of them had the insight or capability to avert.

"Laurie had no value to her life," Russell commented. "This was her way of getting revenge."

Meanwhile, in another part of the house, Floyd Mohr was making an important telephone call.

After putting Philip Andrew in the ambulance, Mohr had been assigned to work with the Emergency Services Team, gathering intelligence. He began by interviewing the Wassermans in an attempt to understand what had happened to Laurie since he last saw her. They told him about her move to Madison, Wisconsin, and about her being seen by a psychiatrist there. Even in this crisis, knowing she had committed murder, they were protective of her privacy and did not volunteer any medical information. Mohr discovered the name of the therapist, Dr. John Greist, from the FBI and got the Glencoe police to find his telephone number. This is Floyd Mohr's recollection of their conversation:

"Doctor, I am Detective Mohr of the Glencoe police and I am working on a case that is making news right now. I am sure you know what is going on here in Winnetka, and I want to ask you some questions about your patient, Laurie Dann. Did you ever think she could be homicidal?"

"Absolutely not."

"Or suicidal?"

"No, I never had reason to believe that."

"Did you ever think she could have more than one personality?"

Mohr was struggling to equate the timid girl he had known with the Laurie Dann he had not recognized at the time of Russell's stabbing, a Laurie who had just viciously killed, and might kill again. A multiple-personality disorder seemed to him the only explanation.

"I never thought about it before, but it could be a possibility," Greist responded.

It would soon be dusk, and Herbert Timm did not want to delay an assault on the Andrew house any longer. There had been no sign of Laurie's existence since Philip was shot, and that made him uneasy. He was worried that during all these hours she might have devised a way to slip out after dark. "And this area is like a jungle at night," he observed.

He considered injecting tear gas into the house, but if that failed to force her out, it would hamper the police who would have to go in and find her. There was also the risk of fire "and I would have a lot of explaining to do to our city fathers if a two-and-a-half-million-dollar structure burned to the ground."

"She won't come out. She'll commit suicide," Norman Wasserman kept saying. Outwardly he was calm but his anguish was palpable.

It was almost 7:00 P.M., time to take Wasserman to the Andrew house, although not for the reason he imagined. Timm had given the order for the police to enter at 7:00, and Gary Stryker had not tried to dissuade him.

"I knew Herb was under a lot of pressure from residents and from the media," he said. "And there was the one percent chance that Laurie Dann had got away, although I felt sure she hadn't. What convinced me was that there had been one incident after another from nine A.M. until the time Philip Andrew was shot, but none since then. If she had gone free, there would surely have been other incidents. So it was evident that she had acted alone, and was still in that house."

Stryker's plan was to have Wasserman engage Laurie's attention by standing in the front yard and calling out to her while his team entered the house. Dan Andrew had already pointed out the basement door whose lock could most easily be broken. Unaware of the second part of the plan, Wasserman still wanted to go into the house alone, convinced that if anyone could influence Laurie it was he.

It fell to Floyd Mohr to take him the short distance to the Andrews' property. As the two of them walked through the hallway of the house at 12 Kent Road, Mohr picked up a leather dog leash which was hanging there and, as soon as they got outside, hooked one end to the older man's belt and grasped the other in his clenched hand. The news cameras recorded the ignominy of Wasserman's situation. A widely published photograph showed him looking defeated and demeaned, a slightly built man with shoulders hunched, head down, hands thrust in his trouser pockets, being held in check like the cocker spaniel to whom the leash belonged. At the other end of the leash the picture shows a grim-looking Mohr, younger, taller, broader, and stronger than his captive, with an unnatural stiffness about his chest from the bullet-proof vest he always wore under his shirt. Mohr was afraid that

Wasserman might make a dash for the house, or that Laurie might shoot at her father as he stood on the Andrews' driveway wailing through a bullhorn, "Laurie, Laurie, please come out."

But the only voice which responded was the echo of his own. "Laurie, please come out."

Norman Wasserman continued to call, unknowingly acting as a diversion while, at exactly 7:00 P.M., a team of eight broke the basement lock and entered the Andrew house. One team member was an FBI technician carrying a kind of electronic stethoscope which he held against various basement walls, listening. Another was a police dog handler, Patrolman Eric Lundahl of Northbrook, who (although he did not remember it) had also been in high school with Laurie. When no sound was heard from the basement, Lundahl sent his German shepherd to sweep around the first floor. Finding nothing, the dog returned to him.

Team members looked in every downstairs closet, then cautiously waited by the backstairs while Lundahl turned the dog loose on the second floor. The animal padded around and, immediately after entering one of the bedrooms, hurried straight back to his handler, without barking.

"Is that a good or bad sign?" Lundahl was asked by his colleagues.

"It means the dog found a body," he replied.

NINETEEN

J ESSICA FELDMAN was tuned in to her television and radio at the same time, avid for news of Laurie. She couldn't stop thinking of this thirty-year-old woman (child, she called her), the same age as her daughter Sandra, barricaded in that house in Winnetka. Horrified as she was about all the shootings, Jessica had only pity for the Laurie she had known, and fantasized that she might somehow elude the police and ring her doorbell, seeking refuge and a welcoming embrace. In this fantasy she would hold the child in her arms, and then, because she didn't want her to do any more harm, go with her to the police. She was so convinced that if Laurie were to escape from the Andrew house she would come to her that she telephoned her village police station to warn that this might happen.

"Do you want protection?" she was asked.

The suggestion shocked her. "Why would I be frightened?" she said. "She would come here because she needs a safe harbor; someone to tell her they love her."

It was to Jessica's ranch-style house, several miles west of Lake Michigan in a less fashionable neighborhood than Glencoe, that Laurie had come in the middle of the night after claiming that Russell had raped her with a steak knife. Both Jessica and her daughter had been as dubious of the rape story as the emergency-room doctor had been, but for slightly different reasons.

"She was shaken up that night and I thought something had happened, but that it wasn't rape," Sandra remembered. "Over the thirteen years I knew Laurie, I discovered that she had different stories every day of the week."

Jessica's was the pragmatic approach of a woman who had lived long enough to experience the frailties of humankind. "There's not a man in the world who couldn't get a girl to sleep with him, plus Russell is not homely and has a lot of money, so he didn't need to force himself on Laurie," she said. "I don't believe he raped her. I think she turned around the story of her knifing him. When she came to our house that night she said in the calmest way, 'He is trying to kill me. I know he is trying to kill me.' But she did not appear to be badly upset or injured.

"I have come to believe she did stab Russell, that it was the first violent thing she did, and it's why she came here after saying he had knifed her. I think she knew she was out of control, and needed to be somewhere where she could feel safe."

Laurie had met Jessica Feldman through her daughter. As classmates at the University of Arizona, Laurie and Sandra had been drawn together by a pair of coincidences: Both were transfer students from Drake University in Iowa, and both had grown up on Chicago's north shore. They did not room together or take the same courses, Sandra graduated and Laurie did not, but their friendship deepened as Laurie supported Sandra through a painfully broken romance, and as Sandra reciprocated through Laurie's divorce. It followed that Laurie would be drawn to her friend's mother, who was warm, insightful, and supportive: qualities which she seemed unable to find in her own parents.

"I felt I knew Laurie better than they did," Jessica remarked. Indeed, it was Jessica to whom Laurie turned when the Highland Park police arrested her for making threatening telephone calls to Russell's sister.

"I went to bail her out," Jessica related. "She drove me to her parents' house, and she went in and gave me the money back. It was a hundred dollars or more because I remember having to cash a check. Her father knew about it because within days he called to thank me. Laurie seemed very upset, more upset than I have ever seen her. She admitted to having made the phone calls but didn't know why everyone was making such a big deal of it.

"I said, 'But, Laurie, why do it? This is something a ten-year-old would do.'"

Laurie replied that she hated Susie Taylor and wished her dead.

"I felt that for a while she was entitled to be in a strange state of mind," Jessica commented. "She was separated from Russell, having all these divorce problems, and she told me that whenever she tried to talk to her father about them, he would merely say, 'Who am I to give advice?'

"I thought to myself: The child needs sympathy. She never grew up. She is like a little girl who read all the fairy stories and thought she could meet a prince and live happily ever after. But when happily ever after doesn't happen, what do you do? No one had explained to her that there is more to life than going to school, looking cute, and grabbing a guy.

"After her marriage Laurie became a typical north shore housewife with nothing to do. For a time she had a job in a shopping mall because women without children are expected to do something, and it's okay to work for a store with cachet like Lord and Taylor or Neiman-Marcus. You get the clothes at discount and you end up spending more than you make, looking better dressed than the customers, but that's all right because you would buy the clothes anyway. It's also all right if your friends come in the store and see you, although it wouldn't do to work behind a counter just anywhere. Laurie did not stay with this job for long. Her heart wasn't in it and she didn't need the money. She only went to work because people were asking her, 'What do you do?' In other ways she wasn't the typical north shore wife. She didn't entertain. She didn't plan parties for her husband's business associates. She didn't cook; she didn't know how to put a meal together. The refrigerator was filled with snacks, and they ate out.

"She wanted to make the marriage work and I know she adored Russell. She was thrilled to death when she married him. But she was not sure whether she wanted children. I think she was afraid of them, or rather, afraid of herself with a child. I think she knew she didn't have any maternal feelings and felt guilty about it. The true princess would want to have children and be a good mother.

"Russell must have seen her mental problems, but they did not show to the rest of us until four or five months after he left her. Then she started telling these stories about what he was doing to her. I don't think she believed everything she said; it was more like she wanted to get attention. And she did not feel she could talk to her parents."

One of the stories Laurie told shortly after Russell left her was that she was pregnant with his child. "Wouldn't it be funny if I gave him a baby, him and his girlfriend?" she asked Jessica.

"I said, 'Laurie, you are not thinking straight. A child deserves more than you are about to give it. And if the only reason you want to have a baby is to get back at Russell, you should have an abortion.'

"I asked her, 'Do you want me to go with you?'

"She said, 'No, no. I will be okay.'"

There was never any suggestion of Edith Wasserman's supporting her. "Laurie never talked about her mother," Jessica said.

"Afterward she said she had the abortion. But I don't believe she was even pregnant. It was just so she could say Russell had done this to her: the ultimate indignity. And when that didn't work, she said he had raped her.

"She was still in love with him, and inventing these stories was her way of trying to hold on to him. Even in an adversarial position she wanted to hold on. When the divorce was final she did not tell us. She let us think she was still having fights with Russell because she wanted to keep up a pretense of being married. She kept building these stories in her head, and as long as she could do that she managed not to fall apart. But somewhere inside herself she was definitely falling apart, except I did not see it until later."

Jessica understood Laurie's need for pretense. She was very familiar with the mores of north shore life, especially those of the Jewish community. "Laurie's whole idea was traditional: Find a husband. She had tunnel vision, was never career oriented. In my time you went to college with the idea of finding a man, and if you found one it was okay to quit school and get married. That was Laurie's outlook too, although her generation of north shore girls was expected to graduate, not necessarily with any particular field in mind, and then to marry well.

"Laurie didn't finish college. And she said her father told her she had really blown it when Russell left her. 'He can't help it,' she would say. 'He had a terrible childhood, and that's the way he is.' I understand that. Most of our generation came from immigrant families. They had the Jewish work ethic, the idea that you give your children more so they can accomplish more. To this day Jewish parents still do that. Holding on to money is important to them because if you have money you can handle everything. The idea is not to spend it. The idea is to have it. So when Laurie was unable to stay married to a rich young man from a prestigious family, she was made to feel she had ruined her life."

Laurie consulted a divorce attorney, and in describing the meeting to Jessica, she revealed that she had used a false name.

"I told him it was Porter," she related. "Wasn't that smart of me? If I had said Dann, he would have recognized the name and charged more money."

Thus Laurie Porter came into being, out of the wreckage of a failed marriage. Over the ensuing months a fictional life story would be woven to fit her, a life so socially acceptable that the Laurie Porter who presented herself to the Rushe family was not only an exemplary baby-sitter but everything that a well-bred young woman on the north shore was expected to be: respectably employed between college and marriage, with a fiancé who had given her an heirloom engagement ring and the promise of a honeymoon on the Virgin Islands, the same gifts that the other Laurie had received from Russell. Only the new Laurie was meant to stay married, and to have children who loved her.

Knowing nothing of this, Jessica Feldman dismissed Laurie Porter as an amusing alias. At the same time she was watching the disintegration of Laurie Dann. "She really let herself go after the divorce. The girl wasn't wearing makeup, didn't fix her hair, and was living in sweatsuits. And this didn't happen so quickly that her parents could not see it. It went on for months.

"In all this time she did not drink to excess. She was not on drugs. She never went for that kind of high. I never even saw her smoke a cigarette. She did none of the things that a lot of rich kids do when they are unhappy. She was looking for help but there was no one to save her. And had someone done something for her, then I think the real Laurie Dann would have stood up."

Laurie confided to Sandra that she was afraid of going mad. She said her maternal grandmother had been institutionalized for mental illness, and she feared it might be hereditary. In this disturbed state, she rented a student apartment at Northwestern University, Evanston, for the summer of 1987. "She thought it was a great place to meet men," according to Sandra. "It was by the lake, there were parties every night, she didn't want to work, and she didn't want to be at the house in Glencoe when her parents were there. And they wouldn't be in Florida during the summer."

One of Laurie's stories was that the man in the student apartment next to hers was crazy, even dangerous; he had guns. Sandra did not know what to make of these remarks. She knew only that the friendship had become too uncomfortable to maintain, and began to let it drift. Not until the following May, that day when her mother sat transfixed between her radio and television sets, did she realize that it was Laurie who had owned the guns, Laurie who had disturbed her nights with all those hang-up telephone calls after she stopped seeing her, Laurie who was crazy.

"She transferred everything," Sandra said.

If her husband had not argued so strongly against it, Jessica Feldman would have driven straight to the Andrew house. She did not know that the Wassermans were already there. Even knowing, she would have gone, believing that if anyone could influence Laurie it was she. It was almost beyond endurance for her to hear the news reporters reiterate, from as close to the house as they could get, that the place was still ringed by heavily armed police with no sign of anyone moving around inside it.

Hours passed like this.

"Either she is dead or in a corner, catatonic, in a fetal position, rocking herself," Jessica told her family.

She kept hoping that Laurie would telephone her. Then she would certainly have gone to Winnetka, regardless of her own safety. She was imagining entering the house (with no thought of the police preventing her), putting her arms around this unhappy child, and saying, "I can't help you but I'm here for you."

She would never have this opportunity. Soon after 7:20 P.M. she would hear a news bulletin that it was Laurie's body which the police dog had found. Subsequent telephone records would show that a few minutes after shooting Philip Andrew, Laurie made a third telephone call to her parents' home and spoke for half an hour. Whatever was said in that conversation, neither of the Wassermans attempted to go directly to their daughter. There was a delay of about two hours until the police fetched them. Jessica could only speculate about Laurie's feelings when she hung up the phone and realized that she was alone in that house, alone in the world, to face the consequences of her actions. And she would always wonder whether the story might have ended differently if Laurie had telephoned her instead.

Laurie is believed to have used a phone in a bedroom shared by Philip's two teenaged sisters. It was the second room she would have come to after going up the backstairs by the kitchen: a pretty, girlish room, mostly lemon and white, with frilly white spreads on the twin beds and a collection of affectionately used toys by the fireplace. Laurie probably spent the next three or four hours there, among the assortment of teddy bears and the scattered items of girls' clothing. She may even have tuned in to some of the news bulletins about her own rampage along the north shore. Halfway through the afternoon she placed the barrel of her remaining gun in her mouth and fired a fatal bullet. The police's German shepherd found her in a pool of blood on the green and cream shag carpet. She was lying near one of the beds like a crumpled doll, her eyes open, the revolver about three feet from her body, looking very dead and very young.

For months afterward Jessica anguished over the fact that Laurie had become nationally known as "that woman who walked into a Winnetka school with a gun."

"Every time I hear the word 'woman' I cringe," she said. "Laurie was not a woman, but a child. She was definitely a child.

A child in need. I don't think I shall ever get over her death. Nor will Sandra. Nor Russell. I have thought about her so much. I cannot help thinking about her."

There was one other woman whom Laurie saw as a mother substitute, although the relationship was not such a close one. Her name was Virginia Dean and she lived in Glencoe, near the Wassermans, in a house of charm and character which reflected her own refined taste. She was a beautiful woman, dark-haired and dramatic, who loved to read, to play the piano, and to talk about her travels. From time to time Laurie dated her son, not seriously but often enough for her to feel very comfortable with his mother.

"Tell me about the isles of Greece," Laurie would ask. And Virginia would describe the Aegean, and the dunes of the Mediterranean, and would lend the younger woman her copies of *The Alexandria Quartet*, sharing her delight in Lawrence Durrell's passionate prose. Virginia felt they were both romantics, and knew Laurie read the books because of the comments she made about them afterward. Her son found this hard to believe. The Laurie he knew was shallow and moody, with a limited attention span. He thought her strange without being able to name a reason, and was never quite at ease with her. It was not a relationship he wished to maintain.

Around the time of Laurie's divorce, Virginia was aware of the younger woman's intense loneliness. When Laurie questioned her about art and literature and music, and when Virginia responded from her store of knowledge, she had a feeling that Laurie was trying to copy her, to establish another identity for herself.

Virginia devoted time to her, feeling she understood her better than her son did, although she was puzzled by some of Laurie's behavior: the fact that she did not like to be touched, and that she would not touch metal, pulling down the sleeves of her sweater to handle cutlery at one of Virginia's barbecues. Otherwise Virginia had the impression of a young woman who was gentle, intelligent, shy, and refined.

"Your children are lucky to have you as a mother," Laurie told her one day. "You are so easy to talk to."

Virginia was touched. She, too, thought of Laurie as a child, in the sense of one who needed to be guided, loved, and protected, who was not yet mature enough to be compassionate and unselfish.

In the latter months of 1987, Virginia's son ceased to be available when Laurie telephoned, and none of the Deans saw her again. On one occasion Virginia had the task of telling Laurie, truthfully: "He is not in." In the early spring of 1988, a few weeks before the Winnetka shootings, Virginia was wakened at 2:00 A.M. by a telephone call.

"Mrs. Dean?"

"Yes."

"You are going to die."

It was a woman's voice which she did not recognize. Feeling sickened and uneasy, she dismissed this as a crank call. But when the story of Laurie's last weeks was put together, it fitted the pattern of the many death threats she made at that time, all of them to people who in some way had disappointed her.

It was in this same period, on a bright Sunday morning, that Laurie hitched a ride from Emily Fletcher and announced she was thinking of suicide. Her response to Emily's question about her name may have been her last attempt at role-playing. She said it was Laurie "but I like to be called Melissa."

Melissa was the Greek mistress of the storyteller in *The Alexandria Quartet*. Durrell described her as a woman of charm, beauty, and intelligence, who loved passionately and died young.

TWENTY

As soon as Laurie was found dead, Commander Gary Stryker's team withdrew and Winnetka Police Chief Herbert Timm took over the suicide scene. Timm was immensely relieved that the bloodshed was over, and would have settled for capturing Laurie dead or alive, but her death robbed him of the chance to make her accountable. "I felt cheated," he said.

When he went into the Andrew girls' bedroom and looked at Laurie's body, he had a sense of anticlimax. He found it hard to equate all the terror of that day with the pathetic remains staining the carpet.

"My God, after all this trouble, here is this girl dead. And that's it," he thought. He loved Winnetka well enough to feel relieved that the community was spared the public agony of a murder trial. "But from an investigator's standpoint it was frustrating. There would always be so many unanswered questions. What horrible thing happened in her life? What else did she plan? And why?"

He had an innate feeling that her suicide was not the end of the story, not because of the things he would yet find out about her but because of the nature of this village. More than a year later, looking back on that night in the Andrew house, he would remark that "Laurie Dann just wouldn't die, isn't dead yet, may never be laid to rest." He got a glimpse of this phenomenon at the time, realizing that in one day she had not only robbed a generation of children of their innocence, but had irrevocably changed the way Winnetkans would think about their village.

"Laurie Dann taught us what we already knew but did not want to acknowledge: that there are no safe places," the Reverend Marcia Heeter would comment later. Outwardly, the scars would seem to heal. But the trauma was so intense that for long afterward Winnetkans would not be able to articulate what really happened. They would stumble over the words, substituting a euphemism which would become lodged in the local vocabulary: the incident of May 20. Not the shooting at Hubbard Woods. Not the murder of Nicholas Corwin. Certainly not the insanity of Laurie Dann, because her name became anathema as soon as the villagers learned it. Simply the incident of May 20. It was as much reality as anyone could deal with. To describe the event any more precisely would bring back memories too painful to be reexperienced.

There were so many details of police work to be thought about after Laurie's body was discovered that a crucial one was forgotten, and Herb Timm took the blame for it. This was generous of him because at that moment he was surrounded by a crowd of reporters outside the Andrew house.

"It's all over. She killed herself," he had just finished telling them, and was now responding to the barrage of questions. ("Yes, as soon as we clear up everything I'll let you guys into the house.") In his relief and exhaustion, he was concentrating on the fact that Laurie Dann could not do any more damage, and that this long day was almost over. Later he realized that he, or someone in authority, should have seen to it that Norman and Edith Wasserman were driven home by a pair of police officers who had no emotional involvement in the case, and who were rested enough to be objective.

The second condition would have been impossible to fulfill since every officer along the north shore had been intensely occupied since morning. But none of them was as stressed as Floyd

Mohr, who in about ten hours without a break had helped to put out a fire, interviewed a woman (Marian Rushe) who had just narrowly escaped death, identified the murderer of Nicky Corwin, seen the carnage in Room 7, risked his own life to save Philip Andrew, and been obliged to treat a grieving Norman Wasserman like an errant dog who might slip its leash. Added to all this, in an agony of self-doubt, Mohr had convinced himself that none of these things might have happened if only he had tried harder to separate Laurie from her gun—forgetting how hard he did try, and that the gun Laurie used on Nicky, Philip, and herself was one he had not known about.

"I had exceeded emotional overload," Mohr recalled. "If I could imagine being in Vietnam, that's how it felt that day. At times I had no idea where I was. I was walking around in a daze, I hurt so bad."

Despite this, or more likely because of it, he volunteered to take Laurie's parents back to Glencoe. Norman Wasserman was in no state to drive his own car. Shortly before Laurie's body had been found, he had said that if she was dead his life was over, and now he looked as though it was: bowed by grief, sobbing, broken. Edith was quietly tearful. Floyd Mohr ushered the two of them into his squad car and asked a colleague to follow in the Wassermans' automobile. However this encounter with the Wassermans might turn out, he felt an obligation to deal with it because he had known them for so long. Theirs had never been a close association, or even a comfortable one, but a certain mutual respect had developed.

During the short drive to Glencoe Norman Wasserman wept openly.

"Why did this have to happen? She loved children. She really loved them," he sobbed.

His wife was silent.

Mohr followed them into the house, intending to search Laurie's bedroom.

"No," Wasserman told him, barring the way. "This is over. It has been the most terrible day in my family's life. Now let us alone."

Quietly, Mohr insisted. He did not have a search warrant, but murder had been committed and he did have rights. He could have exerted them by "freezing" the scene, by radioing his station for reinforcements and a search warrant, and by telling the Wassermans that they were under arrest if they attempted to frustrate his investigation. But he felt too much pity for them, and was too emotionally drained himself. He was also influenced by the unwritten police code of the north shore villages. It simply wasn't done to harass innocent people in grief. If they had to be interrogated, one waited until they calmed down.

Mohr therefore tried persuasion. Finally Wasserman agreed that he could go into Laurie's bedroom for a very brief search.

"I will give you just five minutes," he said. His tears had turned to anger, and he was struggling to hold himself together. Clearly it was he, not Floyd Mohr, who was in charge.

While Wasserman glared at him from the doorway, Mohr rummaged through Laurie's possessions. Unlike the rest of the house, her room was messy: drawers open, clothes scattered around. Within seconds he found an incriminating collection of lethal equipment. On the floor near the window there was a plastic bag containing a gun-cleaning kit and at least fifty rounds of ammunition for Laurie's .357 Magnum. In the second drawer of the dresser there was a hypodermic syringe containing liquid that was later found to be an arsenic solution.

Watching from the doorway, Wasserman demanded: "What are you looking for?"

Still searching, Mohr replied: "I don't know, Mr. Wasserman, but I'll know when I find it."

Whatever "it" might be, he was sure it would be gone by morning. This house was so meticulously maintained that he sensed, rightly as it turned out, that before tomorrow this bedroom would be stripped of every clue to Laurie's character.

"I knew that if there was something of importance to the police in this house I had better find it right now," he recalled. The seconds were ticking by, but it did not occur to him to defy Wasserman. "He kept telling me to get out, get out; that people were coming over to comfort them, and that I was invading their privacy."

Mohr gathered up several bottles of prescription pills, including birth-control medication, and the stub of a bus ticket from Madison, Wisconsin, dated a few days earlier. He needed more time, but his five minutes were up.

"That's enough, that's enough," Wasserman told him. "She's dead. What more do you want?" His voice was breaking.

As he was being hustled out, Mohr noticed a stack of *Penthouse* magazines on the high shelf of a closet. It was an unexpected finding, this collection of male-oriented, sexually explicit photographs in a young woman's bedroom, and it troubled him. This was another aspect of Laurie which had eluded him, and he could not judge its significance. He felt sure that Norman Wasserman also saw the magazines because of his immediate, embarrassed glance in another direction.

Mohr left, and the house door was shut firmly behind him. As he suspected, when the Winnetka police made a follow-up call on the Wassermans, they found Laurie's bedroom tidy, and devoid of clues.

Norman Wasserman's way of dealing with the loss of his daughter was to busy himself with the routine of her death, in avoidance of the reality. Over the weekend he took two actions which surprised the Winnetka police by their alacrity and absence of emotion. In the thin block capitals which he used for personal communications, he wrote a note to the management of the Madison apartment building where his daughter had last lived, arranging for a Wisconsin relative of his to remove her belongings. Subsequently, when the police heard about this, they could only assume that he was trying to circumvent another search. The note read:

Dear Sirs,
As you are probably aware, Laurie Dann is deceased as of May 20, 1988. This is your authorization to release all of Laurie Dann's possessions (which are currently stored in your attic) to Mr. Robert Kahn.

I am Laurie Dann's father.

I would also appreciate your returning her $300 security deposit.

Respectfully yours,
Norman Wasserman.
P.S. Copy of the lease is attached.

Also, on the day after his daughter's death, Wasserman showed up at the Winnetka police station, demanding his white Toyota. He had the air of a man who had every right to be aggrieved by its seizure. When told that the police would like to talk with him and Edith, he pleaded for time.

Looking bleakly miserable, he explained: "My wife has taken this very hard."

He was given his car, but the police were never able to interview him. When they repeated the request after the decent interval of a few days, Wasserman replied that his attorney had advised him to say nothing.

"We were very empathetic to him, and we should not have been," Herbert Timm commented. "We should have been much more objective. The biggest mistake we made was not to get a search warrant for the Wasserman house. That should have been done, and in future it will be done."

It was one of many things which would change in Winnetka after this incident of May 20. In a village where violent crime didn't happen, it had seemed all right, even appropriate, for the police to be deferential. It would never be all right again.

After he left the Wassermans' house Floyd Mohr headed for a bar and gulped down so much alcohol that another police officer had to drive him home. Normally he was not a drinking man, one glass of beer a week was his usual limit, but that night he anesthetized himself so completely that, drunk beyond the barriers of pain, he was eventually able to sleep. When he awoke next morning, groggily as from a bad dream, he tried to convince himself that that was exactly what it was, the worst nightmare he had ever had. The feeling would repeat itself, morning after morning for months to come: a waking remembrance of the horror, immediately followed by the forlorn hope that it hadn't really happened.

TWENTY-ONE

ALONG THE north shore good causes flourish like the gardens of lakefront estates, and are as expertly tended. Organizations are created to serve needs, cultural and emotional, to the extent that whenever a gap is perceived in this caring network, a group is quickly formed to fill it. The Cameron Kravitt Foundation is among the many. It was founded in 1982 by Beverly Kravitt of Glencoe out of her anguish over the loss of her second child, Cameron, who was stillborn. Since then it has done much to help ease the emotional pain of other bereaved parents.

"My husband and I made a lot of wrong decisions when we lost our baby because we were in shock and there was no one to guide us," she related. "We were asked, almost instantly, to sign papers for an autopsy, and it was assumed that we would want the hospital to dispose of the body. We had to fight for a funeral. After the birth I was put in a room with a woman who had just had a baby, and I couldn't deal with hearing this infant crying and having all her visitors around. When I asked to be moved, they did not know what to do with me, and put me on a cancer floor."

After she had recovered, Beverly Kravitt lobbied among mental-health experts for more supportive treatment of parents who lose a child at birth. Over six years her foundation had done much to change attitudes and guidelines on the maternity wards of the north shore, and had extended its work to support bereaved parents of older children. Consequently, as soon as she heard of the Winnetka shootings, Beverly Kravitt knew exactly what needed to be done.

Early on that afternoon of May 20 she telephoned Winnetka's Community House, the village gathering place, and asked for some meeting rooms to be made available that night. She knew better than most that the families who had been traumatized by the bloodshed at Hubbard Woods School would need emotional support, and to have their questions answered, before the day was over. Four rooms were promised, and Beverly Kravitt went to work with professional efficiency. She arranged for a team of counselors to be at the Community House, set up a hot line to deal with emergency calls, spread the word of an evening meeting by having Hubbard Woods parents call one another, and put out announcements on all the local radio stations.

"I didn't know what the response would be," she said. "Laurie Dann was still at large, so I thought many people would want to stay at home with their children, listening to the news."

Many did. It was Pastor David Goodman's recollection that "Domino's pizza delivery in Hubbard Woods was besieged by orders. Nobody wanted to cook, nobody wanted to eat in a restaurant. I had to go and pick one up, they were so busy."

Nevertheless, about two hundred families showed up at the Community House, many more than expected. Reporters were excluded to allow people to talk freely. Therapists who came to lead the discussions included several from the Evanston Hospital trauma team. One of them, Jeffrey Berkson, was struck by the fact that he and his colleagues were accorded "a kind of instant credibility, just because we had been at the school all day."

"I don't want you people to think you are in the presence of a serious expert," he told them. "I just do social work at the hospital among children."

Berkson knew that in normal circumstances, Winnetkans would not have deferred to him. Even being in their presence made him awkwardly aware of having grown up poor, and of a personal appearance which he described, deprecatingly, as "scruffy"—meaning, on this particular day, the combination of his casually trimmed brown beard and his son's Hawaiian shirt. He was used to counseling misfits from emotionally deprived homes, and had already been struck by the difference in the demeanor of Winnetka children: a self-assurance to match the quality of their clothes, a way of looking straight at him when they spoke, instead of in every other direction. He would discover as he continued to work with them over the coming weeks that the most effective counseling for these traumatized children was "the same kind of thing that works for black kids," even though they came from families with different motivations and defenses.

That night at the Community House they were all looking to him and his colleagues for guidance. Parents wanted to know how their children were likely to be affected, how to reassure them, what actually happened, and whether it could happen again.

The meeting began awkwardly with an incident which made people in the room realize how jittery they all were. While School Superintendent Donald Monroe was making the introductions, a folding chair which had been leaning against a wall fell with a loud bang. Everybody jumped, but the strained laughter which followed helped to break the tension.

The audience divided into discussion groups, with a professional counselor assigned to each of them.

"I ended up sitting on the floor with about ten little children hanging on to various parts of my body," Berkson said. "I was talking with them while their parents watched, and I think the adults got a great deal out of it. The children were saying things like 'I'm scared. I'm not going to sleep tonight. I want to be in my mommy's bed.' The parents were picking this up and asking if it might cause a regression to babyhood, and I told them that this wasn't the time to worry about whether their children would regress, but a time to give them comfort and security.

"The children were satisfied with personal contact, but the parents wanted promises. They wanted reassurance that nothing like this would ever happen again. More than anything else, they wanted to be told, 'It's over.'"

That news reached them during the meeting. One of the therapists, the Reverend Richard Augspurger of Winnetka's Institute for Living, had to leave early because of a prior speaking engagement, ironically about the emotional impact upon a marriage of a child's death. He got into his car and switched on the radio with the engine, just in time to hear of Laurie Dann's suicide. He walked straight back into the Community House to pass on the news.

"I was glad she had taken her own life," he said. "I had been hoping and praying that there would not be a bloody ending to this day, like a shootout with the police. Every parent in town was on edge, and Laurie Dann's suicide brought some peace."

A sigh of relief went around the room when Augspurger made his announcement. Some adults rejoiced openly, with remarks like "Good!" and "Great!"

"I minded that, but I didn't say so. I kept it to myself," Jeffrey Berkson recalled. "I was uncomfortable with how excited people were, but I have seen it before in crisis situations. There's an adrenaline rush in response to the fact that a serious problem has been fixed, no matter how, and it comes out with an almost evangelical fervor.

"I did not want the session to end with this rejoicing at Laurie's death. So I talked about the meeting at Hubbard Woods School the next day, and how important it was for parents to be there to learn how to help their children."

Berkson was thinking: Laurie Dann was somebody's child, too. But he knew it would be a long time, if ever, before Winnetka parents could see the tragedy in those terms. The thought came readily to him because of the emotionally disturbed teenagers with whom he worked at the hospital: children from a range of economic backgrounds, many of them so profoundly depressed that self-destructive behavior seemed almost the norm to them. His charges were not substance abusers (there were other programs for them), but the offspring of families who did not seem to have enough time, or the right kind of time, for them. He had often been struck by the parallel between poor and rich parents: how the rich work all hours to stay rich, while the poor do the same to survive. Most of the parents he saw at both ends of this spectrum were decent people, bewildered by the fact that their children had become estranged from them.

In his twenty-two years as a social worker he had been disturbed to watch this threshold of self-destructive behavior fall lower and lower, down into the preteen years. "I have not come up with an explanation that I am comfortable with," he remarked. "In the working-class neighborhood of Chicago where I grew up, we were all pretty mainstream kind of kids."

He left the Winnetka meeting worrying about the adolescents in his charge, and how disturbed they might be about the day's news of Laurie Dann, and he decided to stop by their ward at Evanston Hospital on his way home.

Most of the youngsters in his program were hospitalized from four to six weeks, time for them to become quite attached to him. Although it was after 10:00 P.M. he found them still awake, relieved to see him, and anxious to discuss the day's news.

Two girl patients asked him the same question: "You don't think I could be like Laurie Dann, do you?"

Berkson had not anticipated this reaction. "It stopped me cold," he said. "The thought had not even crossed my mind. These were two nonviolent girls who had depression. After hearing about Laurie Dann they were really worried about what they might do, and that put chills through me. It was one of those moments I shall never forget.

"I spent some time with the girls. I don't know if I dealt with them very well but I told them that they had made the decision to get help for their problems, and that being depressed wasn't a life sentence. And that seemed to calm them."

It was very late when Berkson got home. He was so emotionally drained that he could sleep only fitfully, wishing for morning so that he could get back to Hubbard Woods and be part of the action again.

Dick Augspurger spent most of his evening twenty miles away in Arlington Heights, addressing a gathering of about seventy-five bereaved parents. Experienced as he was in pastoral counseling, this was always a difficult group for him to work with. There was so much pain in it. The divorce rate among such couples was very high, close to 75 percent, and as he drove to the meeting he was wondering whether, on this night of all nights, he had the emotional strength to help them support one another.

223

"I felt I had to be honest with them, so I shared with them that I had come from the school, and this reopened some of the trauma for me," he said. "It was such a paradox that I should have been scheduled to speak to this group on this topic, and it was very stressful for all of us because of the death of Nicky Corwin."

He thought he knew the source of his own stress. Earlier in the day at Hubbard Woods School he had made the connection between his immediate feelings of loss and anger and his old grief over his mother's sudden death, twenty-two years earlier. But there was more to it than that, a recent unhealed memory which would surface over the next few days, surprising him by its strength because he thought the episode had been resolved by ending happily.

Almost three years earlier his son Brett, then aged four, had been critically ill with a rare blood disease. At the suggestion of his nursery-school teacher, Augspurger had visited the school to explain to his classmates why Brett was absent. Although he had been reluctant to do this, he drew comfort from the love and concern which the children expressed. But one little girl's question brought him close to tears. "Is Brett going to die?"

His child's recovery had been complete. "I was so thankful, and after the Hubbard Woods shooting I was aware of being thankful all over again. Then I had some guilt feelings because I was rejoicing that he was alive while another child was dead." That led him to reexperience his agony over Brett's illness, almost as intensely as when the little girl in nursery school asked her piercing question.

It was a poignant reminder to him that there is no shortcut to the resolution of grief. "At one time I thought there was," he said. "I tried to do it by writing a doctoral dissertation on the subject, and by becoming a therapist. What I had yet to learn was that the scars will continue to be a reminder of the wound. But I believe very strongly that our own losses, if we can heal from them, greatly increase our sensitivity toward others who have been hurt. The Christian message is that we can go on and have new life, even though we are wounded people."

After she left Hubbard Woods School that afternoon, Dr. Mary Giffin turned into Hamptondale Road, exhausted, to find that Laurie Dann's car had been moved to her driveway, a few yards from the place where it had been wrecked. A policeman stood on guard.

"You can't go in," he said. "She could be in your house."

The possibility was remote, but the police weren't taking chances. Dr. Giffin went back to her office, then visited with a friend. Only after Laurie was found dead was she allowed into her home. Then, she said, "it was the oddest feeling, going into the house and wondering if she had tried to get in, and whether my two dogs had scared her away."

That night, and over the next several months, she found herself remembering events which she had not thought about in more than half a lifetime. She had been a medical student at Johns Hopkins University in Baltimore during the Second World War, and this day's experience at Hubbard Woods, going from classroom to classroom to help the children deal with Nicky's death, reminded her of the terrible losses among the young doctors who had landed behind the enemy lines at Omaha Beach. Twelve of the sixteen she had worked with were killed.

"It came back to me with great clarity, along with other personal recollections of knifing and shooting victims in the emergency room at Johns Hopkins," she said. "I had suppressed these memories for years."

Some time would elapse before the various therapists would realize how widely this reincarnation of buried traumas was shared. They knew it well as a fact of life among their patients. But the shooting at Hubbard Woods was such an intense experience for everyone involved that the care givers were also ineluctably drawn back into the pain of their own pasts, some so vividly that they needed healing too.

TWENTY-TWO

Patrolman Eddie Benoit thought the evening would never end, and when it did he knew he would never forget it. He had been off duty that Friday morning and heard the news of the shooting on the radio. Finding all the telephone lines to the Winnetka police station blocked, he drove straight there from his home in Skokie. The building was almost empty when he arrived.

"I'll go wherever I'm needed," he told William Saunders, the dispatcher.

He expected to be sent to the school, but was directed to Kent Road instead. Only when he got there and saw the street lined with squad cars was he able to get a vague sense that the person who had done the shooting might be in the Andrew house. Lieutenant Joe Sumner instructed him to drive Ray Andrew, who was still very agitated, to pick up his two daughters at New Trier High School, and his younger son at the Sacred Heart School, then to take the four of them to Highland Park Hospital. There wasn't time for Benoit to ask why, and during the drive Ray Andrew was too tense and nervous to be communicative.

Benoit was struck by the fact that the doors of both schools were locked, with the students inside. He went up to the dean's office at New Trier where the Andrew girls were waiting for him, weeping. On the way to the hospital their father tried to calm them with the promise: "He's going to be okay."

Benoit wasn't sure who "he" was or what had happened to him, and didn't feel it appropriate to ask questions. He communicated with Joe Sumner from Highland Park Hospital's emergency room and was told to stay close to the Andrew family, to relay any information which might be needed about the layout of their house.

Ruth Andrew was already at the hospital with some friends, and Philip was in surgery. The family had a long wait ahead, and their conversation was punctuated by hysterical laughter, which came perilously close to tears. What Benoit picked up was a lot of inconsequential talk about trivia which made him uncomfortable because it seemed inappropriate, now that he knew about Philip's life being in the balance in another part of the hospital. He was unable to recognize the chatter as a mask for feelings which none of these people dared expose, feelings which he could not share because he was on another wavelength.

"It was like they were at a party," he remembered. "A kind of circus mood."

He and the Andrews were moved to a second-floor waiting room where he felt even more like an intruder, trying to look as though he wasn't listening to what he couldn't avoid overhearing. Yet there was nothing for him to do but hang around because by this time Dan Andrew had reached Winnetka, and was briefing the police about his home, more clearly than Benoit could do at second hand.

At about 2:00 P.M. a nurse came into the waiting room. "Are you with the Winnetka police?" she asked him. "There's another officer downstairs who would like to see you."

She led him to a curtained cubicle in the emergency room, and walked away.

"I pulled the curtains back, and there was this little kid lying on an aluminum cot," Benoit recalled. "There were a couple of officers there but I didn't notice them because I was so shook up at the sight of this little kid, lying on a cold table with no clothes on. He had a plastic tube under his armpit and a scar right over his heart. I said to myself: 'Why don't they put a blanket over him? He has got to be cold.' Those were my first thoughts, even though I knew he was dead.

"I was still standing there staring at him when the officer who had called me, Brian Bradfield of Northfield, said, 'Eddie, I have to turn over this evidence to a Winnetka officer.'

"I said, 'Why?'

"He said, 'Because we have to maintain a chain of evidence.'

"I said, 'How long is this going to take?'

"He said, 'I have to inventory—,' or something like that. I was not paying attention.

"I said, 'To be honest with you, I don't want to be here. I can't take this anymore.'

"He said, 'No problem. I just have to make a Winnetka officer aware that I have the evidence.'

"I said, 'Okay, I'm aware of it. But I can't take looking at it. I have to get out of here.'"

Benoit explained: "It was easier for him because he had been at the school. You have to work your way into a case, and he had already done that, but this was the first time I had seen the result of the shooting. I love kids, and to see a child in that condition was very hard for me to deal with.

"When I went back to the second-floor waiting room I was shaking, I didn't know why, and there was all this chitchat going on, Mrs. Andrew talking about how her son was a swimmer and her daughter on the school basketball team, and I didn't want to hear it. All I had in my mind was the picture of that little kid on the table.

"I stayed for another hour or two, felt useless, so I called Joe Sumner on the phone. Philip had just come out of surgery and it had been a success. I used that as an excuse. I said, 'Joe, the Andrew boy is doing fine, no complications.' I knew Laurie Dann was still in the house and I felt that if I could get back there I could be more useful. I was hoping that Joe would forget I was supposed to stay at the hospital. So I said, 'I will be on my way back.'

"He said, 'No, I told you to stay with the Andrew family.'

"I said, 'But maybe if I could come to the house I could be of some help.'

"He said, 'No, I need you there. If we have to charge the house I may want you to relay some more information about it.'

"So I said okay. You have to follow orders."

Eddie Benoit was struggling with emotions which went deeper than shock at the sight of Nicky Corwin's body. The only way he could articulate them was by expressing a need to get away from the hospital. But it wasn't just the sight of Nicky dead which tore at him, or even his initial denial of that death; it was his urge to avenge the outrage upon this innocent child. The feeling was so overwhelming that he did not recognize it as his own. Benoit was one of two black members of the Winnetka police team, a soft-spoken man with such a gentle nature that none of his colleagues would have credited him with murderous thoughts. He had pleaded with Joe Sumner to let him be part of the action, arguing that it was a waste of police manpower for him to hang around the hospital. But there was more to it than that, a primitive impulse which Herbert Timm recognized when he was told about the episode.

"He wanted to get out there and kill," Timm said. "He was so enraged about the murder of this child." And that was the emotion which had shaken his body in the emergency room.

Benoit said nothing about this to the Andrew family. He had no idea whether they knew that a child was dead, no insight into their anxiety about Philip, no information about how gravely he had been wounded.

"I only know how I was feeling," he said. "I was torn up inside. And to be with those people who did not know what I had seen, for all those hours, was almost more than I could bear."

Benoit heard about Laurie's suicide from a television news broadcast in the hospital waiting room.

"Oh, God, I wonder where she did it," Ruth Andrew said, and started worrying aloud about which of her furnishings might have been ruined.

Benoit was thinking: What does it matter? While she was avoiding the reality of yet another act of violence in her home, he could only concentrate on the fact that Laurie was dead. Nothing else seemed relevant. Ruth Andrew's concern about her carpets was beyond his comprehension.

"I thought to myself, 'I have to get out of here,'" Benoit related. "The hospital was going to put up Philip's parents for

the night, so I called Joe again. It was about eight P.M. I said,
'Everything is being taken care of here. Can I come back?' He
said okay, so I went to the station. There were cameras, reporters, policemen all over the place. It was like nothing I had ever
seen before. But although it was the end of the action I didn't
feel completely satisfied. I had been isolated from the whole situation, and I wanted to take revenge on this woman for what she
had done to Nicky. If I could just have seen them bring her out
of the house dead it would have been enough."

After Eddie Benoit left the curtained cubicle in the emergency room, Detective Brian Bradfield covered Nicky's body with
a blanket. It was a tender gesture, born of the denial that was
shared by everyone who had to deal with this child's death.

"It feels kind of funny, to see this little boy just lying there,"
he explained. "You want him to know he is not alone. You want
to tell him that everything is going to be all right."

Bradfield had been with Nicky from the time he was carried
into the ambulance. He had seen the paramedics and doctors trying to revive him; watched the comings and goings of his parents
and rabbi. After Nicky was pronounced dead his body became,
in police terms, a piece of evidence which had to be documented
and protected. But even though he had worked himself into the
case, Bradfield was as distressed as Eddie Benoit.

"It's a policeman's nightmare, dealing with children who are
hurt," he said. "In this job you get used to death, but it's usually
the death of adults who know what they're doing. Here's this
little guy, all he's doing is going to school, and he is the only one
to get killed. You see him lying there, lifeless, and all you have
ever learned about not getting emotionally involved doesn't
amount to a hill of beans."

Nicky had been pronounced dead in both Cook and Lake
counties, most recently the latter, which, as Herbert Timm had
foreseen, created jurisdictional difficulties for the police. Laurie's
crimes had been committed in Cook County, and for the purposes
of his investigation Timm wanted all the evidence kept there.
During the afternoon a compromise was reached: that a Lake
County coroner's officer should accompany Nicky's body to the

Cook County mortuary. After this had been settled, Brian Bradfield waited at Highland Park Hospital to gather one more piece
of evidence: the bullet which had bounced around in Philip Andrew's chest.

He never did get it. Dr. Charles Brown, the operating surgeon, found it lodged in the muscles of Philip's back, and decided to leave it there.

Charles Brown, clinical assistant professor of surgery at the
University of Chicago, had been about to operate on a man for
lung cancer when a nurse hurried into the operating room with
the message: "There's trouble in the emergency room. You had
better go down."

He left the patient, already anesthetized, and arrived in time
to see Dr. Phillip Rosett open Nicky's chest. Brown recognized
the surgery as hopeless but did what he could to help. Like the
other doctors gathered around, he was thinking of his own four
children.

"I have patients dying all the time and it doesn't usually af-
fect me, not if they have had a full life, but here was a child who
never had a chance, and it really got to me.

"I was told there would be more casualties so I telephoned
the operating room about my patient. They woke him up and put
him in recovery. I found his wife and told her I would not be
able to do the operation until Monday. His lung was very bad and
she had been prepared for the surgery, so she was very upset. I
told her, 'Sit down and think about what has happened to these
other people, and maybe you will feel better.'"

His next task was to operate on Philip Andrew, who had just
been brought in.

"It turned out to be a real neat case," he said. "He had been
shot on the right side of the chest but there was no exit wound.
I closed my eyes and asked myself where that bullet might have
gone. We did some tests that showed it had missed the heart but
damaged the esophagus, and that's a very serious injury.

"I opened up the abdomen and found the bullet had gone
into the stomach, spleen, and lodged in the back muscles."

Assisted by Dr. Avram Kraft, Brown repaired the holes in
Philip's stomach. "The spleen was not bleeding so we left that.

Usually when you fix an esophagus you have to do it through the chest. But I had been told that this young man was a championship swimmer, and captain of his college team. When you swim, one of the muscles you use to rotate your arms is the latissimus dorsi. And when you repair the esophagus through the chest you have to cut through that muscle. If I did that I knew it would heal, but never be as strong as before. So I really persisted in trying to repair the hole in the esophagus by going up through the abdomen. In the back of my mind I was thinking that he would never be a competitive swimmer again if I cut that muscle. I would have done it if his life depended upon it, but I managed not to."

Philip was in surgery for six hours. If the operation had been done less skillfully he could have taken months to recover. Instead, he went home after sixteen days, and was back on the college team the following year.

Throughout his recovery his parents, brothers, and sisters took turns to watch at his bedside. Doctors and nurses were impressed by the mutual support within this large and loving family. Denied the active summer he had planned for himself, Philip never once asked the question: "Why me?"

"If any of the others had been shot they might not have pulled through," he commented. "I was the best candidate for survival because I was in such good physical condition. So it makes perfect sense that it was me."

Very few of the Winnetka police officers went home that night. Those who did discovered they had become instant celebrities, their telephone answering machines choked with messages from out-of-town friends who had seen them on the national television news. The rest straggled back to their headquarters, a low red-brick building on Green Bay Road, to face hours of desk work writing reports. A village restaurant had sent in refreshments but no one felt like eating much. The trays of cold cuts sat around, merely to be picked at.

"We had so much to coordinate," Sergeant Patty McConnell stated. "There had been so many evidence scenes: the classroom, the boys' bathroom, Laurie's car, the house fire, the Andrew home. We had five victims being treated at two hospitals, two bodies going to the morgue, and an unbelievable number of witnesses at the school. And all this had to be documented by morning."

Bill Saunders had been relieved at the dispatch desk by Elizabeth Ann Ford, the only person in the building who had met Laurie Dann. Before becoming a communications officer for the Winnetka police, she had done a similar job in Glencoe, where she had heard Laurie's stories about being assaulted by Russell. Liz Ford had found them totally believable.

"She felt victimized by her husband, and appeared to be genuinely threatened and horribly frightened. She was very reserved, rather mousy, self-conscious, and soft-spoken. The last time I saw her she came into the station and asked for Floyd. I told her he wasn't in and she bowed her head and started to walk off. I said, 'Laurie, do you want me to call him and tell him you want to see him?' She did not answer. Just walked away. She could not handle that he wasn't there."

Liz found it almost impossible to believe that "this innocent little girl had been randomly shooting kids."

"It doesn't make sense," she said. "It never occurred to me that she was capable."

After they had finished their reports, the police officers sat around and talked about the horrors they had seen. They were all too tense for sleep, and this was their first opportunity to blend their individual experiences into a comprehensible account of this horrible day. Each of them had been involved in a part of it, barely aware of the rest, and some of the things they had been required to do did not make sense until the others told their stories. Some wept as they recalled events. At about 3:00 A.M. they drifted off to various offices to try to sleep. Those who could find blankets stretched out on the floor. Patrolman John Hamick settled on a narrow cot in one of the holding cells. Patty McConnell lay down on a couch in the exercise room, quietly sobbing.

She could not stop worrying about her baby daughter. Although she had been reassured that her husband, Matthew, was now home and Kristin asleep, the fate of the children at Hubbard Woods School was so vivid to her that she felt an overwhelming need to see her own child. Soon after three o'clock she got in her car and made the seventy-mile round trip to her home in Lake Zurich.

"Matt had come in at midnight and was still up," she said. "I held the baby for a minute, grabbed some fresh clothes, and left."

She was glad to get out of the jeans and sweatshirt she had worn all day, and would never want to wear again.

Back at the station none of the police officers had been able to sleep. By 4:30 A.M. most had given up trying and were sitting around in the main office, retelling their tales.

"Someone should make a movie of this," one of them remarked. The others seized on the suggestion, and the conversation turned to the kind of movie it might be, and how each of them should be portrayed. It was a diversion they all needed, and they tossed names of film stars around, releasing their tension in hysterical laughter as they imagined Burt Reynolds, Paul Newman, Sally Field, even the cartoon character Ricochet Rabbit in the roles of themselves.

"It was such a relief," Liz Ford said.

By daylight they were ready to go back on duty.

TWENTY-THREE

I<small>T WAS</small> very different for the doctors and nurses at Evanston Hospital: They had a sense of victory. Instead of losing a child, they had brought one back from the brink of death—so skillfully that eight-year-old Lindsay Fisher, who had no memory of being shot, would soon be able to resume an active childhood with no physical reminder of the experience but the scars on her body.

When she was rushed into the emergency room, her chances of survival were minimal. Her recovery was widely ascribed to a surgical procedure so unorthodox and daring that no doctor would dream of attempting it if there was any other hope. But it also depended upon the experience and intuition of a chain of people, starting with John Fay, the paramedic who judged correctly that he should break the rule about getting an intravenous line into Lindsay before rushing her into the hospital. If he had taken the time to try, she would have been dead on arrival. It also depended upon a fortuity of timing. Lindsay and three other Hubbard Woods children, all in immediate need of surgery, were brought into Evanston Hospital when most of the senior consultants had just finished their morning operations but were still in the building.

Dr. Stephen F. Sener, thoracic surgeon, had been one of the first to finish. He would already have left for another hospital except that he had stopped to chat with a favorite patient, and this made him the second link in the chain.

"My patient was a lady of about sixty-five, and I had been working with her for three years," he related. "I was always impressed by her. She had an advanced melanoma of the neck, was dying and knew it. She was really courageous, and I spent a lot of time talking to her that morning because she was depressed and relied on me for support."

He broke off the conversation abruptly when the trauma alert, summoning all available physicians to the emergency room, sounded on the loudspeaker system.

"There was a tone in the operator's voice that was distinctly different. I know all the operators, I have been around this hospital for fifteen years, and it was immediately clear to me that this was not the usual kind of emergency. I told my patient I had to go and hurried down the hallway. It was the last time I saw her alive. Later, her death was very hard for me to deal with."

Evanston Hospital, a prestigious teaching institution serving the entire north shore, was in the process of applying for state accreditation as a level-one trauma center, which meant that it had to be ready at all times to accept seriously injured patients.

"We were still testing the system," Dr. Charles Drueck, director of the hospital's trauma program, recalled. "That Friday morning I was in my office with a roomful of patients when my beeper went off, and at first I thought the trauma administrator was doing another test." So did many others, but they all hurried to the emergency room, expecting to be thanked and dismissed. There had been several such drills in the last few weeks.

Dr. David P. Winchester, the hospital's head of general surgery, was taking out a colon cancer when he heard the broadcast announcement. Minutes later a nurse told him that children had been shot.

"I had just finished putting my patient's bowel back together, so the primary part of the operation was over. I asked one of the residents to finish and bolted out of the operating room to the emergency room. The sight there was incredible.

"I had never seen anything like it, not even in four months in Vietnam as a frontline medical officer. There I saw men with parts of them missing, screaming, dead; terrible scenes. But this bothered me more because it was wounded children.

"There were four of them surrounded by qualified people, about a hundred in the emergency room, in response to the trauma call. Yet there was orderliness in the midst of the chaos, with every child surrounded by ten or twelve medical personnel. I went from one to another to assess their condition and reaffirm assignments. We were lucky to have so many staff surgeons in the building; it meant we could assign a couple of them to each child. If this had occurred at two A.M. we might have lost one or two children because it takes time to bring that many more staff in at night."

The youngest victim, Robert Trossman, whom Laurie had shot in the boys' bathroom, had a bullet wound through his chest and stomach. He was nine days short of his seventh birthday, and the most vocal of the group, even in the emergency room. Later, doctors would say that his cheerfulness hastened his recovery.

Mark Teborek, who was eight, kept asking the heartbreaking question: "Am I going to die?" He was wounded in the chest and stomach. Dr. Drueck promised him that he would live. "But I wasn't sure," he admitted later. "His color was ashen but he was a remarkable child, very cooperative through all the testing we did before surgery."

Seven-year-old Kathryn Miller had been shot through the wrist and into her chest; ironically, the fracture of a wristbone turned out to be the most complicated of her injuries. She, too, was quiet and uncomplaining, and firmly corrected an emergency-room doctor who called her Kathie.

Only Lindsay Fisher was unconscious.

"Not only that, she was in a terminal state. She had that look about her," Dr. Winchester assessed. She had been shot through the right upper arm, into the chest, through the right lung, diaphragm, liver, and stomach, causing such severe internal hemorrhage that she had lost almost her entire blood supply. The paramedics had correctly identified her as the most seriously wounded child, and brought her in first.

In the few minutes that they had to prepare, the emergency-room staff repeated all the drills they had previously rehearsed. Nothing went wrong. The speed and efficiency were flawless. Triage stations were set up, with teams of doctors and nurses and batteries of monitoring devices. Operating-room staffs were alerted. Everyone in the system reacted exactly as taught, and the system worked superbly.

"My concern was not as great for the three other children as it was for Lindsay Fisher, but without the immediate care they received, they too could have been in serious trouble," said Felix Mesterharm, the hospital's clinical director for critical care. "I have seen victims die from similar wounds when they were not treated immediately. All the children were in surgery within an hour."

As one of the first surgeons to reach the emergency room, Dr. Sener was assigned to Lindsay. He judged that she had less than five minutes to live.

"She had a pulse but it was very rapid, and she had no measurable blood pressure. When that happens it is a matter of minutes before the heart stops because there is not enough oxygen. Her heart was still beating, but the tank was running on empty.

"The bullet had entered the chest from the right arm, and I could feel it in the left lower abdomen. The route between these two points includes some pretty important real estate: the heart, aorta, vena cava, and the liver, all potential sources of massive blood loss. The abdomen was distended by this internal hemorrhage. I decided that she needed an immediate operation, but first had to figure out whether there was blood in her chest as well as the abdomen. I put a tube in her chest and got back blood, enough to tell me that I had to incorporate the chest in the incision.

"Somewhere in the middle of this the nursing supervisor showed up and I told her I needed an operating room immediately, and all the type-O blood in the hospital. That's a lot of blood. I don't think it's ever been done before. We had no blood left in the patient so we couldn't type her.

"We took her up to the operating room as she was, on the emergency-room bed. In a trauma alert all the elevators are commandeered by security, so there was no delay. In the elevator I said to the resident: 'Buckle your seat belt. This is going to be a rough ride.' We knew that the only chance we had was to get this child on the operating table, make an incision, and stop the hemorrhage.

"There are twelve operating rooms on the third floor, and in the middle of a Friday morning all of them were busy. But in five minutes Dr. Herbert Epstein, the chief of anesthesia, had figured out how to make four of them available. In one room they had just finished a thorascopy and were preparing for another case which had to be canceled. In two of the others patients were having a cystoscopy, and they were immediately transferred to the recovery room. In another room Dr. Richard Larson was doing a hernia, using a local anesthesia.

"Dr. Epstein went into the room and told him: 'You have to finish this operation and get the hell out of here. We need the room fast.' The patient heard all this discussion, and went nuts. He was saying: 'What the hell is going on here? You guys can't do this to me.'"

But they did. Sener recalled: "Richard finished the operation in seconds. He was very quick."

There was no time for Sener to put on a gown or a mask or surgical gloves. He remained in his street clothes—blue pants and a white shirt. He could not think about extraneous details. He did not ask what had happened in Winnetka, who this child was, or how she had been shot. He concentrated entirely on saving her.

Afterward, when he looked back on the experience, he realized that even under this extreme duress he had taken special care with the chest incision, guided by the memory of his own outrage when, years earlier, he had seen a young resident insert a chest tube into the breast bud of a baby girl: an action which would doom her to cosmetic surgery after adolescence.

"I was so affronted by that. It was an unforgivable sin," Sener related. "And somehow the recollection clicked in as I began to make my incision under the chest. I realized why I did it that way only after the fact. With a male it would not have made a difference."

At that moment Dr. John C. Alexander, Jr., the hospital's chief of cardiovascular and thoracic surgery, walked in. He was dressed for surgery even to his headlight, having been summoned from another operation which he had almost completed: a coronary bypass on a seventy-five-year-old man.

He had heard about the shootings from Dr. Herbert Epstein, who had come into his operating room with the bare news that a case of a gunshot wound was being brought into the hospital.

At first Alexander was not alarmed. "That kind of remark does not make a deep impression," he commented. "It could mean that someone shot himself in the foot, called Nine-one-one and said there had been a mass murder. But then Herb came back and said there had been a shooting at a grammar school. I live in Glencoe and I have a child in grammar school and a child in high school, so at this point the whole complexion began to change. The next bulletin was that Steve Sener was bringing a child directly to Operating Room Eight. Herb said: 'They need you there.' The colleague who was working with me on the bypass didn't need me to finish, so I left the table and went straight to Room Eight."

His reaction on seeing Lindsay Fisher was: "There's no point in trying. This one is dead." At the same time he was figuring how best to try to save her; shifting gears, as he put it, from his normal speed of thinking into overdrive.

He and Sener were familiar with each other's operating methods, and as they worked together on Lindsay Fisher, there was very little need for conversation. As the senior surgeon, Alexander completed the incision, from the chest to the abdomen, following the track of the bullet. At the same time two anesthesiologists were desperately trying to get intravenous lines into the child's arm and neck, but having no success because her veins had collapsed.

"I looked at her heart and at that point it was empty," Alexander recalled. "It meant that she had lost her blood volume. The heart pumps blood around the vascular system and if the blood is lost you are within minutes of being dead. This child's heart was still contracting vigorously but did not have any volume to move. The intravenous lines would have given that volume, but it was impossible to get them in.

"We found the major source of bleeding in the hilum of the liver, and Steve physically held it to stop the continued blood loss."

Sener commented: "I did a maneuver that has no name. Using both my hands to clamp off the blood vessels, I lifted the liver up and mechanically squeezed it, and that did control the bleeding." Meantime the anesthesiologists were still struggling with their IV lines. They had just managed to get one into Lindsay's left arm, but it wasn't working properly.

"We still can't get any volume," one of them said.

Alexander and Sener exchanged glances. This case looked so hopeless that there seemed no point in proceeding. Suddenly Alexander had an inspiration. As he described it: "I opened the pericardium and put an intravenous line directly into the heart. I had never heard of this being done before. As a cardiac surgeon, putting a small catheter into the heart as a monitoring device is something I do every day. But this was a trauma situation, and very different. Yet it was such a simple idea that I suppose at some time somebody else must have thought of it.

"Once I put in the blood and intravenous fluid, it refilled the vascular space so that the heart had something to pump. We put in a lot of liters while Steve was still holding the liver. Within fifteen to twenty minutes this child's blood pressure went from negative to an acceptable level."

There was visible relief around the operating table. John Alexander's desperate solution would never be attempted in normal circumstances because it means making a hole in an undamaged heart, an intrusion which carries a risk of serious infection. A general surgeon might never have thought of it, or have dared to take the risk, but just as fate had caused Lindsay to be shot, it had now put her into the hands of a skilled cardiologist, and his unorthodox intervention would be a decisive victory in the battle to save her life. Yet despite all the red cells and plasma and platelets which were being poured into her system, the bleeding continued.

"A massive hemorrhage dramatically alters the blood's ability to clot," Alexander explained. "Also we did not have time to warm the blood we put in. It was room temperature. So the child was getting colder and colder, and that too interferes with clotting." On the other hand, cooling the patient was protective of the brain, so the risk was worth taking.

Stephen Sener was thinking: In these circumstances an adult would die. An adult heart would not sustain this blood loss for so

241

long. And if by some miracle it could, the patient would be brain-damaged. He was remembering how, seven years earlier, he had tried to resuscitate Chicago's assistant police chief after this man was shot in the chest. His heart had been torn and Sener tried to replace the blood loss by putting a catheter directly into the right atrium, but his attempt had failed; the victim was already dead.

"A whole range of emotions went through me, all of them unspoken," he said afterward. "I went from thinking this child was going to die, to maybe she will die, to maybe she will live but be brain-damaged, to maybe, just maybe, she will live and be okay. I was so afraid of us having a patient who would survive but be a vegetable. To me that would have been the worst outcome. So I didn't know if we were doing her a favor or not, and the anxiety surrounding that feeling was incalculable."

Not until well into the surgery did it occur to him that he was still in his street clothes. The only precaution he had taken had been to tuck his blue tie into his shirt. From time to time he also thought of the reason why he had wanted to get home early. His twin sons, Matthew and Michael, were two years old today. "While I was operating it kept creeping into my consciousness: This is my kids' birthday and this could have been my kid."

Of Lindsay's various injuries, two to the liver were severely life-threatening. "Once we were able to generate blood pressure, the bleeding from these two sites, the hepatic artery and the middle hepatic vein, became very significant, even with me still hanging on," said Sener. "I decided to try to repair both vessels. If the repair did not work we would have had to clamp off the vessels and lose part of the liver, but I did manage to repair them."

In the middle of this procedure he made a teasing remark to John Alexander. "Why am I sewing this? You have the magnifying loops on and you are a vascular surgeon."

Alexander had been holding the child's liver while Sener worked on it. Without looking up he mumbled: "I have been watching every stitch go in, and if any of them were bad you would have heard from me."

With blood still being injected directly into the heart, the two men went on to repair wounds in the stomach and diaphragm, worrying all the while because Lindsay's body was getting colder.

"I tried to warm her by putting warm fluid into the abdomen," Alexander related. "The loss of heat when you have a patient open like that is tremendous. So we made the decision to close the wounds and get her out of the operating room and into the intensive-care unit, knowing that we might have to do more surgery after she had stabilized. Because of the lack of clotting factors, there was still some bleeding, and we were worried about that."

All this surgery had taken about one and a half hours.

"That much I know," Sener said. "But we were all so fixated on what we were doing that we had no concept of time. We all commented on this afterward. Everyone behaved magnificently: the anesthesiologists, the residents, the nurses. And everything went right, although none of the stuff we did is in any book."

As they were finishing, Dr. Robert Anderson, chairman of the hospital's department of surgery, came into the room. In mock reproof he asked Stephen Sener: "Could you please put on a pair of gloves and a gown?"

Sener recalled: "I was covered with blood. Afterward I threw everything into the garbage can. The only thing I kept was my shoes. I had to take a shower and put on a pair of greens before I could go out to talk to the parents. But first I said to Anderson, facetiously: 'Yes, now I have finished, maybe I can.'"

The parents of the four injured children had been sequestered in the third-floor surgical library. Sener led George and Karen Fisher out to a corridor, and told them that Lindsay was out of surgery but still in danger. "They were both so stunned that they seemed to have no comprehension of what I had said. All they seemed able to grasp was that their daughter was alive. And this, by the way, was the first time I heard her name."

After he finished checking that the four operating rooms were ready, Felix Mesterharm had caught a glimpse of Lindsay being rushed into surgery. He was struck by her resemblance to his eldest daughter, who, like her two siblings, was born prematurely. At the age of a negative twelve weeks, it had been necessary for her to have chest surgery for a collapsed lung, and the remembrance of that terrible anxiety flooded back to Mesterharm with the sight of this wounded child, now about the same age as his own.

"I suppressed my feelings because I had a job to do," he said. "I think everyone in this hospital did that. But after I had seen all the children into surgery and done everything I could, I got a telephone call from my wife. She had heard the news on television and wanted to know if I was all right."

He took the call on a phone in the hallway near the operating room where, at that very moment, John Alexander and Stephen Sener were working desperately on Lindsay. At the reassuring sound of his wife's voice, Mesterharm felt such a flood of emotion that for a few minutes he could not answer her question. Instead, he turned to the wall and wept.

TWENTY-FOUR

For susan Guilianelli and her staff of forty registered nurses, saving lives was a common event. Losing them, too. Sue was convinced that the women working under her in the intensive-care unit had the most stressful jobs in Evanston Hospital. The best of them allowed themselves to feel the pain of a loss they had tried to prevent, and did not become case-hardened. Those who kept their emotions under control for fear of exposing them tended to drift off into other kinds of work. "Critical-care nurses are known for burnout and turnover," Sue explained. "We do not have a high retention rate."

She was a gentle, motherly woman who encouraged her nurses to share their distress with her, knowing how tension can build up when there isn't time to do the necessary mourning between one lost life and the next. One of her nurses was in this state on the day the Winnetka children were shot, although Sue didn't realize it at the time. After the trauma alert sounded throughout the hospital, she called in several of her off-duty nurses. One declined, making an excuse. Ironically, this nurse's last case had been that of Larry Carney, the former Winnetka fireman who had been electrocuted by lightning and whose funeral procession had just got in the way of Laurie Dann's escape.

"This nurse was so upset about a man of his age dying like that, she felt it was such a waste, that the thought of caring for a child who might also die was more than she could cope with," Sue explained. "She should not have felt guilty about needing time off. The pace and stress here are so ongoing."

There was another factor. "When a patient comes into this unit you can pretty much predict who will live or die. It's more than just knowing the injury. Some of it is intuition. When Larry Carney was brought in we knew he could not make it. But this nurse was still having a hard time accepting the fact that she had not been able to save him."

While waiting for the injured children to be brought to her unit from surgery, Sue watched the television news in a room next to the nurses' station. There she learned that the shootings had happened in a Winnetka school. Immediately she thought of her own eight-year-old son, Paul, at school near her home in Mundelein, twenty-five miles from Winnetka, and at that precise moment she received a telephone call from Paul's teacher. Sue's heart raced.

"This is Carol. I want you to know that Paul is—"

Unaware of the Winnetka shootings, the teacher was about to add "—getting an award." But Sue interrupted. She was thinking: Now Paul has been shot, too. Why else would his teacher call?

"Carol," she said. "Where is Paul right now? Is he there?"

Responding to the panic in her voice, the teacher asked: "Sue, what is your problem?"

She replied: "Some children have been shot in a classroom in Winnetka and I'm waiting for them to arrive here. I have to know if Paul is okay."

"Sure he's okay."

"Then please give him a hug for me. And now I have to hang up."

"I understand."

After she had put down the phone Sue thought to herself: That was pretty irrational. But she explained: "This happened to me once before. We had a child-abuse case, and the nurses who were mothers had a terrible time with it. When you are dealing with a child you cannot displace yourself. And this concern for my own children remained in the back of my mind all day." She also had a ten-year-old daughter, Lisa.

"I wanted to be with them but I had to be here, and I didn't know when I would be able to leave the hospital. So I called my ex-husband and asked if he would pick them up and keep them for the night." That arranged, she was able to concentrate on her job.

She had been warned that one of the four Winnetka children was in serious condition. Lindsay Fisher was the third child to be brought into her ward.

"They came in from surgery pretty close together. We were surprised at how good three of them looked, but Lindsay was so pale, even with a machine breathing for her. She looked as though she could die at any minute."

George and Karen Fisher were given the privacy of Sue's former office. "We shut the door, and even let George smoke there. Periodically we allowed them to see Lindsay, but not to stay with her. I think the doctors were very honest in telling them that she might die." •

At this point the children had become the responsibility of Dr. Joseph R. Hageman, director of pediatric intensive care. To satisfy reporters who were badgering for news of the children's condition, even clogging up telephone lines into the intensive-care unit, he gave several press conferences, the first of them that evening, all memorable for the fact that he was photographed wearing a cervical collar.

"The hospital PR people suggested I take it off, but my neck was so screwed I had to put it back on," he explained. He was suffering from a rare muscle problem which caused painful spasms when he was in any position but lying down, and he should not have been working when he was summoned to the hospital within minutes of the shootings. "I did not have any choice but to get involved," he said.

He had been at the YMCA doing physical therapy when his pager sounded. "Get your ass over here as quickly as possible," one of the head nurses told him on the telephone.

For the next few days he worked all hours, contrary to his own doctor's orders, piling up more stress for himself. He drew some wry amusement from the similar plight of the chief of surgery, Dr. Robert Anderson, who had a painful back condition. When their press conference photographs appeared in the newspapers, "we compared notes as to who looked the lousiest." A year later Hageman's neck still wasn't right.

At the time, his concern for the Winnetka children helped him forget his pain. Watching their reactions after they regained consciousness, he noted that Kathryn Miller came out of the anesthesia with her left hand in a cast and her right hand pointed as though she was firing a gun. "She also complained of shortness of breath, but we found no medical reason for this, so my best guess is that she was reliving the tragedy."

Mark Teborek was fearful whenever a stranger walked past the doorway of his hospital room, while Robert Trossman dealt with his memory of being shot by constantly talking about it. "He was upbeat, verbal, and outgoing," Hageman remembered.

Lindsay Fisher was brought into the intensive care unit on a respirator. At first her condition was fairly stable, and she was still holding her own when Joseph Hageman and Sue Guilianelli left late that evening. Sue had kept her own emotions in check throughout the day, but on the way home her anxiety for her children surfaced, and she drove through two stoplights, thinking about how badly she wanted to hug them. "But I couldn't because they were overnight with their dad."

She had assigned thirty-year-old Karen Halfen, who had an infant daughter of her own, to keep a close watch on Lindsay throughout the night, checking her blood pressure, heart rate, and respiration every fifteen to thirty minutes.

Karen reported: "Between one and two A.M. she became paler. Her heart rate was increasing, her blood pressure was dropping, and her hemoglobin was dropping, indicating that she was bleeding internally. We began pumping blood into the IV but it did not seem to help. Her condition didn't improve and she was getting bloated. Through all this I was talking back and forth with the residents, and they were making suggestions: Try this, try that, give her more oxygen. And I kept telling them that the blood was not doing enough, that her vital signs were still failing."

From her nine years' experience as a staff nurse, Karen was convinced that if this child did not have prompt surgery to stem the internal bleeding, she would die. Lindsay was Dr. Alexander's case, and it was Karen's impression that the residents were reluctant to call a senior member of the hospital hierarchy in the middle of the night. She could hardly defy them, but was sure enough of her own medical judgment to take a bold initiative.

"I decided to call Stephen Sener. I have known him well since he was a resident, and have a lot of confidence in him. At about three A.M. I telephoned him at home and said: 'Steve, you have got to get in here. This child must be got back into surgery.'"

"I'll be right there," he said. And he was, within fifteen minutes.

Karen alerted the operating room, and broke the news to Lindsay's father. George Fisher was sitting at his daughter's bedside while his wife was trying to get some sleep. Sener confirmed Karen's opinion.

"George was quite distraught," he said. "I told him we had to do more surgery. I think he felt he would never see his daughter alive again. His wife felt as badly as he did, but she internalized her anxiety."

In this second operation Sener reexplored the abdomen and was able to control most of the internal bleeding. Back in the intensive-care unit, Lindsay seemed to rally. But when Dr. Alexander arrived for the day, he determined that there was still some bleeding in the area above her diaphragm.

"At about seven A.M. I took her back to the operating room and cleaned out her chest," Alexander said. "I looked at the hole I had made in her heart because I was concerned that it was continuing to bleed, but it was not." To his enormous relief, his tests showed that her blood had developed a clotting factor. "That left us with a child who had been seriously injured, who had gone through three operations and lost an enormous amount of blood."

After twenty-four hours Lindsay's condition became more stable. "From then on she recovered faster than I would have thought," Dr. Hageman said. "Once she woke up more, still on the ventilator, someone gave her a pad and pencil. The first thing she wrote was that she had missed her soccer game. She was one of those children with a real zest for life.

"We were anticipating that she might develop a variety of problems relating to her injuries, but none of them materialized. She was quite remarkable. Most children get more feisty as they get better. Lindsay was not like that. You don't get more stars for being stoic as a child, but she was very cooperative and controlled."

Stephen Sener concluded that she probably did not see Laurie Dann. She was shot from the right rear and may not have been aware of danger. "She has retrograde amnesia from the moment before she was shot until several days later in the intensive-care unit," he observed.

He could empathize with the feeling. "I had a traffic accident in 1980. I was driving down the tollway to work, and the next thing I knew was a week later in the ICU. I still have no idea what happened. Not a clue. I went to court and heard testimony that I had rear-ended a truck. Whether I fell asleep or had an arrhythmia I'll never know. But I have no wish to retrieve the memory. I'm alive, well, and recovered from the injury. And I'm sure that's how Lindsay will feel about what happened to her."

Over the ensuing months John Alexander kept a careful check on her progress. He had a special feeling about this patient, an emotion close to awe at her indestructible vitality. She could so easily have been dead or maimed. He didn't often get introspective about his cases—they came too close together—but his experience with this wholesome blond child gave him an unexpected insight into what his work was all about.

"I have often thought over this episode," he said, months later. "We all came off as heroes at Evanston Hospital. But had Lindsay Fisher not lived, we would have had the same feeling of failure as the doctors and nurses in Highland Park who couldn't save Nicky Corwin. As it is, I look back on that day with a great deal of personal pride, with the feeling that all the time I spent learning my trade was worthwhile, and with the knowledge that a lot of other people would not have been able to pull it off. If it had not worked out I would have been able to tell myself that I tried my best. But I would have kept thinking of a thousand things I could or should have done, and would have been much more entrapped in the remorse and anger of that day."

He was referring to the community's anger, which, by that time, had gone a lot deeper than the immediate outrage over the shooting of children. It stemmed from the violation of a privileged life-style, and John Alexander observed this with the detachment of one who had spent most of his years in other places. He had retained the soft and courteous speech of his native North Carolina, where he had married the girl he met at church when he was in seventh grade, and he had come here four years ago by way of Maryland, New York, and West Virginia. While he valued the opportunities the north shore gave his children, he was struck by the fact that his own professional environment of life and death varied very little from place to place, and was closer to reality than the idyllic neighborhood in which he now lived.

"I stop someone's heart every day, and I get a lot of satisfaction from solving impossible problems," he explained. "I am working on the edge of what can be done in my world. I play the odds against disease, have people's lives in my hands, and get a kick out of winning. I don't come to work just to make a dollar. I operate on people to beat the odds, to try to do things no one else can do, and it can be very rewarding."

Lindsay's recovery was his most memorable reward, and it continued to amaze him how straightforward it had been. He had a mystical sense about his own part in it, as though the lifesaving hole in her heart had been made by another John Alexander, guided by a force above and beyond himself.

"In my mind's eye I can still see that child on the operating table," he said. "A kind of out-of-the-body experience, as though I am watching myself struggling to keep her alive." He shook his head. "I can call up that image anytime."

He felt a need to keep in touch with Lindsay, not just to monitor her progress, but to see how this life given back would be lived. On the Christmas after her surgery she sent him a greeting card and he responded with a letter. In it he expressed his belief that God intended her to do something special with her life, and that when she was older she would find out what it was. He phrased this as though he had a similar vision for himself: that his life hereafter would be more meaningful because of this opportunity so randomly given to him, for reasons which he did not yet understand.

From time to time he would take Lindsay's Christmas card out of his file, and experience a very warm feeling about her. "Most of us get to know our patients, but there is no big deal about it," he remarked. "It's not major league. But this is major league. This child came as close to being dead as anyone I have ever seen."

As head nurse of the intensive-care unit, Sue Guilianelli had a different perspective. "We felt ambivalent about all the attention this brought to the hospital," she said. "We have done a lot of wonderful things over the years, and we wondered why it took this to get recognition. And then most of the recognition went to doctors—they were the ones on TV—not to the paramedic who brought that child to the hospital, or to my nurse who kept her alive in the middle of the night. One who was less experienced than Karen, or less familiar with the medical staff, might not have made that telephone call. People appreciate the loving things that nurses do, but they don't realize how smart they are, how much doctors depend on them to make assessments and suggestions."

Sue's eyes moistened as she added quietly: "You know, a child did die that night, a fifteen-year-old girl with chronic renal disease. She had been in the intensive-care unit a few days and her prognosis was poor, but we did not expect her to die so soon. The nursing staff and doctors and chaplain supported her family. But those parents did not get a room set aside for them, or food sent down by the administration, and their child's name did not appear in the newspapers. That caused some resentment among the nurses. Some of them felt very close to this girl's parents; families will say things to nurses that they will never say to doctors. But we didn't hear much from the parents of the Hubbard Woods children because they were getting special treatment.

"For a long time afterward we were all very affected by that young girl's death. On this unit we go head over heels to save a child's life. Children are wonderful; so resilient and honest. And it seemed so unfair to us that this one should have died unnoticed while those who lived got so much attention."

After Lindsay was out of danger, some of his colleagues suggested to paramedic John Fay that they might go together to visit her in Evanston Hospital. He wished he could have seen her in recovery, but his own sensitivity held him back. "Seeing me might have reminded her of what she had gone through," he said. "And I certainly did not want to be thanked."

TWENTY-FIVE

W INNETKA ON the morning of Saturday, May 21, was like a village hit by a freak tornado. Outwardly it appeared unchanged, but it was as though all the landmarks and signposts and parameters had been removed in the night, leaving its raw edges publicly exposed and propelling it onto the front pages of newspapers across the nation. Winnetkans were shocked to see widely reproduced photographs of their neighbors as participants in the drama, people too proud to show a suffering side of themselves caught by alien cameras in all their anguish: parents with tears streaming down their faces, a visibly traumatized school principal with blood on his shirt. It was not to be borne, the thought that these pictures were being scrutinized over breakfast tables across the nation.

Journalistically, this was a story which had everything: violence, madness, the blood of children spattered on the floor of a little red schoolhouse, weeping parents, a wealthy neighborhood given a glimpse of life on the other side of the tracks. It was the stuff of sensational headlines, of magazine articles and television documentaries yet to be written. There might be no end to the exploitation. And Winnetkans were trapped in the middle of it, unable to get away.

Everyone in the village knew someone directly involved in the tragedy. People whose children did not go to Hubbard Woods School had some association with a school family, went to the same church, belonged to the same social group, knew the Corwins or the Andrews or the Rushes. Winnetka prided itself on its neighborliness, so it was automatic for the grief to be shared. The death of Nicholas Corwin was everybody's bereavement, and the American flag outside the Winnetka Bank was flown at half mast for him. Villagers walked around with taut faces, wordlessly touching one another as they met. There seemed nothing left to say, and only one topic to be talked about.

The shock waves spread up and down the north shore. Although every village has its entity, there is a lot of overlapping. The Danns were known in Highland Park, the Wassermans (less well) in Glencoe. In every community there were people who had gone to school with Laurie. One young woman was "so freaked out that I knew this person" that for the next three weeks she slept with her bedroom light on. She and Laurie had been college classmates in Arizona; now it was horribly clear to her why all those hang-up calls in the middle of the night had continued after she changed to an unlisted telephone number, twice in one year, sharing it only with friends. "From now on I feel like I should get résumés on everyone I talk to," she said.

Some people who had never met Laurie were chilled by the thought of how close they had come. Dr. John Alexander, for one, had almost bought a house near Hubbard Woods School when he moved to the north shore. If he had, his younger son would have been in second grade there, standing, perhaps, in the same spot as Nicholas Corwin. Or replacing Lindsay Fisher on his operating table.

The only people who had nothing to say were those who knew Laurie's parents. Overnight, they seemed to disappear. A north shore rabbi remarked: "I do not know anything about the Wassermans. Nor am I aware of anyone who does." On this day after the tragedy reporters searched Glencoe for someone who had an insight into the family, and came away quoteless.

Meantime, in Winnetka, the police began to organize an investigation to determine Laurie Dann's motives, and whether or not she worked alone. Clergy rewrote their Pentecost sermons before meeting later in the day to plan an interfaith service for Sunday afternoon: one which would bring villagers together in corporate prayer, hurriedly crafted to accommodate those whose faith inhibited any mention of Jesus and those whose faith was incomplete without it. Between them they came up with a formula, and a place for the service: the Roman Catholic Church of Saints Faith, Hope and Charity, the largest in the village. Pastor David Goodman drafted a memorable address: "We gather as a community whose heart has been ripped out of it, to ask God's help in the healing. . . ."

At Hubbard Woods School on this Saturday morning, parents and children were nervously arriving for another airing of feelings, and to be assured that school was again a safe place. School Superintendent Donald Monroe had asked a minister of his own religious denomination, the Reverend Dr. Paul Allen of Winnetka Congregational Church, to open the assembly with an invocation.

"Don took a risk in inviting a clergyman to say a prayer in a public school," Dr. Allen observed. "And yet it was right because this was an event which called for some recognition of people's feelings of helplessness. Religion has always been about things that happen at the edge of life. When you are involved with everyday tasks you do not always understand its relevance. But when you are looking over the precipice it becomes meaningful."

He was struck by the atmosphere at Hubbard Woods School that Saturday morning. "It was more like being in church than being in church," he said. "Some of the parents and teachers embraced. There was a huge sense of us all having been caught up in an awesome event, a feeling of communality and tenderness toward one another. The fact that a child had died was part of it. All the adults were going out of their way to be specially kind to children."

Nobody minded the little ones being fidgety. Parents kept touching them affectionately, smoothing hair already brushed, retying sneakers already laced, every gesture solicitous and grateful.

Quietly authoritative, Donald Monroe was in charge. Paul Allen was impressed. He commented: "Faced with an emergency for which there were no rules, Don instinctively made the right decisions by bringing the school community together, and by having therapists there rather than expecting nature to take its course."

Between seven hundred and eight hundred parents and children crowded into a school auditorium designed to hold half that number. Monroe opened the meeting with the statement that all four children in Evanston Hospital, and a fifth, Peter Munro, who had been taken to Highland Park Hospital, were recovering from surgery. He had dreaded having to break the news of another death.

"Yesterday the children's condition was critical," he said. "Today it is critical but stable. As a school community, we too were in a critical state yesterday, and today we are returning to stability. This is the beginning of the healing process, one which can bring us closer together and even enhance the quality of this community." Calmly reassuring, Monroe displayed no hint of his own shocked state, although he would long be haunted by the memory of the wounded child he had carried to an ambulance, and of the chaos in Room 7.

Some of the Evanston Hospital experts talked about the clinical effects of post-traumatic stress; then teachers, parents, and children went to their appropriate classrooms, with a mental-health expert assigned to every group. Room 7 had been so well cleaned up that there was no sign of Laurie Dann's having entered it. Amy Deuble, the class's regular teacher, was back, unable to forgive herself for taking Friday off. She was more sturdily built than Amy Moses, an athlete and a karate expert, who would feel, perhaps to the end of her days, that she might have been able to prevent the mayhem by overcoming Laurie or by knocking the gun out of her hand. Equally she might have failed and made the children more vulnerable, but she wasn't yet ready to accept that possibility. As it was, her earlier absence became an asset, enabling her students to work through their trauma by telling and retelling her the story in detail, as to one who had missed the action and needed to be informed.

Jeff Berkson, the Evanston Hospital social worker, arrived early for the session. On the drive to Winnetka he had stopped for breakfast at a roadside café in Wilmette. "It was about eight A.M. and everyone there was talking about the shooting," he related. "I didn't say anything. Just listened. Then a doctor from the hospital came in and asked me if there had been any new developments. I told him that I was on my way to another meeting at the school.

"'So you were there yesterday?' he asked.

"Everyone turned around and stared at me. I felt very uncomfortable, hurried my coffee, and left."

At the school he was assigned to the fifth-grade classroom. "The children were worried about Michael Corwin, Nicky's brother, who was absent. They felt crushed about Nicky. I have had some experience of children dying, and usually some lionization goes on, but in this case it was clear that Nicky was an extremely valued child. All the others thought so highly of him. I asked them to tell me about him, and they said he was good at math, a good reader, that he played soccer and basketball. 'I hear you,' I said, 'but what is it you will miss about him?'

"They said: 'He was this really nice guy. He would help people who needed help. If he was asked to choose a team he always knew which kids would be the last to be picked, and he would pick them first.'"

Berkson was impressed. "This is in a community where active sports participation is valued. It seemed clear that Nicky did have those intangible leadership qualities, and that made it so unbearable for the others to have lost him. They were still trying to grasp the reality of his death."

Fourth and fifth graders who had been on a field trip when the shooting happened had a lot of survivor guilt. Dr. Ronald Rozensky, who led the fourth-grade discussion, was astounded by the extent of it. Several children asked him why Laurie had picked on little kids instead of waiting until they were in school.

"I could see parents with tears in their eyes listening to their children saying, 'It should have been me,'" Rozensky related. "My own children were aged ten and six at the time, and I could imagine myself in their place."

The fourth graders asked why Laurie had wanted to kill children she did not know.

Rozensky explained: "I talked about how at times we all have angry and confused feelings, and how some people can't control those feelings because they have an illness which causes their mental wiring to be crossed. I tried to get them to understand that this was an aberration of an illness, and that it was rare. I used the computer analogy to put it into their range. They had no problem understanding about crossed wires. They asked me why this had happened to Laurie Dann, and my response was that I did not know enough about her history or biology."

Rozensky could see that many of these children were deeply affected. "I think they will be dealing with this for the rest of their lives," he said. "It will define who they are—not completely, but they will all have a very different view of the frailty of life."

Outside the school Herbert Timm was giving another press conference. He was beginning to feel easier about this new role for himself, answering questions fluently when Sergeant Patty McConnell interrupted him. Tugging at his sleeve, she whispered: "I have to talk to you."

"Not now, Patty," he told her.

"Chief, it's very important," she persisted. "I have to talk to you now."

He broke off to hear her whispered story. His face blanched. "My God," he said. "This thing is even bigger than we thought. Tell the reporters what you just told me."

Patty had been standing near the police chief when a Glencoe policeman had come up to her. He reported that two families in his village had found sample-sized cartons of fruit juice in their mailboxes. In one family a four-year-old child drank the juice and became mildly ill. A close inspection found that both cartons appeared to have been tampered with. Both families had known Laurie Dann as a baby-sitter. One juice carton contained Hawaiian Lite Punch, the other Capri Sun Cooler. A quick check at a grocery store established that cartons of this size were sold in packages of ten, leading to the conjecture that Laurie may have made at least eighteen more deliveries of poisoned juice before going on her shooting spree.

This put a different complexion on the case. Yesterday the police had thought of her as a woman who had recklessly decided to end her life in a blaze of violence, taking with her as many people as possible, no matter who. Today's poisoned juice cartons told another story: of a systematic, premeditated attack upon people she had known and, for some reason, wished to eliminate. It was clearly of a piece with the poison she had slipped into the Rushe children's milk.

Herbert Timm had never appreciated a crowd of reporters more than at this moment. Minutes after Patty McConnell passed on the news, radio and television programs in the Chicago area were interrupted to warn people to hand over to the police any food or drink samples which may have been delivered to them.

Over the next few days twenty-six packages were turned in. Twenty-two of them had been hand-delivered in north shore villages, suggesting that Laurie was up all night. Most of her deliveries were juice cartons, but some were the Rice Krispie treats made in her mother's kitchen. All of them had been injected with the arsenic solution that Floyd Mohr found in Laurie's bedroom. The juice cartons had a tiny hole near the top, apparently made with the hypodermic syringe which he had also confiscated. Laurie had stolen the poison from a medical laboratory across the hallway from the office of her Madison psychiatrist, Dr. John Greist; unaware that it was heavily diluted, she had not used enough to constitute a lethal dose. A package of doctored Rice Krispie treats which she delivered to a Winnetka family merely caused the dog to throw up.

Other plates of the cookies were found on the doorsteps of fraternity houses at Northwestern University, Evanston. Laurie had become friendly with some of the male students there during the previous summer, and made no attempt to hide her identity. Attached to one of the paper plates was a handwritten note on her father's business stationery (FROM THE DESK OF NORMAN WASSERMAN, CERTIFIED PUBLIC ACCOUNTANT). With her typical misspellings it read:

"I'm going to be in Glencoe when your in town—look forward to seeing you guys. I was going to send you coffee cake, but I was making rice crispy treats for school and decided to send some. Enjoy. Love, Laurie."

A student who ate a cookie was briefly hospitalized for tests, then released. Herbert Timm commented: "The food didn't look that great but fraternity kids will eat anything." He shuddered to think how many people might have died if the samples had been more appetizing and the arsenic solution stronger.

The fraternity house deliveries were probably made late on the evening of Thursday, May 19, before Laurie was seen abstractedly pacing the sidewalk on the opposite side of Evanston. The poisoned packages of fruit juice (all of them stamped SAMPLE) were delivered early the next morning to houses in Highland Park, Glencoe, and Winnetka. Most of the recipients had known Laurie only slightly, as a baby-sitter, a former neighbor, or in high school. Several of them had not heard from her in years, and barely remembered her. She seemed to have picked their names at random from an old address book.

Two people knew the exact time of delivery. At 6:55 A.M. that Friday, a former Highland Park neighbor of Laurie's heard the storm door of his house open and close. A few minutes later he found, between the two doors, a carton of Capri Sun Cooler with a pinhole near the top. Shortly before 7:15 A.M. a Winnetka householder responded to a ring at the doorbell and saw a similar juice carton on the doorstep, and a woman driving away in a white car.

While she was making these twenty-two deliveries, and before picking up the Rushe children, Laurie mailed four poisoned packages. One went to Russell at his post-office-box address in Highland Park, another to Dr. John Greist in Madison. Both juice cartons arrived stickily leaking. A Los Angeles couple at whose wedding Laurie had been a bridesmaid five years earlier received a large Rice Krispie cookie. She had telephoned them on May 17, cheerfully announcing that she was well, that life was beautiful, and that she was sending them a package. Puzzled by its contents, they set it aside.

On May 19 a young mother in Glenview, a village southwest of Winnetka, was telephoned by a woman who said she was a modeling agent. This "agent" told her that if she would take her three children to Hubbard Woods School the following morning they would be signed up as models. The woman did not agree to the suggestion, and later received a package of poisoned cranberry juice in the mail. Her family's only connection with Laurie Dann was that her husband had been Laurie's high school classmate.

All these incidents seem to have been planned with such a mixture of intricacy and oversight that it was impossible to discern a motive. It made a diabolical kind of sense for Laurie to have fire-bombed the Highland Park schools where she expected to find her sister-in-law's children. But why poison all these casual acquaintances? And why had she wanted to eliminate the Rushes? Yesterday her motive had looked like revenge because she felt rejected by them; today it was evident that she began planning her killing spree before she learned about their intended move from Winnetka. Was Hubbard Woods, the school where three Rushe children were enrolled, an afterthought on a list she had already drawn up?

Had she intended to kill herself at the end of the day? Herbert Timm thought not. With two guns and all that extra ammunition, he was convinced that she meant to commit more murders. With a better sense of what she was doing, she could already have eliminated more than fifty people. "Had she succeeded in her plan, about thirty could have died from the poisonings alone," Timm commented. "But for her incredible heroism, Mrs. Rushe and her two children would have perished in the house fire. And if her .357 had not jammed, Laurie Dann could have blown that classroom full of children to pieces."

At Winnetka police station all the pathetic items of children's clothing were laid out and photographed, with their bloodstains showing. Later, when she went through this evidence Patty McConnell was struck by a detail which others might have missed: a lighter stain in the crotch of the blue jeans which one child had been wearing. "I could bear to look at the blood," she said, "but this really got to me: the fact that this little girl was so scared that she wet her pants. It was the thing which bothered me most, the terror that poor little kid must have felt. You can put a Band-Aid on the injuries, but how can you ever restore that loss of innocence?"

There were other difficult pictures to be taken and, as an evidence technician, Patrolman John Hamick was given the job. He was up early this Saturday morning, having failed to snatch any sleep on the cot in the police station's lockup, or on the chair which he tried after that. He had no opportunity to change from the clothes he had worn yesterday, a day in which he had gone from the fire at the Rushes' home to Hamptondale Road where Laurie wrecked her car, to the Andrews' house to collect evidence at her suicide scene, then, late at night, into Chicago to accompany her body to the Cook County morgue. Back at the police station he had been up writing reports until 3:30 A.M. He had not eaten a proper meal in all this time, and didn't want breakfast. This morning's assignment was to go back to the morgue to take autopsy photographs.

Usually he was able to do this mechanically, having recorded more suicides than he could remember. After any violent death, the body and what a pathologist does to it must be photographed for police files; Hamick always dealt with this by keeping busy, concentrating on the evidentiary details of the objects on the autopsy table. The sight of Laurie Dann's body, even with that lethal wound in the head, presented no problems to him. Like the rest of his colleagues who had gone into the Andrew house last night, he had been almost glad to see her dead. Today he was told that he must also photograph the autopsy of Nicky Corwin, but on this second drive to the morgue he pushed that thought to the back of his mind. Arriving there, it came as a shock to him to find both autopsies scheduled to take place at the same time in the same large room.

This is common practice in large city morgues. The Cook County room had four widely spaced autopsy stations, with four pathologists working on separate cases. One of yesterday's victims had been a black woman, one a white policeman bludgeoned to death by a street gang on the south side of Chicago. The other bodies were those of Nicky Corwin and Laurie Dann.

John Hamick was struck by the irony of the scene: the victim and his murderer, unknown to one another, killed by the same gun, ending up in the same place. This child had merely happened to be in her line of fire, and because of this mischance all the bright promise of his life and the defeated hopes of hers had suddenly been obliterated, bringing these two strangers together in the inescapable equality of death. In the end there had been a kind of justice: although he had died because of her, she was here because of what she had done to him. Waiting for the pathologists to arrive, Hamick felt uneasy and overwhelmed.

He had a seven-year-old son who was the same build as Nicky, tall and slender, and in his wearied mind he kept making the transposition between the dead child and his own. Later when a pathologist dictated his notes into a tape recorder, one phrase brought a lump to Hamick's throat. "And the body has the normal scrapes and bruises of an active eight-year-old. . . ."

"I looked at Nicky and saw the kind of bumps that a youngster gets playing soccer, and I thought of my own kid," he said. "It left a memory that will stay with me forever."

He shied away from taking Nicky's photograph, and did not realize he had done so until, back at the police station, he compared his records of the two autopsies. "To me, photographing Laurie Dann was just part of the job. They cut her open, recovered the bullet, gave it to me, and sewed her up. I did not have any feeling about this. All the passion was on the other side of the room. Afterward it struck me that my photographs of her were very professional and matter-of-fact, and that there were many more of them. I took only a few pictures of Nicky, and did them very delicately. It was so much easier to focus on her."

Two days later, on a gray Monday morning, Nicky Corwin was buried. Temple Jeremiah in Northfield can seat more than a thousand; despite heavy rain, about fifteen hundred showed up for the funeral service. Some were children, anxiously clutching the hands of parents and teachers. Rabbi Robert Schreibman had sat up late the previous night, trying to find words for a eulogy that might make sense to all these bewildered people, as well as to himself.

"I hate funerals, I really hate them," he admitted. "When I know the person it tears me to shreds. I feel as though I am burying a little of me. And when a child dies, it's the hardest thing in the world."

Over the weekend he had organized a special program at the temple, bringing in therapists to help his congregation deal with the tragedy. Three questions had been asked, repeatedly. From parents: Could it happen to my child? From children: Could it happen to me? From everyone: Why Nicky?

There was no straight answer to any of them. A memory which came to him, as he put his eulogy together, was of the rabbinic belief that when a child dies during the lifetime of its parents, God grieves with them. On this drenching Monday morning the weather matched his thought. The address he finally wrote at about midnight on Sunday was quoted in newspapers across the nation: "So deep is our sorrow, so great is this loss that we know that God too is weeping. . . . Nicky was loved because of who he was and what he accomplished in eight short years, and the pain is great because the joy was immense. . . . He lives on in the timelessness of time, and in all of our hearts and memories."

In this bitter downpour, at approximately the same time, Nicky and Laurie were buried in separate Jewish cemeteries. His funeral service was a media event. Hers was a well-guarded secret, attended only by her parents and a few friends.

TWENTY-SIX

In OTHER times, and even now in less enlightened places, debriefing for the police meant a single session of self-assessment, determining the lessons learned and the actions which might be handled better in another crisis. Herbert Timm did that, and realized it wasn't enough. His staff needed the kind of debriefing which, since the Vietnam War, has been judged necessary to soldiers coming out of combat; the opportunity to acknowledge their fears and anger and, in doing so, to reduce the tensions. This was the concept which Sue Guilianelli instinctively understood about her intensive-care nurses: that those who allow themselves to experience their feelings are less likely to become burned out.

That Friday morning, in the emergency room at Evanston Hospital, a member of the trauma team had told a pasty-faced paramedic that it was all right to cry; given permission to do so, the man was able to return to the scene at Hubbard Woods School. There is a fiction that people in jobs like his aren't supposed to hurt; in an attempt to break through this, the Evanston team called a meeting of policemen, ambulance workers, and nurses at Winnetka police station on Sunday, May 22.

More than fifty attended. Although none of them had been to anything like this before, under expert guidance they talked about experiences in a very personal way. Patrolman Eddie Benoit was able to admit to his urge to kill Laurie Dann, after agonizing over it alone for hours. "I had thought my feelings were not normal," he said. "So I took my time before telling my story and I have to admit I cried. Others cried too, and nobody looked down on anyone for showing emotion. It was such a relief. After that one debriefing I could go home and talk about it to my family, and I had not been able to do so until then."

"We all sat around in a big circle, and it was very intimidating at first because most of the others were strangers," Sue Guilianelli remembered. "I didn't say anything until the end because it was apparent to me that the people who needed help most were the police and paramedics."

It took several more debriefing sessions before most of them could comfortably speak out. "By that time people on the periphery were wishing we would stop talking about it," John Fay said. "But they had not had the children's blood on their clothes."

Months later Fay was still dreaming about Laurie Dann. "She was pounding at the door of my house. I went to the front door to answer it, but she was not there. So I went to the back door and saw her, but then she disappeared."

Floyd Mohr was deeply traumatized. As well as his own feelings of guilt and inadequacy, the school shooting recalled an earlier tragedy in his own life, one he had not fully dealt with when he was a freshman in college: the sudden death of his little sister from a rare virus. She too had been in second grade, and the renewed pain of her loss was almost unbearable. His nightmares and mood swings would continue for months. "I am so lucky to have such a supportive wife," he acknowledged. "A lot of people wouldn't be able to live with me."

Patty McConnell hesitated to talk about her feelings in front of her male colleagues. Her recent promotion put her in charge of the Laurie Dann investigation, and she was overwhelmed by the enormity of the task. Heading investigations in Winnetka usually meant tracking down burglars and car thieves, with an occasional mention in *Winnetka Talk*. This was murder, and national news. How could she appear authoritative if she were to admit, in the presence of men about to work under her, that the biggest emotional stress of this job would be the long hours of separation from her baby daughter? She was torn between the career opportunity of the assignment and her urgent need, shared by every parent this tragedy had touched, to keep reassuring herself about her own child.

"I can't handle this alone," she admitted to Herbert Timm. "It's a massive undertaking. May I call in people from other departments?"

"He said yes," she recalled, "and the first person I thought of was Mike O'Connell. I felt comfortable with him and trusted his expertise. There's a lot of pressure here being a woman, but I could say to Mike, 'I don't know how to do this,' without being made to look stupid."

Together she and Sergeant Michael O'Connell, the Glenview police detective who had worked with her on Friday, put together a task force. At the outset he told her: "In order to close out this case and satisfy the curiosity of the public, we have to find out everything we can about Laurie Dann. Even though she's dead, people are going to demand to know."

They drew up a team of eighteen, including federal investigators and detectives from several north shore communities. For the next two weeks the group met daily in Winnetka police station's basement classroom. Some of Laurie's case history was already in police files: her allegations against Russell and his against her, the telephone threats and baby-sitting stories. But little else was known about her, which left dozens of people to be interviewed. Every morning assignments were handed out, and every evening the investigators shared that day's information with their colleagues. Working hours were from 7:00 A.M. to midnight, sometimes longer.

The investigation focused on the last year of Laurie's life, the period when she was divorced and mentally unraveling. She had no home of her own in this time; despite a settlement from Russell which would have bought her one, she drifted between her parents' house in Glencoe and the campuses of Northwestern and the University of Wisconsin, choosing for herself, at almost thirty, the cramped student accommodation which most people are glad to leave behind at twenty-two. She made a feeble attempt to enroll for some classes as though still trying to graduate, but mostly she hung around fraternity houses, looking for eligible men.

During the summer of 1987 there had been a lull in the baby-sitting incidents, then, briefly, a resumption of them in the early fall; after that Laurie had slipped out of the north shore police's sight. Now the Winnetka investigators were able to fill in the gaps, and they discovered a tale of her steady disintegration, matched by her father's failure to recognize the seriousness of the problem.

The local police had not known where she was that summer, but they found an ex-policeman who had traced her. Franklin Bullock, private investigator, was interviewed in his office in Waukegan, across the street from the Lake County courthouse. He had been hired by Russell's attorney, Richard Kessler, after Russell was stabbed and accused of rape; his assignment was to watch Laurie and to protect the Dann family.

"They were scared of what she might do next," he said. "Why else would they pay me? I worked on the case for a good year and that would have cost in the thousands."

Bullock was true to his name, large and beefy, with sandy hair and a tattooed arm; not a man to be trifled with. He recalled meeting with Laurie in May 1987, a month after the divorce.

"I walked up to the Wassermans' house at about ten A.M., rang the doorbell, handed her a card, and told her I was a private investigator hired by Russell Dann's attorney, and that I would like to talk to her." Although alone in the house, she invited him in but avoided touching his visiting card, letting it fall. He was surprised at her lack of curiosity about him "because mine is a kind of odd profession."

They sat down at the kitchen table. He noted that her hair was unkempt, and that she was wearing a long, dowdy sweater which she kept clutching at the throat. She was calm and polite, but strange. He asked her about her allegations that Russell had twice broken into her parents' house, once to vandalize the place and once to rape her, and got an unexpected response. "The police are taking care of that," she told him. "It's all up to my family. I don't have to worry about it. I don't want anything else to happen. I just want to be left alone."

He noticed a change in her manner as she spoke. An insurance investigator who had handled her arson report had warned him about this. "When you go to see her, Frank, talk to her for more than half an hour," he had said. Bullock did, and felt he was watching her psyche shift gears.

"As I talked to her she changed," he said. "It's hard to describe just how, but it made me feel uncomfortable. It was the inflection in her voice which struck me. Her answers came more slowly and she seemed to get distant, and it was obvious I was not going to get any more from her. As I saw these warning signs I thought I had better get out of there. It's always a delicate situation when you interview a female alone, and this one had already filed three false police reports."

He left hurriedly, without the information he sought, surprised that he wasn't stopped by the Glencoe police before he left the village. He continued to watch the Wasserman house and, after a while, concluded that no one was living there. It was hard to get information from neighbors. Eventually, "some people she sat for agreed to give me some background information if I would then get lost." But they couldn't help him with Laurie's whereabouts.

By this time Russell had a girlfriend named Pat, who had been receiving anonymous, threatening phone calls at her office. Bullock guessed how Laurie had discovered the number: Pat had left her car parked near Russell's home, with some business cards on the front seat. He traced the calls to Northwestern University in Evanston and discovered that Laurie had rented a student apartment there for the summer.

The Winnetka task force followed up by interviewing people on campus. From Mark Boney, administrator of the university's Kellogg apartment building, they learned that Laurie arrived there in June, presenting herself as a summer student. Kellogg is a residence hall for graduate students, and Boney's first impression of Laurie was of a bright, youthful north shore preppie who would be a desirable short-term tenant. In his experience women took better care of apartments than men. At his first meeting with her, she was attractively dressed in a pale-green designer sports outfit. She looked scrubbed and well groomed. "You could have lined her up with all the other co-eds taking summer classes."

She took a three-month sublet from a male graduate student, but before long she was in Boney's office, complaining. She said she had expected to have the suite to herself, and was dismayed to find a man sharing it. The apartments were built in pairs, a studio on either side of a common bathroom and kitchen. In term time this dual accommodation was rented only to couples of the same sex, but the rule was not enforced during vacations. Laurie's roommate was a man of her own age, alienated like herself from a comfortable north shore family, who had also drifted down to Northwestern for the summer. It was an attractive place to be, with its lakeshore campus and its proximity to Chicago. The roommate was indifferent about sharing the suite. He didn't mind her being there but didn't want to get romantically involved.

Over the next few weeks some strange reports reached Mark Boney's office. He was told that Laurie spent hours in the student common room watching television; one of the building's receptionists referred to her as "that little lost soul who sits around the lounge all day." Another employee saw her wearing rubber gloves, fingering other students' mailboxes. Then a passkey was unaccountably missing and she was found in the apartments of several other students, on one occasion asleep on the bed, on another rummaging around in the refrigerator. She always had a ready explanation; she was looking for a friend, or somebody had let her in. In one of these rooms a small fire had been set on the floor, and Laurie was suspected.

Boney related: "At about the same time I got a call from the building superintendent to say that his staff had been discovering large pieces of spoiled raw meat in the common areas, under cushions in the lounge, under a rug, in a corner of the hall. He showed me, and it was the most bizarre thing I have ever seen. The meat had not just been dropped. Someone was putting it there. And it wasn't ground chuck. It was huge quantities of top-quality steak."

His account recalled complaints made to the Glencoe police of meat missing from the freezers of two of Laurie's baby-sitting employers, but the dates didn't jibe. This was August, and the freezer meat did not disappear until September, after Laurie had left Northwestern and returned to her parents' home. What happened to all that stolen meat remained a mystery, along with the origin of the rotting steaks in the common room. Now that Laurie was dead, Mark Boney had a theory about her obsession with raw steak. "She may have had murderous fantasies. This partially hidden meat is like bodies being stowed by a person who really wants the crime to be discovered, who has a lot of inner rage yet wants to be controlled."

But that was hindsight. At the time he was baffled.

Using his own passkey, he went up to her fifth-floor room. "It was a complete shambles," he said. "There was a big cardboard box which seemed to be the place for clothes, and there seemed to be boxes of chocolate-chip cookies on every surface, some of them open, some empty. Strewn all over the room were quantities of plastic hospital gloves. The mattress was exposed, the sheet pulled down to the end of the bed. The place smelled strongly of urine, and the main source of it was the mattress, but it also came from the carpet. There were a few copies of *Penthouse* around, and I was standing there looking at all this when she walked in."

They got into an argument about the state of the room and its overdue rent. "Laurie, why are you here anyway?" he asked. He had just discovered that she was not registered for any classes.

"I'm auditing them," she told him. She always had a ready response.

Boney conferred with the student director, who had been wondering whether it was Laurie who left the rotting meat around.

"We went to her room together when she wasn't there," Boney said. "This time we went into the kitchen. I looked in the refrigerator and saw the most disgusting sight, a lot of spoiled meat dripping blood all over the place. It smelled awful."

Laurie reacted to this inspection by filing a report with the Evanston police that her room had been broken into, and that she suspected Mark Boney. This report reached the university police, who called Norman Wasserman. He responded by telephoning Boney.

"He asked me why I was harassing his daughter," Boney recounted. "He was angry, and talked to me as though I was some boy making a nuisance of myself."

They scheduled a meeting for Labor Day, September 7. "When I first saw Wasserman I felt sorry for him," Boney said. "He had the defeated look of someone dealing with problems that would not go away, yet he was also defensive and belligerent. I told him, 'Look, Mr. Wasserman, I am responsible for this building and some very disturbing things have been happening here, all of which have been traced to Laurie. I don't want to cause embarrassment. I just want her out.'

"He said: 'I thought this was America. People have rights. What is my daughter supposed to have done?'"

Boney began to list the allegations: the missing passkey, Laurie's unauthorized appearances in other students' rooms, the disturbed mailboxes, the spoiled mattress, the rotten meat.

"I did not get through this," he said, "when Wasserman dismissed it by saying that Laurie had some emotional problems and was getting help for them. But he still acted as though she had a right to be there, and I was harassing her."

Wasserman was told that the university police would prosecute Laurie for theft if she stayed. No longer protesting, he helped her to pack. Her last month's rent went unpaid, and the mattress had to be replaced.

Her roommate was interviewed but had little to add. He talked of her odd habit of wearing yellow latex gloves whenever she came in or out of the building, of her slamming in and out of the apartment all day, and aimlessly riding the elevator at night, up and down for hours.

"She was a slob in the kitchen," he reported. "There were opened cans of spaghetti all over the place, and raw meat left around, bleeding off the plate." The freezer was stuffed with more steaks, which Laurie told him had come from her mother. "It was way too much for her to eat. And with so much of it out there rotting, I told her she would get salmonella." One day he was sure that had happened. He found her on the floor of her room writhing in pain, with garbage bags wrapped over her clothes despite the hot weather. He offered to drive her to Evanston Hospital but as they neared the building she refused to go inside, so he drove on to Glencoe and left her with her mother, where she stayed for the next two days. He remarked to Edith Wasserman that Laurie seemed to have no purpose in life, and received no response.

272

His own casual approach to life made him unusually tolerant
of his strange roommate. "I did not notice the bad smells because
I had allergies and my sinuses were stuffed up all summer," he
explained. "And I didn't need to use the kitchen much because
I was into health foods."

Other campus residents told the police investigators that
Laurie had spent much of her time around fraternity houses, the
same buildings where nine months later she would leave poisoned
food. She dated a few male students, none of them seriously. To
one of them she confided that she had an incurable disease,
to another how bereft she had felt since her brother moved to
Texas, to others that she did not get along with her parents. The
phrase "My father is a wimp and my mother is a yes-woman,"
first told to Floyd Mohr, recurred. These men were all meant to
feel sorry for her, and to an extent did. But none of them felt
impelled to develop a relationship.

After her eviction from the Kellogg building Laurie returned
to her parents' house. The meat-stealing incidents and her story
of Russell's alleged sexual assault in a parking lot happened over
the next two months, closely followed by her purchase of a second gun. Later that fall she moved to Madison.

TWENTY-SEVEN

The winnetka task force picked up Laurie's trail at The Towers, a student residence in Madison, close to the University of Wisconsin campus. Laurie was just thirty when she moved there but gave her age as twenty-three and described herself as a graduate student in journalism.

She did not attend classes. Norman Wasserman did not seem to expect it of her, but made these new living arrangements so that she could be treated by Dr. John Greist, who worked out of the university hospital. As a specialist in obsessive-compulsive disorders (OCD), Greist had the expertise to help Laurie with the mindless compulsions which had been taking over her life: her fear of touching metal (hence the rubber gloves) and her obsessive repetition of routine actions. People who suffer from OCD are not generally violent, and the Winnetka task force learned that Greist was not told of Laurie's police record, or of her treatment by two previous psychiatrists. He came into the case late, taking on a patient who was uncooperative, skilled at deception, and severely disturbed.

Similarly, the management of The Towers was not warned of Laurie's disastrous tenancy at the Kellogg building, and before long she was repeating the pattern. Student residents told the Winnetka investigators about her aimless riding of the elevators, nude on occasion; about her roaming the hallways at night, unnerving students by turning the doorknobs of their rooms; about her sitting in front of the large television screen in the common room, flipping from channel to channel in a self-prescribed sequence, and repeating the sequence hour after hour. It was infuriating to those who wanted to watch a program. They nicknamed her Psycho and The Elevator Lady. A male student who called her Psycho to her face found a lighted toothpaste carton pushed under the door of his room.

A poignant detail reported to the investigators: Increasingly careless about her appearance, Laurie invariably wore a pink sweatsuit, Russell's last birthday gift to her. She owned several copies of it in various shades of pink, and wore them alternately. At mealtimes she added red woolen gloves to avoid touching cutlery.

After the Christmas break, the period when she went home and bought her third gun, her condition worsened visibly. She became puffy-looking, potbellied, and unkempt. One of the advertised attractions of The Towers was its All-U-Can-Eat food service in the basement cafeteria; she was often seen there, lining up for meal after meal, disappearing to the washroom, and coming back for more. Several students reported their suspicion that she was bulimic, and were assured that her father had been told.

Jami Halperin, one of the freshmen, recalled two of Norman Wasserman's several visits. "There were six or seven of us sitting around a table eating breakfast when he walked in. He pulled up a chair and introduced himself as Laurie's dad. He said, 'Hi, honey, I'm here for the day.' He seemed like a nice guy, but she was very cold to him, and he didn't seem to know how to react. He just sat there, looking out of place. Another time she was by the front desk when he came in at the door, and she took off before he could see her."

Students who tried to befriend her soon gave up. The few who saw her room were appalled by its scatterings of half-eaten food, its assortment of unwashed silverware stolen from the cafeteria, and the stench of its urine-soaked carpet. "It was just gross," one young woman said.

"In that second semester it was obvious to all of us that she was ill," said Kristen Peter, another freshman. "One of the resident assistants was constantly trying to get her help. But Laurie wasn't the college's responsibility, and the building management didn't seem to know what to do."

Unlike the Kellogg building at Evanston, The Towers was privately owned, so it was not the management's concern whether or not she attended classes. Most of the 475 residents were freshmen and sophomores from wealthy families, and in the fall of 1987 Laurie looked youthful enough to fit into their environment, one which was "rather East Coast and snooty," in Kristen Peter's description. Later, when her looks and mental health began to deteriorate, the building staff tended to ignore her problems, knowing that she would move out when the academic year ended in May. "Nobody thought she was dangerous, and all of us assumed that someone in her family was getting help for her," one student remarked.

The management's last encounter with Laurie was at about 9:00 P.M. on May 15, 1988, when a building employee was shocked to find her lying in the corner of a trash storage room, curled in a fetal position inside a plastic garbage bag. Startled by him, she removed the bag and ran off, muttering that she had been looking for something among the trash. She was sweating profusely as though she had lain in the bag for some time. Later in the evening the building manager checked her room and found her asleep on a bare mattress, surrounded by a muddle of possessions. The muddle was searched for weapons and suicide notes. None was found and she was left to go back to sleep. The building manager tried to telephone her father in Glencoe, but was unable to reach him. Once again the Wassermans were in Florida.

Laurie moved out of The Towers on the following day. Nobody questioned her departure because it was an appropriate time for her to leave, the end of the semester. Four days after that she was dead.

Winnetka's deputy police chief, Lieutenant Joseph Sumner, reached Madison just in time to prevent a Wasserman relative from removing all the goods Laurie had left in storage. Sumner saw this as a further attempt to destroy evidence, and was doubly annoyed with himself for having been so considerate to the Wassermans a few days earlier. Sorting among Laurie's rescued belongings, he found a recent letter from her father, written from Florida, urging her to become a voluntary patient in a psychiatric ward. So her parents knew how bad it was, he thought. Evidently Dr. Greist had not thought Laurie dangerous, or he would have had her committed. Norman Wasserman's pen-printed note was pleading rather than directing, the letter of a caring and troubled father who had long since lost control. His tone was so apologetic and conciliatory that, given her state of mind, it was predictable that she would ignore it.

Dear Laurie: This is probably the most important and the hardest letter that I will ever have to write. I am going to ask you to do me the biggest favor that anyone could do for me. (You know how hard it is for me to ask anything from anyone). I am going to ask you to go against all your instincts and let yourself be hospitalized and treated by Dr. Greist. I DO realize how hard this will be for you. I DO realize what I am asking you to do for me, but I would do anything for you. . . .

PLEASE set it up with Dr. Greist. For me, if not for yourself. I love you, Dad.

Wasserman's letter made no mention of his wife. She sent Laurie a separate greeting card with the words already imprinted: "Everything is going to be alright—I believe in you." It was the warmest expression on that piece of paper. Edith Wasserman's written message was about a grandchild's tonsillectomy ("she is recovering great"), a visit to a boat show ("interesting but not our cup of tea"), and a projected outing in a friend's Rolls-Royce ("how's that for class?"). It read like a duty letter from a distant acquaintance who wasn't sure what to say.

Laurie had also saved pages of her own scribblings; unrelated phrases scrawled by a disturbed hand, most of them angry fantasies about her breakup with Russell.

"Want divorce & want you out of this house by the time I come home—ran to phone naked—very afraid—raped twice—bag lady—scum—paraplegic—hurt me—break me—I'll teach you a lesson—I know you hate pain—I'm going to make you suffer bitch." And more like it.

In a neater hand she had made her last attempt at revenge on her former boyfriend, the Arizona doctor. The Winnetka investigators found a copy of the unsigned letter which had been received by the administration of his hospital, proof that this had indeed been written by Laurie. She described herself as a nineteen-year-old student who had recently consulted the doctor professionally. (In fact, she had not seen him in years.) She alleged that he delivered a prescription by making a personal call to her home where he immediately undressed and tried to assault her. There was a cruel touch at the end of her letter: as proof of her story, she offered the information that he had a birthmark on his penis. "How would I know this unless it was shoved in my face?"

In addition, Laurie had kept two recent news clippings, both uncannily prophetic. One was about a nineteen-year-old Madison man who had walked into a public building with a gun and randomly killed two people. "I'm going to kill everybody, and I don't care if you kill me," he had said. The other was a bizarre medical tale of a depressed young man who tried to commit suicide by putting a gun in his mouth and pulling the trigger, just as Laurie would do. He survived to discover that the injury to his brain had cured him of OCD, doing no other damage and making it possible for him to function normally.

Students at The Towers thought that Laurie never left the building, but police records disproved this. On March 14 she was arrested for stealing four wigs from two Madison stores. Caught in the act, she gave her name as Karen Glass. In the same week she stole chemicals, including arsenic and material to make incendiary devices, from a university laboratory. At Madison's public library she helped herself to four reference books on the subject of poisoning, removing the catalog cards to avoid discovery of the theft.

The more Lieutenant Joe Sumner and his Winnetka colleagues learned about Laurie's life in Madison, the clearer it became that her murder attempts of May 20 had been systematically planned over several weeks. But they were unable to discern a motive. Their attempts to find out about her medical condition were frustrated by the refusal of Norman Wasserman, her executor, to sign releases for the three psychiatrists who had treated her.

"He could have opened a lot of doors for us," Sumner complained. "We wanted to talk to her doctors, to know what she was being treated for. We wanted to know about that half-hour telephone conversation with her mother after she shot Phil Andrew, whether she gave a reason for what she did. It might have helped us to understand, to prevent someone in future from getting so out of control."

Police investigators speculated that the prescription drugs Laurie had been taking—clomipramine (sold under the trade name of Anafranil) to control the OCD, lithium carbonate for her manic depression, and birth-control pills for her sporadic sex life—might have had a dangerous synergistic effect. These drugs were prescribed by different doctors who did not have access to the others' records. In the spring of 1988 Anafranil had not yet been licensed for general use. Although Dr. Greist was one of the few American psychiatrists permitted to prescribe it, Laurie was being supplied the drug by her Chicago psychiatrist, who was importing it from Canada. Meantime, Dr. Greist was giving her lithium carbonate as a stabilizer, and becoming increasingly concerned about her ability to cope with life.

The Winnetka task force also gathered into its net a sad relic of the extended Dann family: Sheri Zilligen Taylor, Laurie's contemporary and a distant relative by marriage. Sheri's ex-husband, Scott, was the brother of Jeffrey Taylor, who was married to Russell's sister, Susie. Sheri had lost the custody of her children to Scott in a bitter divorce which happened at about the same time as Laurie's. For a time the two women were friends; unsympathetic relatives thought of them as companions in misery, griping about their ex-husbands.

Early in May of 1988 Scott told Glencoe police that Sheri had threatened him on the telephone after he refused to let her take their children to Boston for a weekend. Less than three weeks after this incident, Laurie went on her killing spree. Fearing that Sheri might copy her, Scott Taylor asked the police to take his ex-wife into protective custody.

Some members of the task force thought he was overreacting. But they understood his fear of a copycat crime, given the fact that Laurie had just attempted to kill his brother's children, and that Sheri owned a gun. The tension was so great in his family that when the news broke that an unknown woman had gone into a school and shot children, Jeffrey Taylor, sitting in his executive office at the Cole Taylor Bank, had the immediate reaction: "That could be one of my ex–sisters-in-law."

After much debate the Winnetka task force came up with a devious but legal way to part Sheri Taylor from her gun. The previous November she had been arrested for driving while intoxicated, and had failed to show up for her court hearing. As a result the police had a warrant for her arrest, but had not yet served it. Now this omission could be turned to advantage. They could pick her up on the outstanding drunk-driving charge, then, on the basis of her ex-husband's complaint, have her committed to a mental institution for psychiatric evaluation. In Illinois a person who is committed loses the right to own a gun for the next five years, which was the entire purpose of this exercise. On an involuntary commitment Sheri could be held for up to ten days, and rather than have his ex-wife spend this time in a public institution, Scott offered to pay for treatment in one of Chicago's best private hospitals. While she was there her firearms license was revoked.

Patty McConnell described this incident as the most exhausting part of the investigation. It involved complex arrangements between the police and the judiciary in two counties, and hours of work for several team members. Sheri had come down in the world since her divorce, and was living in a cheap motel in Highwood, "a rough little town," in the description of one of the police investigators, immediately north of the north shore. Its main function is to serve the recreational needs of men at two nearby military bases, providing all-night bars and garish entertainment. Sheri had a menial job there in a grocery store, working the late shift. She had been a model before her marriage, and her professional photographs show a beautiful girl with red-gold hair, hazel eyes, and a wide, even smile. The arresting officers found it hard to recognize this earlier Sheri in the emaciated and carelessly dressed woman whom they took into custody on the night of May 25 as she left work.

"She looked pale, her eyes were sunken, and her face was drawn," recalled Detective Mark Anfenson of the Deerfield police. "I don't think she meant to do any harm. I think she had been through a bad divorce, it had been rough on her, for a time she had abused alcohol, and now she was doing the best she could. She had a gun but I don't think she intended to use it on anybody. I believe her story that she had bought it to send to her brother. I don't think she was in league with Laurie. She just happened to be in the wrong place at the wrong time."

Reluctantly Sheri led the arresting officers into the shambles of her motel room where, from beneath a pile of clothes, she produced a .357 Magnum. She realized that she was being associated with Laurie Dann, and said she had not seen Laurie in more than a year. The task force had intended to keep Sheri's arrest quiet, and was shocked at the speed with which the media ferreted it out. DANN FRIEND ARRESTED, SURRENDERS GUN ran a prominent headline in the *Chicago Tribune*, its reporter making the point that this was the same kind of high-power revolver Laurie had owned. A subsequent story referred to "chilling similarities" between Sheri and Laurie. In public opinion a link had been established, and the fearful question was being asked: How many more madwomen are out there, plotting to kill?

"It was a terrible, terrible emotional experience," one north shore mother related. "We were still in shock from the Hubbard Woods shootings, and after this news about Sheri Taylor, many of us kept our children locked indoors for days. We were all so frightened."

Sergeant Michael O'Connell was enraged by the sensationalism. On the night of Sheri's arrest he had been at the Winnetka police station until 2:00 A.M. "At about seven A.M. I was on my way back there, and I heard on the radio news that a woman had been arrested in connection with the Laurie Dann case. I know the press has a job to do, but how could they, without official notice from this police station or the task force, put a person's reputation in jeopardy? It was so unethical."

As the investigation grew, so did the task force. "We had more investigators working on this case than Winnetka has policemen," one detective remarked.

"We would sit around after work, in the police station, in restaurants and bars, brainstorming," said Sergeant Michael Blackburn, an investigations officer in Cook County sheriff's office. As an intelligence officer specializing in organized crime, he was used to working in rougher neighborhoods, and like others brought into the task force from beyond the north shore, he was struck by the comparison. "If Laurie Dann had walked into a school on the south or west side of Chicago, or in any city of the USA, yes, there would have been anger and frustration. And there would have been a police investigation. But not a task force, and not such an extreme reaction from the press and public."

A lot of the brainstorming was punctuated by "if onlys." If only Dr. Greist had seen enough of Laurie's behavior to have had her committed . . . If only the Arizona doctor had not withdrawn his complaint of telephone harassment, and had let the FBI arrest her . . . If only some of her baby-sitting employers, or the authorities at Northwestern or in Madison had prosecuted her . . . If only Norman Wasserman had practiced tough love, instead of enabling, excusing, and covering up . . .

One lead which the task force did not follow, because it didn't seem to matter anymore, was Russell's earlier suggestion that the police interview Kirsten Mundy, his former neighbor at the Highland Park townhouse where he was stabbed. Two weeks after the stabbing he had urged the Highland Park police to talk to her, but they never did. "She was a witness," he had insisted. "She'll tell you what she heard."

Had she been asked she would have told this story: "Russell's scream woke me up. Our bedroom was next to his stairwell, and the next thing I heard was someone in his house running downstairs. Then the front door was slammed. It was a hot night and our windows were open, so I could hear the person run outside, away from the house. It could not have been Russell because shortly after that I heard the police arrive, and then I heard him talking to them as they were leaving. They did not seem to be believing him, and were saying: 'You must have had friends in, or a party, or maybe someone was playing a trick on you.' I didn't know what it was all about until Russell told me two weeks later."

If only Russell had not antagonized the police by swearing at them . . . If only they had not dismissed him as a stereotype of north shore arrogance . . . If only he had seemed more credible . . .

These thoughts led to a task-force discussion about the lie-detector tests, taken after Laurie's allegation of rape. At the time Laurie had convinced the polygraph expert of her veracity; now Patty McConnell could understanding why. "Lie detectors don't work on pathological liars," she explained. "That's why they're not acceptable in court. They measure physiological reactions: the heart rate, perspiration, breathing. If you don't know you're lying, you have no reactions. Russell, on the other hand, was so tense and irritated when he took the test that he came across as guilty."

In a detailed report the task force concluded that "in all instances Laurie Dann acted independently and after a period of significant premeditation." The team noted that although she was treated by three psychiatrists, "little if any information was transmitted among these mental-health practitioners to adequately diagnose the full extent of her condition."

"Laurie had a delusion of some sort, but what and why we shall never know," Sergeant Michael Blackburn commented. "Maybe if her room had not been tampered with, we might have some idea. We would like to have asked Mr. and Mrs. Wasserman why they kicked Floyd out of their house, why they cleaned out Laurie's room before the police could get back, why they wanted all her possessions in Madison picked up.

"There is a secret, and Laurie Dann died with the secret, but that secret did not die with Laurie Dann. For whatever reason, the Wassermans decided not to talk to the authorities, and that leads one to believe that they know what the secret is. Or maybe the only thing they are guilty of is ignoring the problem. Maybe as a result of that they have decided to suffer in silence. And that is their right. Laurie did the shooting, not Mom and Dad."

Quietly, Blackburn added: "My mother committed suicide when I was sixteen. I shall never know why. She too died with a secret. All I have to go by is what my father and other adults in her life told me. But it's why I feel the way I do about Laurie Dann. We may never know all the answers, and there comes a time to let go. We did what we could with this investigation, and now I think we need to close the book."

TWENTY-EIGHT

Less than four weeks elapsed between the shooting and the end of the school year. In that time lessons were set aside for group-therapy sessions at all schools in the neighborhood, and children were encouraged to work through their feelings instead. They told and retold the story, remembering it (as traumatized children often do) a little differently every time, so that Laurie Dann was sometimes like a mother and sometimes a monster, and the horrors which they had seen became embellished by their own fantasies and by the memories of other classmates.

"I'm very glad that Laur dan is dead!!!! I also wish that before Laur dan had come to Hubbard Woods she had jumped in a VOLCANO," a small child wrote beneath a drawing of a woman walking up a steep and smoking mountain. Insightfully, one child drew a line down the middle of her portrait of Laurie Dann, one side of the face a devil, the other that of a weeping woman. Another drew a tombstone with the epitaph: "Laurie Dann a very very mean and terrible person." But most children pictured her as alive and threatening, with a gun almost as large as herself.

Children too young to understand the finality of death continued to imagine Laurie Danns all over Winnetka, poking guns into their bedroom windows, catching them alone in dark places.

"What if she could fly?" a four-year-old asked. This child was one of the pre-kindergarten group which had heard the screams from Room 7. She had also seen one of the wounded children running terrified into the hallway. As she talked about it at home, "I could see the television reports and the storybook fantasies getting mixed up with her memories," her mother said.

The mother tried to reassure her daughter that the danger was over. "But it was hard to explain to her what dead meant when her only experience of death had been a goldfish. She felt that even locking the doors would not prevent this woman from coming back, and she wanted her dad to become a policeman so he could protect her. For some time she imagined Laurie Dann as a man because she couldn't conceive that a woman could kill people. A killer had to be a bad guy."

Even older children had difficulty struggling with the concept of death. They knew murder only as the stuff of soap operas. "What does dead mean when you can see the same actor in another television show next season?" a father asked. And how could they deal with the mixed emotions about Laurie's death and Nicky's? In a group-therapy session Dr. Ronald Rozensky was impressed by "some very existential stuff coming from fourth graders." One of them confided: "I'm confused. In church they asked us to pray for Laurie Dann, but how can we when we're glad she's dead?"

Repeatedly, for weeks afterward, questions were asked about Nicky: Will he wake up? Is he sad? Is it cold and lonely for him under the ground? If he's in heaven, how did he get there? Does he mind being separated from his mom and dad? Does he know how much we miss him? Does he miss us?

Problems were wrestled with at all levels. A teenage group discussion on capital punishment at the Church of Saints Faith, Hope and Charity inevitably led to a debate about Laurie Dann. If she had lived, should she have been sentenced to death? If so, would the state be a killer too? One girl had known her as a baby-sitter, and remembered that although she seemed troubled she was kind and friendly. Why hadn't someone got help for her?

Why, when it was so fashionable for north shore people to be in analysis, was it so shameful to be mentally ill?

At New Trier High School a meeting was announced for those students who had siblings at Hubbard Woods. "I expected about ten," said Diane Juneau, director of student services. "But between thirty and forty showed up, all of them very concerned."

In recent years New Trier, which prided itself on being one of the best public high schools in the country, had been shocked by a variety of student deaths, from suicide, drunk driving, and natural causes. As recently as the 1970s such things were not talked about. Now there were no taboos, and the school community faced up to having a murderer among its alumni. As soon as she saw the newspaper photograph, Mindy Nadell, a home economics teacher, remembered having the teenage Laurie Wasserman in one of her classes.

"I knew the face right away. It kept haunting me. Something about the eyes . . . And I remembered her name because it was Jewish like mine, and there weren't many Jews at New Trier at that time." Her recollection of Laurie's personality was less distinct. "She was a waiflike creature. I remember well those students who are outstanding and those who cause trouble, and she did not fit into either category." A review of Laurie's school records produced an unexpected finding. In her senior year she took an advanced course in child development and got an A for it. It was one of the few subjects at which she excelled.

The memory set off a lot of introspection among teachers. Did Laurie have problems back then, and were they missed? A more sophisticated system of advisers and counselors had developed since she was at New Trier. And yet there seemed to be even more troubled teenagers.

"There are a lot of powder kegs: students ready to explode because of anger, loneliness, and lack of attention," Mindy Nadell commented. One of her colleagues had recently asked a class of juniors and seniors how often they ate with their parents; half the students had said about once a week, the other half couldn't remember when it last happened. In many north shore homes the pressure upon adults to stay successful left little time for family.

Nevertheless, the belief prevailed: that the comfortable and protected life-style was worth the price breadwinners paid. Laurie

Dann had shattered that equilibrium, leaving Winnetkans two disasters to deal with: the shock of the shooting, and the demise of their dream. Overnight their village had become as vulnerable as anywhere else, and the aftereffects would paralyze and divide its people for months to come. An Evanston Hospital doctor likened the trauma to that of rape. "You think you are protected, and then some lunatic comes along and violates you in the most outrageous way."

Given the unexpected insight, some Winnetkans observed that this is what life must be like for impoverished parents in the Chicago projects. Two days after the Hubbard Woods tragedy a nine-year-old black youth was critically wounded by a stray bullet in the dangerous city neighborhood where he lived, an event which merited a few paragraphs in the Chicago newspapers only because of its proximity in time to the Winnetka shootings. Ironically, the boy's mother had a menial job at Evanston Hospital, where the Winnetka children were getting special care; her son, meanwhile, was in a public hospital in Chicago. Editorial comments were made about the juxtaposition of the two events, but it took a black mother from the projects to put it in context. "I feel so sorry for Winnetka parents because they didn't expect this to happen," she told a researcher. "We do."

Some Winnetkans tried to distance themselves from the tragedy by arguing that Laurie Dann was an outsider. "She came from Glencoe," they said, as though Glencoe were another country and not the next village. There was a sense of surprise that the killer had not been poor and black; as one long-term resident remarked, "People find it hard to believe that the chronically unemployed would not be so angry that they would not come here with a gun."

If that had happened, Winnetka would have responded by strengthening its defenses, increasing police protection, and being even more suspicious of strangers. Poor and black can be subdued. The insanity from within was another matter.

In the aftershock of May 20 some community leaders were emboldened to speak out. In the Congregational Church on the Sunday after the shooting, Dr. Paul Allen ventured: "We build walls around ourselves, our families, our communities, hoping to keep evil out. In other places, we say, violence and disorder live.

In other places lives turn out distorted and terrible things happen. Here we can be safe. Here we can keep innocence protected. But that's not so. As last Friday proved, the root of evil is everywhere. Our only defense is not to distance it, push it away, and thus turn a blind eye to ourselves, but to confess its presence and seek our safety elsewhere than in walls."

"Laurie Dann is the child we all might have had," a Hubbard Woods mother acknowledged. It was a rare comment. Most found it easier to treat her as an aberration, to respond with the confident assurance of one father at the Hubbard Woods meeting of May 21: "We shan't let this happen again. Anyway, lightning never strikes in the same place twice."

And that was the promise most parents gave their children when asked: "Is she really dead? Can she come back?" Yes, honey, we're safe. And no, it won't happen again. It was so tempting to return to the myth.

Since there were not many evangelicals in Winnetka, Pastor David Goodman drew most of his congregation from less affluent areas, allowing him a critical view of the village where his Bible Church was prominently sited. What he saw in the summer of 1988 troubled him deeply.

There had been an intensity of emotion at the ecumenical service on the Sunday after the shooting, felt rather than seen because exhibiting feelings isn't the Winnetka way; then, all too soon afterward, people became impatient to put the tragedy behind them and move on.

"They wanted to do this at too fast a pace because on the day of the shooting they lost autonomy, and the wealthier people are, the more important it is for them to be in control," Goodman observed. "In communities like this there is drug and alcohol abuse, child abuse, sexual problems; a lot of unhappy people. But Winnetkans manage to hide all that behind a facade of living in the right place, wearing the right clothes, belonging to the right club. Laurie Dann stripped the facade away and exposed their vulnerability, but not for long. After the school broke for summer, some parents took their families to the Bahamas or wherever, didn't talk about the shooting anymore, and behaved as though it hadn't happened. But you can't deal with these things by forgetting. For those who try to work through it, it can take years. For those who don't, it can take forever."

He spoke of Winnetka in general, but Hubbard Woods parents reacted differently. Unable to forget, they clung to one another for support, believing, like all traumatized people, that only those who had shared their experience could understand.

"I did not want to go outside the Hubbard Woods area," a mother related. "Two days after the shooting I had to take my child to a birthday party in another part of Winnetka. It was good for her to go, but I was uncomfortable. This family had not experienced it the way we had, so I did not want to talk to them about it. And yet I did not want to talk about anything else."

A mother whose child had been in Room 7 described going to a business luncheon with some women whose company she usually enjoyed. "This time I couldn't deal with it because they weren't talking about Hubbard Woods, and right then it was the most important thing in my life."

It also worked the other way. "I felt the bottom had been taken out of the world, and yet I did not have a right to talk about it because my child was at Greeley School so it wasn't my tragedy," a Winnetka woman remarked.

There was resentment about this. "It was a community tragedy, and for the Hubbard Woods people to try and own it isn't fair," another woman said.

Even those with a personal attachment to the school began to feel like outsiders. Shelley Galloway had lived in Winnetka since she was five, and had attended Hubbard Woods School in childhood, but now she felt alone in her grief. There had been a discussion about the shooting at her little boy's nursery school, and he had come home asking her to show him where it happened.

"We walked around the outside of the building and I held him up and showed him my old classrooms. Nothing seemed to have changed. As a child I had such a positive experience in that school, and had always thought of it as a warm and comfortable place. In first and second grades I had a wonderful teacher who was Pennsylvania Dutch. She taught us German, and took us to her house to make Concord grape jam, and let us sleep over. There was an art teacher who gave us some really exciting projects—I can still remember a drawing I did—and a great gym teacher who was well known in the Boy Scout community, a kind of Pied Piper. The principal was a tall, thin man who was so warm and kind."

She was near to tears when her little boy became bored with peering through windows and wanted to run around the playground. "I kept thinking, 'This is my school and it has been violated.' For years I had all these wonderful memories of it, and now they had been spoiled. It was like my school was a person, and that person had been wounded."

During the summer the Hubbard Woods parents drew closer to one another, and more estranged from the rest of the village.

"It was hard for us," a Hubbard Woods mother acknowledged. "The kids needed to talk about it over and over, while we were beginning to feel that we ought to get on with our lives." As a professional, she was shocked to find that she couldn't. "I used to be supermom. I was highly organized and very disciplined, and I put pressure on my children to keep up with the pace. I followed a schedule that two people would have had difficulty maintaining. The events of May twentieth put me outside all this. For several months I was numb. I kept thinking about the shootings and could not focus on my work. It was a shattering experience. Finally my boss said to me, 'Go home and take as much time as you need to get over this.'"

She was describing a well-documented symptom of post-traumatic stress. Her child, who had been more directly traumatized, showed others. "She came out of school that day crying hysterically. At first she didn't say much and I thought she was being very resilient, but now I realize she was frightened. In the weeks that followed we saw anger, frustration, temper flare-ups, insecurity, nightmares, and a loss of self-confidence. It's still hard to know what is going on inside her. I cope with it one day at a time."

The mothers' immediate therapy was to busy themselves helping those who were worse afflicted. They took casseroles and flowers to the families of the wounded children, hoping to minimize their hurt. This could be done with a brave smile because all five children were getting better. Comforting the Corwins was another matter.

"We wanted to help but felt uncomfortable meeting them, not knowing what to say," one mother acknowledged.

Another excused her awkwardness with the belief that "Linda needs to be given her space."

It was distressing to see Linda Corwin shopping in the village, pale and unsmiling, with that terrible pain in her eyes. She looked lost and inconsolable. At home she channeled some of her grief into assembling a collection of Nicky's drawings and schoolwork, which she would show to visitors with the heartbreaking comment: "What is so sad is that this is it. When I think of what he would have gone on to do . . ."

Joel Corwin was overwhelmed by his own helplessness. "He keeps saying, 'I am a father and I couldn't protect my own son,'" Linda related.

Other fathers shared his sense of failed responsibility. Theirs was not merely the misplaced guilt of having been safely in their offices when the horror happened, or even the knowledge that their children had narrowly escaped being shot. Facing those realities was within their range. It was the death of their ideal they couldn't deal with; the realization that there were no longer any safe places, even in this Camelot they had created for themselves.

This caused them to wonder whether the struggle to raise their families here was worthwhile. The answer had never been in doubt before; now it was. Thoughtful Winnetkans had long known, but been reluctant to concede, that the American dream seemed likely to end with their generation. In terms of worldly success there was little left for their children to strive for beyond what they, the parents, had already achieved. Given the tenor of the times, their children would probably not live so well. Now, prematurely, Laurie Dann had forced the question: Did all the pressure to succeed pay off? Maybe it would make more sense to work less hard and live in a place more like the rest of America. Maybe that would be a better preparation for children to face the real world.

Dr. Willard Fry was one of a few Winnetkans entitled to some positive feelings about the outcome of May 20 because he had saved a life; nevertheless, he was troubled by the thoughts it aroused. As a Northwestern professor of clinical surgery, he had successfully operated on Robert Trossman, the youngest victim of the shooting, who was wounded in the chest and stomach. Over the years Fry had treated many gunshot victims, but this was the first from his own village. "I would have been wrecked if the kid had died," he said.

Fry, a kindly, genial man, had grown up on the north shore and it gave him what he called "an ego massage" to have his daughter come home from New Trier High School and tell him that he was regarded as a hero there. He was a New Trier alumnus, and had been under pressure to succeed from that time on. "One day my daughter asked me what life was like in the sixties. I couldn't tell her because through all those years I was programmed to work. There was no way you could be part of the protest movement and be a surgery resident, starting at six in the morning and finishing between nine and midnight. And in my field, which is very competitive, a mediocre surgeon isn't going to cut the mustard here. So you start working in high school to get into a good college, and then into a good medical school, and the pressure never stops."

TWENTY-NINE

FROM THE beginning, Dr. Ira Sloan and his trauma team warned parents that the events of May 20 could have long-term consequences. "Events like this play hell with individuals, marriages, communities," he told them. "Anything that hurt in the past will hurt again, from stress headaches and backaches to marital problems and alcoholism."

Nobody wanted to hear this, much less to admit that these problems existed. Alcoholism was widespread on the north shore: the life-style supported and excused it. Marriages were stressed. Some children felt lonely and neglected, left in the company of maids who barely spoke English.

After May 20 many parents rearranged their family lives, allowing more time for children. Laurie Dann had made baby-sitters suspect, which reinforced the reason for parents to stay at home. But there were unexpected new feelings to deal with. In their efforts to atone for past neglect, some fathers became overly protective of their children, more by talk than action. Young mothers felt abandoned, because although their husbands had rushed home on the Friday of the shooting, they went back to work the following Monday morning, leaving them to cope with terrified children alone. A typical comment, weeks later: "My husband is sick to death of hearing about the shooting. He had to repress his feelings and get on with his job, so all he wants to do now is forget it, and all I want to do is talk about it."

And from a child: "I knew it had to be bad because Daddy came home early that day."

By midsummer the rest of Winnetka was also tired of the topic. Jealousies were surfacing. Of the village's three elementary schools, Hubbard Woods had the strongest reputation as a warm and caring place, but the others were more prestigious—Greeley because it was in the old-guard section of Winnetka, and Crow Island on account of its innovative landmark building. Now Hubbard Woods had become the focus of attention, and the village school board seemed preoccupied with how to minister to its children, how to support its faculty, how to restore its sense of security. Children in the other schools had been frightened, too. What about them?

The dynamics of the school board hinged, to a considerable extent, on the fact that Linda Corwin was one of its elected members. She said it was painful for her to sit through these meetings after Nicky's death, but she attended faithfully, and other members deferred to her to avoid compounding her hurt. She didn't have to say anything; they read the look on her face, knew where she stood, and voted her way. None of this was conscious on her part, but the effect was powerful.

Before the schools reopened in September the board discussed security measures and decided upon closed doors and a strict monitoring of all visitors, putting an end to the charm of an open school system. None of the schools along the north shore would ever again leave their entrances unattended. At about this time Evanston Hospital's department of psychiatry proposed a study which would identify and treat the most traumatized people.

"We went before the school board and explained that now the crisis was over, we would like to do an assessment of the entire community," Dr. Sloan stated. "We wanted to look at all the children and all the parents. It seemed do-able, but there was a lot of resistance."

He had not expected this. Members of his team had been working with the Hubbard Woods community since the morning of the shooting. They had been trusted and appreciated; now, to their surprise, they were suspect. In part, Ira Sloan recognized, this was because of the intrusive questions they would need to ask, like whether there had been any family problems before the shooting. But the resistance went deeper than that; it was more like antagonism, and he was baffled by it.

In 1988 the medical literature on the psychological effects of community disasters was very limited. Turning to it, he came upon a phrase which was new to him: the trauma membrane. It had been coined by three mental-health professionals from the University of Cincinnati College of Medicine (Dr. Jacob D. Lindy, Mary C. Grace, and Dr. Bonnie L. Green) who worked with survivors of a devastating fire which raged through a night-club on the outskirts of their city. They observed that most of the severely traumatized people were quickly surrounded by a protective circle of trusted friends who determined (not always wisely) what was, and was not, beneficial for their recovery. All other influences were firmly excluded. Outsiders, however competent and well intentioned, found it impossible to penetrate these tight circles.

"Trauma membranes around individual survivors may fuse together to form an inclusive community-wide trauma membrane," the researchers noted.[*]

Suddenly it became clear. Trauma membranes had been drawn over Hubbard Woods School like concentric circles, with the Corwin family at the heart. The next circle surrounded the five injured children and their parents; beyond that were the children of Room 7, and in the outermost circle, protecting all those within as well as themselves, was the rest of the school community. These groupings had formed, unalterably, during the summer vacation while the school administration's control was relaxed. When classes resumed in September and the Evanston

*"Survivors: Outreach to a Reluctant Population," *American Journal of Orthopsychiatry*, July 1981.

team was ready to intensify its efforts, this large encompassing trauma membrane was firmly in place, with Ira Sloan and his staff outside it. In May the parents had gratefully welcomed the Evanston team; by September they wanted to dismiss it and to handle their own healing process. The issue for many parents was not what kind of therapy their families should receive, but whether they needed any at all.

It was easier to focus on ensuring that the shooting would never happen again, and some of them began a movement to ban gun ownership in the village. Political action helped to restore the parents' lost sense of power, and was a classic reaction to the kind of disaster which leaves people feeling impotent and vulnerable. Thus groups like Mothers Against Drunk Drivers and Parents of Murdered Children were born. A local gun-control law could have only a limited effect so long as the state of Illinois allowed all its legally sane and law-abiding citizens to assemble arsenals of handguns, but in the hope of influencing the state legislature, several suburban Chicago municipalities had recently enacted local antigun statutes. The rationale of Hubbard Woods parents was that if there had been gun control in all the north shore villages, Floyd Mohr would not have been obliged to plead with Laurie Dann to give up her revolver. He could have seized it, and all the horror of May 20 would have been averted.

George Fisher, Lindsay's father, was in the forefront of this movement, a persuasive public speaker who took his campaign to Washington, testifying before congressional committees about the need for national gun control. Most of it, however, concentrated on the local issue, and most of its proponents were mothers. "My husband thinks it is a nice thing for us to do, but he's too busy to get involved," one of them remarked.

In the meantime, Ira Sloan's proposal for a five-year study of the community was stymied.

"A lot of parents were asking why Dr. Sloan would want to do this study, what was he going to get out of it, why put the children through any more questioning? People who I thought would be the first to cooperate were strongly opposed," Dr. Abby Adams related. As a Hubbard Woods mother who was also a physician she saw it differently. "I had a hard time with their point of view because I understand the importance of medical data, and know that the more you talk about a trauma now the less it will hurt later."

She did not minimize the damage to her own family. "This has affected every aspect of our lives. My daughter still has nightmares about it. She is old enough to know that it is irrational to think that Laurie Dann can come back, but she now knows that there are other Laurie Danns out there."

The first of them surfaced on September 26, four months after the Winnetka shooting. James William Wilson, a nineteen-year-old recluse who had been undergoing psychiatric treatment, walked into an elementary school in Greenville, South Carolina, carrying his grandfather's pistol, and opened fire. Two eight-year-old girls died; seven other children and two teachers were wounded. Wilson made the chilling statement that he had been inspired to kill by Laurie Dann. He had clipped a magazine article about her, and read it daily. "I could understand where she was coming from. I think I may have copied her in a way."

A week later a gunman in a camouflage outfit fired into a third-grade gym class in the playground of a school in Mascotte, Florida, seriously wounding a nine-year-old girl. On December 16 a teacher was killed and another wounded in a shooting spree by a sixteen-year-old student at a school in Virginia Beach, Virginia. On January 5, 1989, a sixteen-year-old student was fatally shot by a nineteen-year-old man in a school yard at Little Rock, Arkansas.

Then the Stockton shooting happened.

The earlier copycat crimes had received scant national coverage, but the massacre in Stockton, California, was heavily reported by the television networks and major newspapers. It was an appalling story. On January 17, 1989, Edward Purdy, a twenty-nine-year-old drifter with an extensive criminal history, took an AK-47 assault rifle, a weapon with a rapid-firing mechanism, and sprayed gunfire into a crowd of children who were playing in the yard of an elementary school. Five of them were killed and twenty-nine people wounded before Purdy, who was dressed in army fatigues, fatally shot himself.

His crime shocked the nation, but in Winnetka its impact was profound. Once again the helpless terror of screaming, bleed-

ing children intruded into living rooms of villagers, forcing them
to relive the horror of Hubbard Woods. Inevitably, newspapers in
the Chicago area ran sidebar stories recalling the Winnetka shooting. George Fisher was called upon to comment and, welcoming
the opportunity to put his case for gun control, told a Chicago
television audience: "I don't know what it is going to take for the
American people to stand up and say, 'Enough is enough.'"

Some Winnetkans wished he had not brought attention back
to their village. It disturbed them to be reminded that, eight
months earlier in Hubbard Woods, Laurie Dann had set off a
chain reaction which had run so wildly amok that it might never
be contained. It was as if she had given permission to the crimi-
nally insane to tote their guns into schools and slaughter innocent
children: as if she continued to wield an evil power from beyond
the grave. Could she fly? Would she come back? In a way, she
could and did. And the worst part of this was explaining to their
children.

"We were able to shelter them from the earlier school shootings, but not from Stockton. It was of such magnitude that we
couldn't keep it from them," said a Hubbard Woods mother. "My
own child was very angry at me because I had told her it wouldn't
happen again. All I could say was, 'I'm sorry. I didn't believe it
would.' One of the problems is geography. She's too young too
understand how far it is to California. Stockton might be Evanston to her.

"She didn't say very much about it, but a lot of the behavior
which we had seen at the beginning recurred. She was sensitive,
raw. But it did open the door for her to tell us more about what
she had seen that day, things she had not talked about before."

On the morning after the Stockton shooting a crowd of anxious Hubbard Woods mothers held an emergency meeting with
school officials. Dr. Mary Giffin, the school's consultant child psychiatrist, had already alerted Superintendent Donald Monroe to
the likelihood of an "anniversary reaction" to their own tragedy
in May. After the mothers' meeting she observed: "Stockton
made it happen four months sooner. The parents were right
back to their original thoughts. There was a lot of discussion
about whether the new security measures at the school were
enough, whether we shouldn't have armed guards. They also

wondered whether it might be better for our children if we helped them to face the reality of living in a violent society."

No decision was made on either issue. Instead, as if by silent agreement, the parents tightened their trauma membrane. Few of them recognized it for what it was, much less admitted to its existence, although one mother noted that "there is an unconscious control over the entire community." Another observed: "After Stockton the message went out to the school administration loud and clear that neither the media nor any other outsiders were to be let in."

As she left the school that day, Dr. Giffin was asked by a reporter if she would appear on a nationally televised interview program. She declined, and hurried back to her office.

It was an immensely difficult school year for the Hubbard Woods teachers. Still traumatized themselves, their priority was to facilitate the children's recovery. Not a day passed without some intrusive memory of the shooting forcing them to abandon a lesson plan in order to lay it to rest. Children who used to be secure and outgoing were terrified of strangers and of loud noises. For several weeks they needed teachers or friends to accompany them to washrooms to reassure them that another Laurie Dann wasn't lurking. They were fearful of new situations, of being left alone, and of the amorphous threats and monsters which formed the substance of their dreams.

"These children are different," their principal, Richard Streedain, agreed. "The world has changed for them. It is not as safe as it was."

Among themselves, teachers admitted to equally unexpected fears and reactions. One woman was as afraid as the children to go to a public bathroom. Others wept again on the day of the Stockton shooting. Some very dedicated teachers began to doubt their choice of profession. Amy Moses, the substitute teacher who bravely defied Laurie Dann in Room 7, left Hubbard Woods at the end of the school year and took a clerical job in Evanston.

This excluded her from the trauma membrane and the healing process. Thereafter, her status in the parent community fell from that of heroine to outsider, and a fiction developed that if

the regular class teacher had been in Room 7 the shooting might
have been averted. Amy Deuble's survivor guilt fed into this. "If
I had been there I would have given her a karate chop," she is
reputed to have said. Or maybe a parent thought she said it, and
the legend grew in the telling. In any event, Amy Moses ceased
to be part of Winnetka's group-therapy sessions, and was rarely
seen in the village again.

Even among the children there was a protected inner circle.
Teachers with the best of intentions saw to it that the five who had
been wounded received class gifts of drawings and stories and vid-
eotapes throughout their hospital stay. When they returned to
school they were given special treatment. For months afterward
they continued to be a celebrity group and, like the inner circle of
their own parents, wielded an unsought power in class. Bound by a
common experience, they clung to one another and, to the dismay
of other children, let earlier friendships drift. As time passed, some
of them felt uncomfortable about being the focus of attention.
"Look, I didn't ask to be shot," one of them told a therapist.

After months of negotiation a limited version of the proposed
Evanston Hospital study was set in place. At the parents' insis-
tence it was restricted to volunteers, and the questioning done by
social workers. Psychiatrists and psychologists were rejected on
the assumption that they were motivated by a desire to advance
their careers. Dr. Sloan had hoped to produce a comprehensive
piece of scientific research which would serve as a guide in treating future child victims of disasters. But he understood the resistance. "These people have been violated in a way they never
expected, and are trying their damnedest to regain control," he
remarked.

They didn't know it, but he too was traumatized. He kept
intending to write a professional paper about the Hubbard Woods
disaster, but couldn't bring himself to start. "I find myself backing away from it because it brings back such a vivid memory of
that bloodied classroom," he said. It was some time before he
realized why that memory caused him such anguish. It recalled
an event of thirteen years earlier, the death of his father from a
massive hemorrhage.

"The nurse who was with him described the scene to me in
intense detail, several times over. Although I did not see it, my

picture of what happened was so vivid that I could believe I was there. And although I was an adult, my father's death was effectively the end of my childhood."

"You can never put trauma to rest if there is a reactivating factor," Dr. Mary Giffin explained. "It's like having a trick knee. Most of the time it holds you up, but then it lets you down when you least expect it. And that's how it is for those who were closest to the shooting. People farther away were merely stressed, and those who master stress can be stronger for it, but trauma is overwhelming.

"One of my most startling experiences was when I was in the village shopping district, dropping off some material at the cleaner's. Suddenly a car door slammed and my dog barked. A little girl who was a second grader at Hubbard Woods School started to scream hysterically. I told her, 'It's all right. It's not a gun,' and then she calmed down."

As to stress: "Every day the four-thirty A.M. train rumbles through Winnetka. Most of us had never noticed it, but now it wakes us up because we are all more sensitive to sound."

Soon after the shooting, Police Chief Herbert Timm hired a media consultant to advise him on problems which the police might face during the recovery process. At that stage there was a strong communal pride about the villagers' response to the crisis, and Timm was a local hero. It was almost embarrassing, the way people would come up to him on the street, or after Sunday Mass at Saints Faith, Hope and Charity, and congratulate him on a job superbly done. Before the Laurie Dann crisis some villagers undoubtedly shared Russell Dann's view of the police: that if they were better qualified they would be earning more money elsewhere. But on May 20 Herbert Timm's team had proved its professionalism, and now Winnetkans were as proud of its officers as of themselves for having staffed the village so well.

Timm's consultant warned him that the euphoria would not last. He recalled: "She said the village would split apart, that there would be movements to construct memorials for the dead boy and that this would be controversial. She also said that some people would try to find scapegoats. We could not believe this, but it all happened. One of the scapegoats was Amy Moses; another was me."

For months after the shooting, Timm was in demand as a lecturer. Law-enforcement groups, social workers and school administrations called upon him to describe his department's handling of the crisis, and the lessons learned from it. He always accepted the invitations, with a sense of mission about making people aware of the importance of gun control, school safety, and police access to the mental-health records of people as disturbed as Laurie Dann. It was painful for him to keep reliving the events of May 20, and on a couple of occasions he told his wife: "It is physically impossible for me to give this talk one more time." Yet he always managed to do so, and in the process surprised himself by his newfound skill as a public speaker. He was fluent, persuasive, and patently sincere. Without realizing it, he was trying to make sense of a trauma which, for him, went back through the bloodshed of Room 7 to the death of his own child eight years earlier.

"I want to see some good come out of this," he insisted. For months he kept speaking engagements around the country, on his own time and often at his own expense. He had a film made to reinforce his talk, and rumor spread that he was getting rich on the proceeds.

"I could not possibly make money out of this tragedy," he said. Those who knew him personally did not doubt this. But the rumor fed on the fact that he was publicly talking about an event which villagers wanted to forget.

The proposal to memorialize Nicky Corwin came from within the trauma membrane. There were some sports fields near his home where he used to play soccer: Edgewood Park, named after an adjoining street. It would be a comfort and support to the Corwin family, so the thinking went, if this land were to be renamed the Nick Corwin Park. The suggestion received wide support in the Hubbard Woods School community. Beyond that there was opposition. Other parks in the village were named after public benefactors. Should a murdered child be memorialized in this way? Translated, the question meant: What shall we tell our children, and our children's children, when they ask who Nick Corwin was?

Few villagers said this publicly for fear of offending his parents. Those who did risked hostility. Mary Giffin, long beloved at Hubbard Woods School, was surprised to find herself among them. "People went from house to house with a petition for renaming the park," she said. "When I was asked my opinion, I suggested that perhaps there should be a simpler memorial. There had been several child deaths in recent years, all from illness, and I questioned whether it was appropriate for a murder death to be singled out. Afterward I got several nasty letters accusing me of anti-Semitism."

Linda Corwin was deeply touched by the park proposal. "I want him to be remembered for the beauty of his life, and not the horror of his death," she said of her son. That clinched it. The Nick Corwin Park was dedicated at the opening of the 1989 soccer season, and a close-up photograph of Linda at the ceremony occupied the front page of *Winnetka Talk*. MRS. CORWIN SMILES it was captioned, implying that it was now all right for the rest of the village to smile too.

Within Hubbard Woods School there were more prosaic signs of a return to normalcy. Halfway through the school year spitballs began to reappear on the ceiling of the boys' bathroom: a welcome sign that washrooms were again seen as places to slosh around in, rather than to be used hurriedly, in fearful groups.

"We still get parental requests to stop all this discussion of the shooting," a school official commented. "But we never hear children say that they don't want to talk about it. They have been working hard to incorporate the experience into their lives." Many of the children continued to act out their feelings in playground games, with Laurie Dann as the villain. There was also a positive effect: "While those close to the shooting will always carry the emotional scars, they already have a sympathetic understanding of other victims of violence."

Meantime Winnetka's gun-control campaign had developed into a bitter battle in which all the unexpressed frustration of the park opponents found release. An issue which would normally have been resolved in the village council was forced to a referendum, with arguments raging back and forth for weeks. George Fisher's group, Winnetka Citizens for Handgun Control, was joined by a newer grass-roots organization, Mothers Against Guns.

Villagers for a Safe Winnetka, a pro-gun lobby, formed a vociferous opposition.

On one side it was argued that the slaughter of innocents had to stop; on the other, that depriving law-abiding citizens of their right to bear arms would attract more criminals into the area. No way could there be a meeting of these minds, although everyone wanted the same thing, a crime-free village. Mothers Against Guns waged the most visible campaign, going from door to door with their children and urging people to vote. Several of these women received anonymous calls accusing them of child abuse. Jeanne Pence, one of the group's most active members, said that some villagers reacted to her anti-gun lapel pin by demanding, "Who do you think you are?" and "Why don't you stay in your kitchen and bake cookies?"

"Don't make waves, Jeanne," a neighbor warned her. But in April of 1989, the same month as the park dedication, the wavemakers triumphed by a vote of 2,125 to 1,407. Legally no one could ever again bring a handgun into Winnetka.

Philip Andrew, by now recovered from his wounds, ran his own gun-control campaign. In the hope of influencing some pending anti-gun proposals before the Illinois state legislature, he called a press conference at his home on Kent Road, one year to the minute from the time Laurie Dann shot him there. He asked the parents of the five wounded children to join him, but they opted out, urging him not to invite reporters into Winnetka for this first anniversary. They agreed with what he was doing, but wanted him to do it elsewhere. Many Hubbard Woods families were so unnerved by their memories that they left the village for the weekend. Only the Andrews seemed at ease in their surroundings, this rambling old house where Laurie Dann had killed herself.

After speeches from Philip and several other gun-control proponents, Ruth Andrew served refreshments. She was obviously proud of her son, who already had the easy grace and fluency of the politician he hoped to become. He had recently returned to competitive swimming and was almost back to championship level. It was a lovely spring morning, just as it had been a year earlier when a stranger walked into their kitchen and disrupted their lives.

At first neighbors had assumed that the Andrews would sell their house and move elsewhere, as the Rushes had moved to New York, and the Wassermans, permanently, to Florida. But none of the family considered this.

"Does it bother you that Laurie Dann died here?" Philip was asked.

"Not at all," he replied. "I spent most of my conscious life growing up in this house and there are too many good memories. The fact that this deranged woman was stopped here only makes it a greater place. It is now part of the history of the house, part of the history of our family, a point for us to move from rather than to hide from."

Catherine and Patricia Andrew handled the crisis as calmly. They never saw the bloodstained carpet in their bedroom; after Laurie's suicide their older brother Dan ripped it up and took it to the village dump.

"We bought a new carpet, which was a big deal for them," Ruth Andrew said. "All the other carpets in the house were secondhand. I offered to buy them new furniture but they said no. They wanted their room back the way it was. These are tough little girls, let me tell you, although they've had their share of jokes about it.

"It's the people in the house who make the place, not what happens. I hope we handled it well. None of us went to a shrink. Since there were so many of us we just sat around the table and talked about it. I had assumed that everybody else was doing just as well until this first anniversary; then I realized that all those Hubbard Woods children and their parents were still having a very hard time. I guess our own experience protected us from seeing it."

Within the trauma membrane memories kept resurfacing. After the first anniversary the children seemed to be recovering better than their parents. Jeffrey Berkson, the Evanston social worker who continued to visit Hubbard Woods School, noted a shift in their concerns. They stopped asking whether Laurie Dann could come back and talked about how the shooting had affected them. "There is no one theme," Berkson said. "What I see most is a loss of confidence in their ability to go on and be successful. This class of children has seen something that no others have ever witnessed, just like Holocaust survivors and Vietnam veterans, and the event has overshadowed everything in their lives. The rest of us can never know what it was like to be in that room. And the difficulty for parents is that they did not share the experience."

One day, at about this time, a Winnetka father was standing by a school yard watching his children at play. He was enjoying the carefree scene when a thought crossed his mind which was so disturbing that he did not share it with his wife until much later.

"You know," he eventually said, "I have this strange feeling that our children will never again be completely safe."

INDEX

INDEX

INDEX